OLD SOLDIERS' HOME

A HISTORY AND NECROLOGY
OF THE
NORTHWESTERN BRANCH
NATIONAL HOME
FOR
DISABLED VOLUNTEER SOLDIERS

WAUWATOSA, WISCONSIN

1864–1900

Dr. Jeanette L. Jerger

HERITAGE BOOKS
2012

HERITAGE BOOKS

AN IMPRINT OF HERITAGE BOOKS, INC.

Books, CDs, and more—Worldwide

For our listing of thousands of titles see our website
at
www.HeritageBooks.com

Published 2012 by
HERITAGE BOOKS, INC.
Publishing Division
100 Railroad Ave. #104
Westminster, Maryland 21157

International Standard Book Numbers
Paperbound: 978-0-7884-1731-3
Clothbound: 978-0-7884-9225-9

PREFACE

I did not know all of this was here – in the area I have lived in most of my life. A genealogical search for one piece of data and then a discovery of information in a place where one would least expect. Who would think that an *Annual Report,* usually a statistical summary, would contain vital information about Civil War soldiers? The *Ladies* of Milwaukee in their *First Annual Report of the Wisconsin Soldiers' Home in Milwaukee for the Year Ending April 15, 1865* included in their report identification of those who died in the Home. Also given was the veteran's company and regiment, where the veteran lived at time of enlistment, date of death, cause of death, and cemetery where buried. These records of deaths of veterans continued over the three years that the *Ladies* managed The Wisconsin Soldiers' Home in Milwaukee. All subsequent Annual Reports from *the Board of Managers of the National Home for Disabled Volunteer Veterans* also contain substantive data on veterans as well as statistical information. The *Ladies* of Milwaukee set the stage that launched a search for further data on deaths of veterans in the *Northwestern Branch,* the National Branch that replaced *Wisconsin Soldiers' Home.* The necrology collection includes data through 1899.

The history of the *Northwestern Branch* could not be overlooked as it reflects the life of veterans who became members - data obtained has become part of this text.

Thus from an unexpected discovery comes a time framed picture of life of veterans and the social structure that provided for their needs and a memorial to their deaths.

The illustrations are generally photocopies of archival material. Letters and newsprint items are dated. Lithographs and photographs are reproductions found in government materials documenting the history of *Old Soldiers' Home.*

Sections on *Medical Terms, Military Terms and Related Abbreviations* and *References* are included in this text.

TABLE OF CONTENTS

THE WOMEN

The problems afflicted on the soldier during and after the Civil War left civilians with an unsettling view of a changing society. There was no social institution designed to provide support for soldiers returning home temporarily or permanently. They returned to Wisconsin without the wherewithal for food, clothing, lodging, and medical care.

Many saw the need some acted – the women of Wisconsin. These women were activists who not only publicized the need for help for soldiers but actually set up the process by which the care could be provided in a timely manner. And then they provided the care. Their place in history is limited to archival holdings and is minimal in amount.

Mrs. Louis P. Harvey (Cordelia A. Perrine Harvey) was one of the first leaders. The widow of Governor Harvey of Wisconsin, she was appointed Sanitary Agent for Wisconsin, Western *Sanitary Commission, at St. Louis in 1862 and visited hospitals and hospital boats in that area that were responsible for the care of the sick and wounded from Wisconsin. From her observations she concluded that Wisconsin veterans should convalesce in *northern air*. She was successful in several attempts to return veterans to northern hospitals. On her return visits to Wisconsin she shared her experiences with other concerned women giving guidance to their activities And she spent time in conference with President Lincoln convincing him of the need to establish more institutions in Wisconsin. The hospitals and convalescent home opened under President: Lincoln's mandate were: Harvey United States Army General Hospital located in Madison in 1863, Swift Hospital located in Prairie du Chien in 1864, and an. officers' convalescent home located in Milwaukee in 1864. They were closed soon after the war ended – by the summer of 1865.

*Sanitary commissions were temporary adjuncts to the War Department. Their main function was to assist in the provision of basic needs to soldiers on a volunteer basis. They provided supplies, food, clothing, and medical treatment as they saw the need.

Milwaukee Soldiers' Home opened March 31, 1864 at 207 W. Water Street. *The Milwaukee Daily Sentinel*, March 7, 1864, page one editorial, noted that there was an urgent need to establish a Soldiers' Home in Milwaukee and ... *Should the ladies who are moving so energetically in this cause succeed... they will be the means of accomplishing a great amount of good.*

The Milwaukee Daily Sentinel, May 16, 1864, printed on the front page, the following:
Soldiers' Home – The women of Milwaukee have founded a Soldiers' Home in that city for the purpose of administering to the wants of the wounded, diseased, or penniless soldiers passing through the city and make appeals to our people to help sustain them. It is a holy work, in which they are engaged, and one in which all should feel a common interest. We hope to see some of our men and women take hold and do something
Whitewater Register.

The *Milwaukee Daily Sentinel*, May 25, 1864, printed a thank you message to *the ladies of Milwaukee,* from *J. H. Hauser, Capt. 'Lawrence Guards,' Appleton.*

Other newsworthy items of interest during the month of May 1864 include *Morale of Our Army,* Col. Webber's visit, and ...*smallpox in the State Prison*

The *Charter and By-Laws of the Wisconsin Soldiers' Home, February 2, 1865,* show a name change and the process of incorporation of the *Home.* A report would be sent to *The Legislature of the State* yearly in the month of February. Board membership was to be limited to women. The first board was as follows:
Mrs. G. P. Hewitt, Jr., Mrs. E. L. Buttrick, Mrs. J. H. Rogers,
Mrs. J. J. Talmadge, Mrs. S. S. Merrill, Mrs. A. J. Aikens,
Mrs. D. A. Olin, Mrs. S. T. Hooker, Mrs. Charles Bigelow,
Mrs. G. P. Gifford, Mrs. James Holton, Mrs. A. Vedder,
Mrs. Byron Kilbourn, Mrs. Walter Burke, Mrs. Charles
Townsend, Mrs. Fred Wardner, Mrs. Charles Moody,
Mrs. H. O. Green, Mrs. Riley Smith, Mrs. A Maxfield,

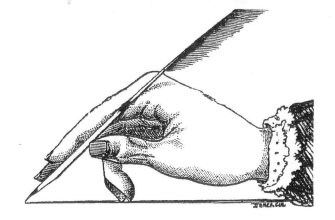

Soldiers' Home.—An effort is being made to establish a Soldiers' Home in this city. The urgent need of one has been demonstrated repeatedly. Should the ladies who are moving so energetically in this cause succeed in establishing such an institution, they will be the means of accomplishing a great amount of good.

Soldiers' Home Association.—It will be noticed in our telegraphic columns that a bill was introduced in the Assembly yesterday to incorporate the Milwaukee Soldiers' Home Association.

Soldiers' Home.

Names of soldiers arrived and entertained at the Soldiers' Home, on Tuesday, the 24th:

Capt. J. H. Hauser, Privates M. A. Lathrop, Geo. C. Metcalf, Egbert J. Blood, F. A. Bailey, Edward O'Neill, Geo. F. Schilley, Dwight C. Pelton, John Ham, Wm. McHelmbagh, Wm. A. Metcalf, M. C. C. Burnside, A. J. Barron, Thos. Logan, F. O. Wilson, E. W. Smith, Geo. F. Turner, E. Smith, J. W. Young, N. Benont, H. Allen, J. H. Heath, J. B. Mann, A. A. White, Asa A. Preston, Lorin Sanborn, Caspar Church, H. W. Martin, Chas. E. Hunter, Melancthon Fish, M. A. Eggleston, W. H. H. Himebagh, J. S. Case, A. W. Lamb.

The warmest thanks of the Company are returned for the dinner, and a "God bless the enterprise of the ladies of Milwaukee."

J. H. HAUSER,
Capt. "Lawrence Guards" Appleton.

CITY MATTERS.

MORALE OF OUR ARMY.

General Meade has had exclusive control of the troops, and in carrying out General Grant's plans has handled the army with consummate skill, notwithstanding the shifting of divisions and the temporary disorder which occurred from time to time. The army is in fine condition, in complete order, and confident of success. Our wagon trains are all safe in the rear of the troops, with plenty of supplies, and, except in the loss of men, the army is as formidable as ever.

PERSONAL.—Col. Watson M. Webber, of the 51st U. S. Infantry, is spending a few days with friends in town.

THE Waupun *Times* says there is a case of small pox in the State Prison. Bad place for the small pox, as the next we shall hear will be, that the prisoners are "breaking out."

Mrs. Chas. H. Larkin, Mrs. M. A. Wolf, Mrs. G. G. Dousman, Mrs. Levi Kellogg, Mrs. John S. Ricker, Mrs. E. O'Neil, Mrs. R. M. Forsbee, Mrs. O. H. Waldo, Mrs. Chas. Andrews, Mrs. J. M. Durand, Mrs. B. B. Jones, Mrs. E. Terry, Mrs. Robt. McCarter, Mrs. A. Green, Mrs. J. M. Kimball, Mrs. S. B. Scott, Mrs. Samuel Vose, Mrs. H. C. Crocker, Mrs. A. J. Langworthy, Mrs. G. C. White, Mrs. E. J. Hill, Mrs. A. Ely, Mrs. Elizabeth Goodwin, Mrs. D. W. Richardson, Mrs. W. G. Fitch, Mrs. John Plankinton, Mrs. J. M. Northup, Mrs. L. A. Henry.

Their mission was to permanently locate the *Home* in Milwaukee, *...for the purpose of providing and caring for the sick, wounded, and disabled soldiers temporarily sojourning in the State of Wisconsin, and to do and perform such other acts of charity and kindness as they in their judgment may deem right and proper.*

In the *First Annual Report of the Wisconsin Soldiers' Home, Milwaukee, For the Year Ending April 15, 1865,* they noted that the *enterprise* began with one building of *limited capacity.* (Two more buildings were added – the City of Milwaukee Directory for 1865 lists three addresses for the *Soldiers' Home, 203, 205 and 207 W. Water.*) This location became part of which later became known as *Downtown* Milwaukee – the Milwaukee River is adjacent to *Water* Street.

In a digression from the usual fiscal concerns found in annual reports, deaths at the *Home* were listed along with information about the soldiers' company, regiment, place of enlistment, cause of death, place of death, and place of burial. The *remains* were sent to their family and those *friendless* were buried in *our beautiful 'Forest Home'* – Forest Home Cemetery in Milwaukee, Wisconsin.

The *ladies* also noted that they would be holding a *State Fair* to raise money to support their work. They had appealed to the people of Wisconsin to help with contributions. The contributors

8

were listed in the *Report* and some are named below with their donations – they gave what they could:

Alcott, J. M.,	medicine, vegetables, cologne, camphor, farina, and eggs.
Bondway, J.,	bale of hay.
Christian Commission,	pickles, canned and dried fruit, quilts and books.
Decker, Mrs. I. B.,	dried and canned currants.
Empire Store,	flannel.
Foote, Mrs. E.,	bandage and linen.
Goodwin, Mrs. Wm.,	potatoes.
Town of Hartford,	barrel flour, pork, sausage, cheese, potatoe turnips, beans, onions, butter, horseradish, jelly.
Judd, T. H.,	100 feet lumber.
Kendrick, Mrs. Wm.,	rice pudding.
Lalumiere, Rev. S. P.,	dressing gown and rocking chair.
Melrose, Andrew,	pig's feet.
Nazro, John,	shelf brackets and hammer.

Ogden, Miss Fanny,	tea spoons.
Plymouth Church,	milk and biscuits.
Raymond, Frank,	ice, fresh fish, and doughnuts.
Sheldon, A. C.,	foot tub.
Travis, I. N.,	washing machine.
U. S. Express Co.,	transporting packages during year.
Valentine, E.,	barrel soap.
Whitmore, H.	oysters.

The *Fair* included an exhibition of paintings and sculpture produced in America, a first for Wisconsin. In addition to her leadership skills, President Hewitt was an artist and an advocate of art appreciation.

The net receipts of the State Fair held at Milwaukee in the months of June and July, 1865 totaled $102, 874.62, according to the *Second Annual Report of the Wisconsin Soldiers' Home, 1866*. Part of the money, $12,000, was spent for a site for a permanent home in the City of Milwaukee. Mrs. G. P. Hewitt, Jr. was president.

The final report, the *Third Annual Report and Memorial of the Wisconsin Soldiers' Home to the Legislature, 1867* was printed in its entirety in the *Milwaukee Daily Sentinel*, February 20, 1867. President: Mrs. C. K. Watkins. The Board of Directors clearly state the change in management and resources from local to national. *The Board of Directors ... was informed that the corporation created by Congress, called 'The National Asylum for Disabled Volunteer Soldiers,' and endorsed by Congress with an ample fund to provide, and to permanently maintain suitable Asylums or Homes for all the*

Madison Wis

Aug 17 1865

Mrs G. P. Hewitt Jr
Pres Soldiers Home
Milwaukee Wis

Respected Lady

It becomes a pleasant duty for me
to return my hearty thanks to you
for you kindness to me. I cannot
express in words how thankful I am to
you. I am happy to think that
there is a chance for me to get an
education

I shall be very happy to revisit
Milwaukee as soon as we are discharged

Very Respectfully
your Obedient Servant
Thomas W Alger

Wisconsin Legislature
Assembly Chamber,

Madison Jan 26 1865

Mrs G. P. Hewitt Jr,

Dear Madam,

I am happy
to inform you that the Bill to Incorporate
the Wisconsin Soldiers home, passed the
Senate yesterday. It was reported back
to the Senate by the Committee on Incorporations
with a recommendation that it be passed.
When Senator Wilson [of] Janesville City paid
a most handsome tribute to the noble hearted
and generous ladies of Milwaukee who
have promptly and efficiently, as far
as any means defied nothing, so promptly
ministered to the wants of the sick and
wounded soldiers passing through our City.
The ladies of the home have a favorable consideration
of the Legislature. Their efforts have
been appreciated and their future usefulness and
prosperity assured. I will send you a copy
of the Bill when it is it will be
signed by the Governor. With the
highest respects to the Ladies of
the Home, I am truly,

Your Friend

J. Hadley

THE WISCONSIN SOLDIERS' HOME.

Third Annual Report and Memorial to the Legislature.

The following report and memorial of the Board of Directors of the Wisconsin Soldiers' Home, has been submitted to the Legislature.— Our readers are all interested in the condition of this institution and we cannot give them more interesting matter to peruse:

To the Legislature of the State of Wisconsin:

The Board of Directors of the Wisconsin Soldiers' Home are pleased to present to your honorable body now assembled, their third annual report for the year 1866 and 1867.

The ladies comprising the Board of Directors, inspired by love for our country, our soldiers and our Savior, have never faltered in their duties to the Home. Their enthusiasm is as fresh, their hearts as warm, and their hands as willing in this work as at the commencement.

In the management of this Home, the board have never deviated from their original idea, that of making this institution approximate as nearly as possible in its comforts and pleasures for the inmates to the true christian home.

We feel that we have been sustained during the past year by an ever kind and watchful providence.

disabled volunteer soldiers of the country, including those of Wisconsin, had decided to erect and maintain three principal Asylums for this purpose, to-wit: One in the east, one in the center, and one in the west, and that they were willing and desirous to locate and erect one of those principal Asylums at or in the immediate vicinity of Milwaukee, on condition that this corporation would turn over and merge its fund and property in that of said National institution, to promote the same general purpose for which the Wisconsin Soldiers' Home was created, on a greater scale.

Dr. E. B. Wolcott was appointed a member of the National Board in December 1866 and appointed Manger of *The National Asylum for Disabled Volunteer Soldiers in Wauwatosa, near Milwaukee,* in 1867. In April 1867, he selected a site in Wauwatosa that included four farms plus a piece of land from the Milwaukee Railway Company, totaling 382.7 acres. The cost was $70,721.24. The City of Milwaukee Directory, 1867, lists *Soldiers' Home, Wauwatoso (sic), Dr. E. B. Wolcott, Supt. Office, 134 Wisconsin.* In May 1867, the veterans were moved from the *Wisconsin Soldiers' Home* in Milwaukee to farmhouses on the site - their care was now under the guiding hand of the Federal government.

THE HOME

In the 19th century and into the 20th century the sick and unfortunate were given institutional care in an asylum. The asylums were generally poorhouses or almshouses. Congress in response to the needs of volunteer veterans of the Civil War passed the *National Asylum of Disabled Volunteer Aid Act* March 3, 1865 for the incorporation of a national asylum. The corporation was to have 100 members and a quorum of 50 to do business. This proved difficult and March 21, 1866 another Act was designated to supersede the original Act. The administration of the institution was placed under the authority of a Board of Managers.

The Board was made up of nine citizens selected by the Senate and House of Representatives, not members of Congress, for a six-year term. Ex officio members were the President of United States, the Secretary of War, and the Chief Justice of the Supreme Court. Their task was to create the *National Asylum for Disabled Volunteer Veterans.* This lengthy title was subject to other versions. The 1870 Federal Census, Wisconsin, County of Milwaukee, City of Wauwatosa, cites the institution as the *U. S. M. Asylum.* The mailing address for most branches was *National Military Home* followed by city and state location. And *Old Soldiers' Hone* was the affectionate, familiar phrase used by families and friends of veterans. The name was officially changed in 1873 to *National 'Home' for Disabled Volunteer Veterans. Home* better reflected the country's concern for the well being of the veteran.

The Managers selected the sites for the first three branches. According to VA Historic Preservation data the following sites were established: Eastern Branch, Togus, Maine, 1867, Northwestern Branch, Milwaukee, Wisconsin, 1867, and Central Branch, Dayton, Ohio, 1867. Annual Reports of the Northwestern Branch list the *Eastern Branch near Augusta, Maine,* the *Northwestern Branch, near Milwaukee, Wis.* and the *Central Branch near Dayton, Ohio* * The Northwestern Branch was located in Wauwatosa, Wisconsin.

In the beginning, admission was limited to disabled volunteers of the Civil War. An exception to this occurred at the Northwestern

Branch, as all members of the *Wisconsin Soldiers' Home* were to be admitted and this included a veteran of the War of 1812. In 1871, veterans of the War of 1812 and the Mexican War were able to apply for admission. An Act passed July 5, 1884 opened up admissions - ...*all honorably discharged soldiers and sailors who served in the war of the rebellion, and the volunteer soldiers and sailors of the War of eighteen hundred and twelve and of the Mexican War, who are disabled by age, disease or otherwise, and by reason of such disability are incapable of earning a living, shall be admitted into the home for disabled volunteers. Provided such disability was not incurred in service against United States*

Subsequently members of the Home were veterans of the U. S. Army, U. S. Veteran Volunteers, U. S. Veteran Reserve Corps, U. S. Marine Corps, U. S. Navy, and the Florida War, Indian War, Seminole War.

In 1866, the Board of Managers setup the rules and regulations for the Home using the military paradigm of the time. They also had been given the authority to take pension payments from members of the Home – except from members with dependent children. In all Branches, staff and veterans wore uniforms made available from military surplus supplies, veterans provided the work force, and farms were operated for subsistence and profit. And large military field pieces, left over from the war, were used as decorations on the grounds.

The site of the Northwestern Branch Home was located about one mile west of the City of Milwaukee limits and about four miles from Lake Michigan in Milwaukee County. There were three natural lakes on the land, a grove of trees, and gentle sloping hills and ravines. Many came to the site over the years to picnic in the park-like setting. The Home was accessible to the public via the electric streetcar. Two of the lines entered the Home grounds from the City of Milwaukee, the Grand Avenue Electric Street Railway and the National Avenue Electric Street Railway. (The first street railway opened in Milwaukee, May 30, 1860.) There were two depots in central locations on the grounds. The Milwaukee and St. Paul rail-

STREET CAR DEPOT AND TRESTLEWORK, NORTH SIDE OF GROUNDS.

ON THE GROUNDS

MAIN BUILDING NORTHWESTERN BRANCH, NATIONAL HOME FOR DISABLED VOL. SOLDIERS.

way ran through the center of the grounds on an east/west track.

The first members to move to the site, the soldiers from the *Wisconsin Soldiers' Home* in Milwaukee were housed in the farmhouses. The sick were cared for in the Mitchell farmhouse- it was used as a hospital for the first two years.

During the summer of 1867, the first building to house the veterans was constructed. It held about 200 members. The second building to house members, the *Main Building*, was constructed in 1868-1869. The architect was E. Townsend Mix. It also held a kitchen and mess hall, a chapel, a library and lecture room, offices and a small recreation area. The basement held an icehouse, bathing and lavatory facilities, and storage space. Ice was taken from the *Ice Lake*, later named *Lake Wheeler*. Water was drawn from the springs n the *Ice Lake* to the top story of the tower of the building and distributed downward by gravity. The first building was used as a hospital. It functioned in this capacity until the completion of a new hospital in 1880, and thereafter became known as the *Old Hospital*. The new *Hospital*, with the attachment of convalescent wards, called *T. B. Camps,* in 1886, remained the main hospital until 1930.

A glimpse of life in the Northwestern Branch for the period of December 1, 1875 to December 31, 1876 may be framed by selected data from the *Annual Report National Home for Disabled Volunteer Soldiers, Northwestern Branch, Milwaukee County, Wis., January 10, 1877.* Veterans living in the Home were noted in this document as *beneficiaries.*

Beneficiaries *cared for or aided* during the year totaled 1115. The average number of men living there was 553. The ages of those veterans who were present in the Home during that time were... *Under 30, 28; between 30 and 50, 632; between 50 and 70, 431; over 70, 36.* The greatest number of these veterans enlisted in New York, Wisconsin, Illinois and Pennsylvania, respectively. There were twice as many foreign born as native-born members. The greatest number of foreign-born came from Ireland and Germany. The number of colored was one.

ON THE GROUNDS

The members were quartered in the *Main Building*. Men who had been married and men who presently had wives and/or minor children numbered 201.

Over 80 % of the men had been laborers or farmers. Less numerous were those who had been blacksmiths, coopers, carpenters, shoemakers, and tailors. A few lawyers, physicians, and surgeons were included as members.

The number of disabilities from wounds received in the service was 560, slightly less than disabilities from sickness contracted during service, 567. The most common causes of need for hospitalization were alcoholism, bronchitis, consumption, fever, paralysis, rheumatism, senility, and ulcers. There were 37 deaths; consumption caused the greatest number. Nine were judged to be *totally or partially* insane and were transferred to the Government Insane Asylum in Washington.

During this time the *Main Building* was the Home for the members their quarters were there as well as amenities usually found in a small town. It had a library, post office, store, chapel, and a recreation area.

Religious services had been held at regular intervals since January 1, 1876. Visiting chaplains provided services in the Chapel. Protestant services were held Sunday afternoons. Roman Catholic services were held every Monday evening and Tuesday morning at times that did not *interfere with the order of the day.* The Grand Army of the Republic and a Temperance League had assigned areas in which their meetings were held.

The Home Library had a reading room and held over 3.000 books, newspapers, magazines – including publications in English, French, German, and Danish.

The Post Office mailed 18,000 letters and received 18,000 letters. Newspapers were sent and received. The postmaster was selected from the membership.

A recreation area provided indoor games, e.g., billiards. Outdoor activities included croquet and boating. Concerts were given outside in the summer by a cornet band in the *Pavilion* built in 1875. In the winter concerts were given in the Chapel. The costs, except for the band, came from the *Contingent Fund (Post Fund)*, i.e., money accruing from fines imposed upon offenders against the discipline of the Home.

The kitchen and mess hall was in the *Main Building*. The bill of fare was sparse except the Fourth of July dinner...*Roast Lamb, Mint Sauce, Cold Ham, Mashed Potatoes, Green Peas, Lettuce, Onions, Radishes, Prune Pie, Ice Cream, Crackers, Cheese, Bread, Butter, Coffee.* An example of the usual fare is noted by the total meal plan two days earlier, July 2: *Breakfast:...Beef Stew, Potatoes, Bread, Butter, Coffee. Dinner:...Boiled Pork, Baked Beans, Potatoes, Stewed Prunes, Bread, Tea. Supper:...Cheese, Bread, Butter, Tea.* The members were assigned a seat at long tables in the mess hall.

A Home store was available in which members could purchase... *underclothing, summer-wear, tobacco, weiss beer, cider, and other necessary and desirable articles.* It made a profit of $4000.48. It was believed to be a good thing in another way. *The influence resulting from the establishment of the store, and especially from the sale of weiss beer and cider to beneficiaries, has been beneficial, as it is instrumental in keeping many men at the Home, who otherwise would loiter about the groggeries in the immediate vicinity of the Home squandering their money, clothing, and credit, for intoxicating liquors.*

On admission to the Home for the first time, the member was provided clothing. The clothing was given in stages, some on admission and the rest six months later. This *admission suit* was free to all veterans. All members were required to bathe once a week, and the Company Sergeant was responsible to see that it was strictly enforced.

Pensions were held in trust by the Home for 458 pensioners. An accounting lists the retention of some funds for the Home Store, fines, and for the ...*benefit of dependent wife, child, mother, or sister.*

PAVILION & PROMENADE

READING ROOM

The total number of members employed and paid was 414. They worked in Mechanical Trades, on the Farm and Garden, and in the Home Laundry. The Trades included a blacksmith shop, carpenter shop, harness shop, paint shop, printing office, shoe shop, tailor shop, and tin shop. (*The Legislative Manual for the State of Wisconsin, 1872,* records average wage at *40 cents a day.*)

During the year a new building was completed. A brick building *20x20, five stories high, for Water Closets, each story being connected with the Main Building by a covered way.*

A greenhouse was built this year and a plat laid out for a flower garden; completion was too late for a report on its operation. Costs to build it were paid by money from the contingent fund and from profits of the Home Store.

Discipline was strict and offenders paid for their transgressions, they were fined or assigned days of labor. The most noted *offence* was *Absence without leave. Drunk* and *Under influence of liquor,* were separate categories. And they made up, respectively, the second and third most noted offences. Fourteen men were dishonorable discharged.

Of the 1115 beneficiaries cared for 734 *committed no offense against the discipline of the Home or the laws of the land....*

There had been 3, 117 registered visitors to the branch, and it was estimated that about 40,000 visited the grounds during this time period.

A comparison with *The Annual Report of the Governor of the North-Western Branch, National Branch for Disabled Volunteer Soldiers, For the Fiscal Year Ending June 30, 1885* notes an increase in the population in the Home. The total number of *soldiers and sailors cared for or aided* at this Branch during the year *was* 2347. The average number present was 1256. Members were older, no one under 30 years, and 137 over 70 years including three, 100 years and over. There were twice as many foreign born as there were native born members. The countries from which they emigrated were Germany and Ireland. States from which most enlisted were Wisconsin, Illinois, New York, and Pennsylvania respectively. Six members were colored.

Those who had been married and those who had living wives and/or minor children numbered 606. Most members were quartered in the *Main Building* and a few were quartered in the *Hospital*.

Over half of the members had been laborers or farmers, the farmer being the lower in numbers cited. Others had been blacksmiths, carpenters, clerks, painters, and tailors, etc. Included were several actors, dentists, physician & surgeons, teachers, and veterinary surgeons.

The members with disability from wounds numbered 1014; those with sickness contracted while in the service numbered 1333. The most common illnesses treated in the hospital were phthisis pulmonalis, rheumatism, old age, paralysis, and alcoholism. There were 96 deaths. The greatest cause of death was phthisis pulmonalis (consumption). Eighteen members were judged to be insane, five were sent to the Government Insane Asylum in Washington, D. C., five went to the Milwaukee County Insane Asylum in Wauwatosa, five were at the Home, two died in the Home Hospital, one escaped from the Hospital.

The Home had two chaplains, one Protestant and one Roman Catholic. Services were held in the Chapel in the *Main Building*. The *Bill of Fare* was omitted in the report.

The volumes in the library, in the *Main Building*, now totaled, 534. Newspapers and periodicals totaled 206, and were in English, German, French, and Scandinavian languages. The Post Office added registered mail and money order services.

The Farm and Garden and the Home Store made a profit. This year the manufacture of underwear and bedding by members and their families were reported to have made a profit. On first admission clothing was issued up to the value of $34.00, thereafter yearly to the value of $15.35. The member was also allowed one dress coat

26

every three years and one great coat every five years – each at the cost of $6.00. Free to all. All members of the Home bathed weekly as reported by the Sergeants in the *Sanitary Regulations* report. Pensions were still under the aegis of the Home. Federal Acts of 1881 and 1882 required that pensions be paid to the treasurer of the Home and was to be used for the benefit of the member. The 1885 report itemized cashed paid to pensioner, cash paid to pensioners family, and money retained by the Home for payment to the Home and Home Store. Any balance remaining was given to the member on discharge or his heirs on his death.

The members employed for pay, now noted to be *pay for Extra Duty*, were averaged to be 254. Money paid to families of members for the manufacture of underwear and bedding was included in the report.

The first barracks had been built. It accommodated 240 members.

Absence without leave and *Drunk* were, respectively, the most common offences. There had been 34 dishonorable discharges. A Post of the Grand Army of the Republic managed by members had been maintained. Members and their families conducted a Sunday School. Amusements and recreations...*have been continued as far as practicable during this year.* An elevator had been installed as it was reported that the number of members and visitors using the elevator totaled 43,862, average per day 266.

And in summation for the year ending June 30, 1885:
... a large number of persons, representing every part of this country and many foreign nations have registered at the office and been shown through the buildings, expressing admiration of the cleanliness and order, which they have observed... .

In the 1880s and 1890s, in order to accommodate the increasing numbers of veterans, barracks (domiciliaries) were built. *The Old Men's Barracks* was built in 1895. It was supplied with rocking chairs and smoking rooms. Later it housed colored members only. A small beer hall was opened, date unknown, and in 1888 a large

27

beer hall was built. The beer halls were major source of funds. These *Post Funds* were used to build the chapel, social hall, theater, and library. Drum and bugle calls were sounded as in garrison life in the army. The routine was up at 6:00 A.M. and to bed by 9 P.M. Each member was assigned to a company the criterion dependent upon like disability. Each company had a Captain, Sergeant and Corporal who were in charge of the members.

The Chapel was built in 1889. An organ and a bell were added later - gifts from friends in the Milwaukee area. Protestant and Catholic services were held several times a week. And the Woman's Christian Temperance Union held services in the Chapel weekly

The Social Hall was built in 1894. The basement was set up as a billiard hall for use by all members. The first floor was set up as a meeting and reading room for members of the Veteran's Social Club, it had comfortable furniture and a piano and card tables. The upper floor was set up for meetings of other group, e.g., veteran associations.

The Memorial Hall was built in 1881 and initially served as a multiple use facility – it was a store, chapel, amusement hall, and railway depot. It was renovated in 1889 to become the Ward Theater and weekly entertainment was provided for the members. The theater is now listed on the National Register of Historic Places.

The Library was built in 1891. The building contained a gallery for books, a reading area and a gaming area for card tables, pool tables and such. It was open to all members of the Home at no cost. Books could be withdrawn and taken to the members quarters to be read. It would later be named after Major James S. Wadsworth the President of the Board of Managers in 1905.

There was a Guard House on the grounds where those who committed offences were placed. The offender would be given a *trial*, the Commandant was the judge and those found guilty of an offense *against the peace and dignity* of the Home were fined. The money went into the Post Fund.

HOME STORE

BARRACKS COMPANIES *F* and *H*

OLD MEN'S WARD

THE HOME CHURCH

WARD MEMORIAL THEATER

SOCIAL HALL

A 12-room house was built for the Commandant in 1868. The house later became known as the Governor's Quarters reflecting the change in title of the administrator of the Branch. It was also called the *Governor's Mansion*. Quarters were also built for officers, e.g., Chief Engineer, Adjutant, Chief Clerk, Treasurer, Surgeon, and Quartermaster. These were homes most often occupied by the officer and his family. Women were not allowed in any of the other *regular Home buildings*.

The Cemetery was located on the northeast section of the grounds near one of the lakes. Each grave had a marble head stone with the soldier's name, company, regiment and date of death. John K. Afton, Civil War veteran, was the first soldier buried in the Home Cemetery - May 22, 1871. Prior to that time veterans were interred in Forest Home Cemetery, Milwaukee, Wisconsin or their remains were returned to their family. In 1876, the Archdiocese of Milwaukee donated gravesites in Calvary Cemetery for the burial of Catholic veterans – these sites were on land adjacent to the Home grounds.

*Other branches: Southern Branch, Hampton, Virginia, 1870; West ern Branch, Leavenworth, Kansas, 1885; Pacific Branch, Santa Monica, California, 1888, Marion Branch, Marion, Indiana, 1888; Danville Branch, Danville, Illinois, 1898; Mountain Branch, John son City, Tennessee, 1901; Battle Mountain Sanatorium, Hot Springs, South Dakota, 1902; Bath Branch, Bath, New York, 1929 (formerly New York State Soldiers' & Sailors' Home, 1877)

SURGEON'S QUARTERS

GOVERNOR'S QUARTERS

NECROLOGY

The collection of data covers the time period of late 1864 to 1900. It begins with information collected by the *Ladies* of the *Wisconsin Soldiers' Home* in Milwaukee, Wisconsin and continues through the years - with changes in format reflecting variations in governmental data collection.

The Annual Report of the Commandant and Treasurer of the Northwestern Branch, National Home for Disabled volunteer Soldiers, 1878 included a supplement listing veteran deaths from May 1, 1867 to December 31, 1877.

Yearly reports directly from the Northwestern Branch noting deaths of veterans continue through the first half of 1885. Thereafter Reports of the *Board of Managers of the National Home for Disabled Volunteer Soldiers* include a *Record of Disabled Volunteer Soldiers; Who Were And Had Been Members of the National Home for Disabled Volunteer Veterans.* This is a National Report and all Branches are included. Information is given regarding the status of all members of National Homes for a particular fiscal year. They may be found in the *United States Serial Set* of *The Miscellaneous Documents of the House of Representatives.* (See references following each section). The volumes for the years 1891 and 1892 were missing from the Set. The *Reports* for the years 1891 and 1892 were located at the Wisconsin State Historical Society by the reference librarians at the Milwaukee Central Library.

Data were selectively retrieved to provide genealogical information about veterans who died at the Northwestern Branch.

Deaths from 09/19/1864 to 12/31/1977 are listed in one section. Deaths from 1878 to 1900 are listed separately by the year. Each section has a format at the top of the page to indicate type of information generally found in that section for each veteran.

Unless otherwise noted in the data following the soldier's name, his rank is *Private*. And unless otherwise noted the soldier's regiment is

Infantry. For example: *ANDERSON, George – H, 28 Wisconsin,...* is a Private in the 28 Wisconsin Infantry.

The veterans of the U. S. Navy are identified by rank not by company and regiment as are other veterans. For example: *BUTLER, Michael – Seaman, U. S. Navy....*

Where an underline appears__the data was not readable or was missing in the record source.

The data has been copied as given in the records, if any question arose it is noted in parentheses.

THE RIDERLESS WAR-HORSE

FORMAT: NAME, COMPANY & REGIMENT, DATE OF DEATH, CAUSE OF DEATH, PLACE OF BURIAL (Additional data may be given as found relevant to soldier's history.)

ADAMS, George W. – G, 7 Iowa, 09/13/1872, died when on leave, cause of death unknown, Nevada, Iowa cemetery.

AFTON, John K. – H, 6 Michigan Cav., 05/22/1871, Cancer of head & face, Home Cemetery.

ALLEN, James - C, 1 Michigan Light Art., 12/11/1868, Dropsy, Forest Home Cemetery, Milwaukee, WI.

ANDERSON, George – H, 28 Wisconsin, 11/__/1871, Fistula, died while on leave, cemetery unknown.

ANDERSON, Ole – K, 8 Wisconsin, 08/04/1874, Consumption, Home Cemetery.

ANDERSON, Peter – E. 90 Pennsylvania, 01/21/1972. Lung fever, Home Cemetery.

ASHTON, James – D, 122 Illinois, 01/23/1872, Spinal disease, Home Cemetery.

ATWOOD, H. H. - War of 1812. First soldier admitted to the Northwestern Branch, 02/29/1868, Senility, Forest Home Cemetery, Milwaukee, WI.

ATZ, Henry – L, 1 New York Cav., 05/02/1874, Uraemia, Home Cemetery.

BADGER, James S. – H, 4 Minnesota, 03/31/1873, Consumption, Home Cemetery.

BAKER, Joseph – E, 13 Wisconsin, 02/20/1873, Apoplexy, body taken by his friends, cemetery unknown.

BALDERSON, William – H, 1 Ohio H. A., 11/03/1872, Congestion of brain, Home Cemetery.

BALTHAZAR, Martin – G, 72 Pennsylvania, 08/02/1874, Consumption, Home Cemetery

BARANOWSKI, Francis – K, 8 & 16 Pennsylvania, 05/14/1872, Railroad accident, Home Cemetery.

BARE, Henry – A, 5 Pennsylvania Cav., 06/11/1877, Cancer of stomach, Home Cemetery.

BARNEY, James R. – 2 U. S. Dragoons, 03/30/ 1877, Senile decay, Home Cemetery.

BAUER, Ferdinand – E, 58 Illinois, 10/11/1870, Inflammation of the bladder, Forest Home Cemetery, Milwaukee, WI.

BEARD, George W. - A, 8 Ohio, 03/12/1877, Pneumonia, Home Cemetery.

BECHER, Charles – B, 1 New York, 03/17/1877, Consumption, Home Cemetery.

BECKWITH, Joseph – I, 4 Wisconsin, 11/15/1877, Albuminuria, Home Cemetery.

BEHMER, Gottlieb – G, 5 Missouri, 08/23/1876, Disease of the spine, Home Cemetery.

BEYNES, Jacob – B, 1 Wisconsin, 05/03/1872, Dropsy, Home Cemetery.

BIELERICH, Adam – F, 58 New York, 08/01/1870, Paralysis & Lung disease, Forest Home Cemetery, Milwaukee, WI.

BIRD, Louis – F, 68 N. Y., 05/07/1871, died on leave, cause of death unknown, cemetery unknown.

BISHOP, Charles – C, 86 Indiana, 03/20/1870, Hemorrhage-lungs, Forest Home Cemetery, Milwaukee, WI.

BJOIGUSON, Sven – F, 13 Wisconsin, 05/22/1867, Consumption, Forest Home Cemetery, Milwaukee, WI

BORUN, Theodore – __, 12 Massachusetts Battery, 02/13/1871, Cancer in stomach, Forest Home Cemetery, Milwaukee, WI.

BOUGHTON, Hart – G, 12 Wisconsin, 06/05/1874, Railroad accident, Home Cemetery.

BRADLEY, James F. – C, 2 New York, 09/30/1869, Hemorrhage-lungs, Calvary Cemetery, Milwaukee, WI.

BRADY, Patrick – D, 6 Wisconsin, 07/24/1875, Apoplexy, Home Cemetery.

BRENNAN, Michael – F. 20 Indiana, 03/22/1871, died on leave, cause of death unknown, cemetery unknown.

BRESLAND, Niel – K, 16 Wisconsin, 12/27/1872, Senility, Home Cemetery.

BREWER, James M. – F. 1 Maryland, 03/20/72, Frozen, Home Cemetery.

BRIER, Fred. A. - I, 6 New York Art., 09/03/1869, Epilepsy, Forest Home Cemetery, Milwaukee, WI.

BROWN, Isaac – I, 77 Illinois, 03/12/1872, Epileptic fit, Home Cemetery.

BROWN, Lyman W. – D, 1 Indiana, 12/19/1875, Dementia, Home Cemetery.

BRUNO, Andrew – H, 3 Pennsylvania Lt. Art., 05/26/1870, Phthisis pulmonalis, Forest Home Cemetery, Milwaukee, WI.

BURCHELL, Benj. I. E. - D, 141 Illinois, 10/01/1876, Heart disease, Home Cemetery.

BURDEN, Chas. B. – A, 144 Illinois, 12/21/1869, Consumption, died on leave, cemetery unknown.

BURNS, Michael – A, 105 Ohio, 06/09/1876, Congestion of lungs, Home Cemetery.

BURNSIDE, John – G, 13 Illinois, 09/23/1875, Enteritis, Home Cemetery.

BUTH, Aug. F. W. – F, 20 Wisconsin, 04/02/1877, Consumption, Home Cemetery.

CAMERON, John – K, 31 Maine, 11/29/1868, Phthisis pulmonalis, Forest Home Cemetery, Milwaukee, WI.

CANLEY, Michael – A, 21 New York, 06/15/1875, Pneumonia, Home Cemetery.

CARPENTER, Thomas – H, 24 Wisconsin, 09/26/1872, Consumption, Home Cemetery.

CARTER, Henry W. – G, 24 Wisconsin, 08/25/1872, Dropsy, Home Cemetery.

CASE, P. C. – C, 41 Wisconsin, lived in Berlin, WI at time of enlistment, died in *Wisconsin Soldiers' Home, Milwaukee, WI, 09/24/1864, cemetery unknown.

CATIN, John – H, 31 Wisconsin, 04/22/1877, Typhoid pneumonia, Home Cemetery.

CAVANAUGH, Patrick – C, 1 U.S, Art., 01/14/72, Frozen, Home Cemetery.

CHAFFER, George – Company & Regiment unknown, at time of enlistment lived in Detroit, Michigan, died in *Wisconsin Soldiers' Home, Milwaukee, WI, 07/31/1866, cemetery unknown.

CHAPIN, John E. – K, 132 Illinois, 06/17/1876, Ossification of heart, Home Cemetery.

CLARK, Thomas – B, 1 Wisconsin, 06/06/1871, Bleeding from lungs, Home Cemetery.

COLBOURN, Dan. L. C. – Staff, 5 Vermont, 06/06/1877, Dropsy, died while on leave, buried Baraboo, WI

COLE, Sylvester - D, 12 U. S. Infantry, 12/11/1877, Consumption, Home Cemetery.

COLLIN, John E. – C, 165 New York, 01/13/1876, Ishuria, Home Cemetery.

CONFREY, Patrick – H, 1 Michigan Cav., 05/02/1877 Railroad accident, Home Cemetery

CONNELLY, Thomas – A, 69 New York, 01/13/1875, Hemoptysis, Home Cemetery.

CONNOR, John A. – G, 39 Wisconsin, lived in Pewaukee, WI at time of enlistment, died in *Wisconsin Soldiers' Home, Milwaukee, WI, 09/22/1864, cause of death unknown, cemetery unknown.

COONAN, John – A, 18 New York, 02/24/1876, died on leave cause of death unknown, buried in N. Y. City cemetery.

COWDRY, Eugene M. – H, 124 Ohio, 03/31/1874, Apoplexy, Home Cemetery.

COX, Thomas E. – F, 132 New York, 06/10/1876, Opium eating, Home Cemetery.

CRANWELL, Thomas S. – A, 1 Illinois Cav., 12/22/1869, Cancer of stomach, Forest Home Cemetery, Milwaukee, WI.

CUTSHALL, William – Company & Regiment unknown, at time of enlistment lived in Madison, WI. died in *Wisconsin Soldiers' Home, Milwaukee, WI, 03/24/1866, Consumption, cemetery unknown.

DATHE, Charles – Company & Regiment unknown, at time of enlistment lived in Oconomowoc, WI, died in *Wisconsin Soldiers' Home, Milwaukee, WI, 10/06/1866, Congestion of brain, cemetery unknown.

DAVIS, Thomas B. – A, 10 Minnesota, lived in Medford Minnesota at time of enlistment, died in *Wisconsin Soldiers' Home, Milwaukee, WI, 01/30/1865, cause of death unknown, cemetery unknown.

DAWSON, Ulrich S. – I, 23 Michigan, 03/02/1877, Consumption, Home Cemetery.

DE CLERCY, John B. - H, 24 Illinois, 04/09/1874, Congestion of lungs, Home Cemetery.

DELANY, Michael – A, 6 New York Heavy Art., 03/28/1870, Heart disease, Yonkers, New York cemetery.

DEREGAN, Caesar – C, 2 Minnesota, 08/15/1870, Hip joint disease, Calvary Cemetery, Milwaukee, WI.

DEVLIN, Patrick – K, New York, 09/07/1871, Heart disease, Home Cemetery.

DIMMICK, Edward – H, 41 Wisconsin, died in *Wisconsin Soldiers' Home,* Milwaukee, WI, 09/26/1864, cause of death unknown, cemetery unknown.

DIXON, Darvin – A, 3 Wisconsin Cav., 04/19/1870, Consumption, Forest Home Cemetery, Milwaukee, WI.

DOWNEY, Patrick – F, 14 New York S. M., 08/28/1875, Consumption, Home Cemetery.

DOWNEY, William – E, 17 Wisconsin, 12/27/1869, died on leave, cause of death unknown, Milwaukee, WI cemetery.

DRAPER, Alvin – D, 1 New York. M. A., 04/06/1873, Hydrathorax, Home Cemetery.

DUDEA, Jacob – __, 9 & 19 Wisconsin, 08/12/1872, Dropsy & Asthma, Home Cemetery.

DUERR, Jacob – __, 2 Wisconsin Cav., died in *Wisconsin Soldiers' Home,* Milwaukee, WI, 05/23/1865, Typhoid pneumonia, cemetery unknown.

DUNN, David – K, 11 Pennsylvania. 06/03/1877, Railroad accident, Home Cemetery.

DUNN, Wm. – F, 12 New York Cav., 05/22/1875, Suicide, Home Cemetery.

DURBIN, Levi – K, 41 Missouri, 07/19/1872, Typhoid fever, Home Cemetery.

DUXBURY, Robert P. – E, 61 Pennsylvania, 04/16/1870, Heart disease, Forest Home Cemetery, Milwaukee, WI.

DWYER, John – G, 59 New York, 10/22/1872, Railroad accident, Home Cemetery.

EDINBERGER, Fred. – D, 1 Illinois Light Art., 05/05/1875, Renal disease, Home Cemetery.

EDWARDS, Charles – B, 1 Illinois Light Art., 01/16/1872, Softening of brain, Home Cemetery.

EGAN, John – E, 19 Wisconsin, 12/06/1872, Dropsy-cellular, Home Cemetery.

ENDERS, Casper – F, 16 Illinois, 04/10/1872, Consumption, Home Cemetery.

EPNER, Charles – A, 170 New York, 02/14/1876, Collapse of lungs, Home Cemetery.

ERENBURG, Arthur – __, 1 Kentucky Independent Battery, 09/17/1873, Opium eating, Home Cemetery.

EVANS, James – B, 39 Wisconsin, died in *Wisconsin Soldiers' Home*, Milwaukee, WI, 09/19/1864, at time of enlistment lived in Pewaukee, WI, cause of death unknown, cemetery unknown.

FARRATER, Morris F. – H, 11 Missouri Cav., 06/14/1874, Consumption, Home Cemetery

FINK, Wm. – War of 1812, 11/30/1874, died on leave, cause unknown, Drakesville, Iowa cemetery.

FISH, Elijah B. – E, 75 New York, 12/15/1871, Chronic diarrhoea, Home Cemetery.

FLYNN, Patrick – A, 1 Illinois Art., 01/16/1876, Consumption, Home Cemetery.

FOGAROTH, August – B, 1 Wisconsin Heavy Art., 03/18/1869, Frozen, Forest Home Cemetery, Milwaukee, WI.

FONDERSQU, Henry – 2 U. S. Dragoons, 12/15/1873, Peritonitis, Home Cemetery.

FONTIER, Joseph – D, 93 New York, 05/01/1875, Renal disease, Home Cemetery.

FORD, Lawrence – G, 19 Illinois, 05/05/1872, Cancer in mouth, Home Cemetery.

FOSSELL, Fred. – B, 175 New York, 07/17/1871, Railroad accident, Home Cemetery.

FREELY, John – B, 51 Indiana, 10/12/1874, Gangerus, Home Cemetery.

FREY, John – F, 15 Missouri, 07/23/1874, Inflammation of bowels, Home Cemetery.

GALLAGHER, John – K, 140 New York, 09/14/1874, Suicide by hanging, Home Cemetery.

GALLISDORF, Matthias – I, 54 New York, 09/24/1870, Lung disease, Forest Home Cemetery, Milwaukee, WI.

GAPEN, Otho W. – K, 1 Indiana Cav., 03/28/1868, Phthisis pulmonalis, Forest Home Cemetery, Milwaukee, WI.

GAULT, David M. – F, 12 Illinois, 09/28/1870, Epilepsy, Forest Home Cemetery, Milwaukee, WI.

GEGAN, John – C, 14 Michigan, 06/_/1871, died on leave, cause of death unknown, cemetery unknown.

GILLBERG, Alfred – A, 198 Pennsylvania, 11/18/1873, Ulcers on lungs, Home Cemetery.

GILMARTIN, Mark – H, 20 Wisconsin, discharged from Home 01/02/1877, died 04/14/1877, Drowned in Milwaukee River, Home Cemetery.

GLEASON, John – G, 14 U. S. Infantry, 02/07/1875, Typhoid fever, Home Cemetery.

GLIDDEN, J. W. – H, 39 Wisconsin, lived in Mauston, WI at time of enlistment, died in *Wisconsin Soldiers' Home, Milwaukee, WI, 09/29/1864, cause of death unknown, cemetery unknown.

GOLLAR, John – C, 65 New.York, 04/14/1871, Consumption, Home Cemetery.

GORDON, Sam. – K, 12 Iowa, 12/03/1868, Phthisis pulmonalis, Forest Home Cemetery, Milwaukee, WI.

GORMAN, Matthew – F, 37 Illinois, 02/24/1877, died on leave, cause unknown, Muskegon, Illinois cemetery.

GOSS, John – D, 23 Ohio, 03/01/1873, Consumption, Home Cemetery.

GOULD, Abner – A, 94 New York, 03/24/1875, Lumbar abscess, Home Cemetery.

GRAY, Lyman – E, 67 Ohio, 05/17/1872, Typhoid fever, Home Cemetery.

GREEN, George – H, 27 Wisconsin, 02/20/1872, Anaemia, Home Cemetery.

GRIESER, John – L, 5 NewYork Cav., 02/13/1874, Senility, Home Cemetery.

GRASSLER, Johann – G, 15 Wisconsin, 04/11/1873, Consumption of bowels, Home Cemetery.

HACKERSON, Ole – B, 25 Wisconsin, 12/02/1877, Found frozen, Home Cemetery.

HAFFEY, Dennis – D, 3 New York Art., 05/05/1877, Hemorrhage-lungs, Home Cemetery.

HAGEMAN, August – D, 21 Illinois, 03/09/1871, Epilepsy, Forest Home Cemetery, Milwaukee, WI.

HAIGHT, James A. – E, 48 Indiana, 08/13/1875, Renal disease, Home Cemetery.

HALEY, Daniel J. – D, 1 Kentucky, 08/19/1872, Consumption, Home Cemetery.

HANIFER, Francis – D, 2 Delaware, 03/16/1871, Fit caused by drink, Forest Home Cemetery, Milwaukee, WI.

HANNAN, Michael – K, 76 New York, 05/23/1870, Typhoid fever, Calvary Cemetery, Milwaukee, WI

HARDIN, Augustin – K, 13 Wisconsin, 09/21/1877, Renal & Cystic disease, Home Cemetery.

HARRINGTON, Cornelius – F, 8 Illinois Cav., 06/19/1877, Paralysis, Home Cemetery.

HASTINGS, Robert E. – H, 17 Wisconsin, 12/11/1873, Apoplexy-cerebral, Home Cemetery.

HAUBER, Augustin – G, 75 Pennsylvania, 11/25/1873, Congestion of lungs, Home Cemetery.

HAWKINS, George – 1 Wisconsin Heavy Art., 06/03/1873, Congestion of brain, Home Cemetery.

HAYS, Martin – B, 15 Illinois, 10/02/1875, Cancer, Calvary Cemetery, Milwaukee, WI.

HEALEY, Thomas – F, 17 Wisconsin, 10/01/1869, Rheumatism, died on leave, cemetery unknown.

HEARD, Sylvester D. – E, 1 Wisconsin Cav., 03/11/1870, Cancer in throat, Forest Home Cemetery, Milwaukee, WI.

HEFFRON, Thomas – E, 30 Wisconsin, 07/29/1874, Peritonitis, Home Cemetery.

HEIMGARTNER, John – E, 17 Missouri, 09/05/1876, Consumption, Home Cemetery.

HEMPLE, George W. – H, 28 Pennsylvania, 12/15/1877, Consumption, died on leave, Pittsburgh, Pennsylvania cemetery.

HERRON, Michael – K, 68 Illinois, 10/03/1870, Inflammation of bowels, Forest Home Cemetery, Milwaukee, WI.

HESSEMER, Chas. A. – B, 29 New York, 04/19/1873, Small pox, Home Cemetery.

HIGHLAND, Patrick – B, 161 New York, 01/15/1877, Drowned, Home Cemetery.

HIMMAH, Charles – War of 1812, 10/06/1871, died on leave, cause unknown, cemetery unknown.

48

HOOPER, John – D, 35 Wisconsin, 09/27/1871, Dropsy, Home Cemetery.

HOUGHTON, Thomas G. – B, 65 Illinois, 06/01/1872, Apoplexy, Home Cemetery.

HOVEY, Geo. W. – D, 13 Indiana, 06/17/1868, Phthisis pulmonalis, Forest Home Cemetery, Milwaukee, WI.

HUNT, John – B, 1 New York, 10/05/1876, Renal hemorrhage, Home Cemetery.

HUNT, John – E, 4 Rhode Island, 10/02/1877, Railroad accident, Blackstone, Massachusetts cemetery.

HURLEY, Patrick – D, 16 U. S. Infantry, 02/28/1874, Consumption, Home Cemetery.

JACKSON, Robert – C, 10 U. S. Inf., 10/18/1874, Heart disease, Home Cemetery.

JACOBS, Gottlieb – B, 2 Missouri Light Art., 10/19/1873, Consumption, Home Cemetery.

JEWELL, John – E, 35 Wisconsin, at time of enlistment lived in Milwaukee, WI, died in *Wisconsin Soldiers' Home, Milwaukee, WI, 01/29/1865, cause unknown, cemetery unknown.

JOHNSON, John – H, 39 Wisconsin, lived In Oconto, WI at time of enlistment, died *Wisconsin Soldiers' Home, Milwaukee, WI, 09/20/1864, cause unknown, cemetery unknown.

JOHNSON, Mark –K, 26 Pennsylvania, 09/02/1870, Lumbar abscess, Forest Home Cemetery, Milwaukee, WI.

JONES, Lewis J. – C, 7 Ohio, 02/09/1877, Consumption, Dayton, Ohio cemetery.

JOSEPH, Joseph M. – K, 66 New York, 05/03/1875, Pneumonia, Jewish cemetery place unknown.

KAHLER, Louis – I, 13 New Jersey, 0913/1873, Fall from roof of Home, Home Cemetery.

KEEFE, John – D, 13 New York, 09/22/1876, Pneumonia, Home Cemetery.

KELLY, Edward – I, 35 Wisconsin, 11/22/1864, lived in Ironton, WI at time of enlistment, died in *Wisconsin Soldiers' Home, Milwaukee, WI 11/22/1864, cause of death unknown, cemetery unknown.

KELLY, John – B, 67 New York, 03/07/1874, Pleuro-pneumonia, Home Cemetery.

KENENWAY, John – I, 6 Kentucky, 11/21/1872, Consumption, Home Cemetery.

KENNEDY, Wm. – I, 2 Pennsylvania Heavy Art., 08/06/1872, Railroad accident, Home Cemetery.

KIFFEL, George – G, 9 Wisconsin, 01/12/1869, Consumption, died while on leave, cemetery unknown.

KILLIAN, Wm. – A, 2 U. S. Art., 04/20/1871, Consumption, Forest Home Cemetery, Milwaukee, WI.

KIMBALL, Henry F. – __, 37 Illinois, died in *Wisconsin Soldiers' Home*, Milwaukee, WI, 04/27/1865, Consumption, cemetery unknown.

KIMBALL, Henry F. - __, 2 Wisconsin Cav., died *Wisconsin Sol diers' Home*, Milwaukee, WI 05/23/1866, Typhoid fever, cemetery unknown.

KIMBALL, Joseph – D, 17 Wisconsin, 09/01/1867, Remittent Fever, Forest Home Cemetery, Milwaukee, WI.

KIMBALL, Will. L. – A, 12 Massachusetts, 09/19/1868, Phthisis pulmonalis, Forest Home Cemetery, Milwaukee, WI.

KINNEY, Thomas – E, 19 Wisconsin, 02/21/1871, Bronchitis, Home Cemetery.

KIWOSKY, Gustavus – L, 4 Missouri Cav., 09/22/1876, Ulceration of bowels, Home Cemetery.

KLAGES, John C. – F, 37 Iowa, 04/10/1876, Apoplexy, Home Cemetery.

KLEAHR, Fred. – D, 1 Louisiana Cav., 03/16/1876, Dropsy, Home Cemetery.

KOCHER, John – A, 18 Wisconsin, 06/23/1871, Consumption, Home Cemetery.

KOELPIN, John – H, 24 Illinois, 04/30/1874, Lumbar abscess, Home Cemetery.

KOERNER, Hugo – D, 1 Wisconsin, 12/14/1872, Hemorrhage-lungs, Home Cemetery.

KOESTER, Frank – A, 52 Wisconsin, 08/11/1876, Consumption, Home Cemetery.

KOSTMAN, Carl – C, 3 Iowa Cav., 12/10/1877, Consumption, Home Cemetery.

KRATZSOH, John – F, 9 Wisconsin, 02/24/1868, Inflammation of stomach, Forest Home Cemetery, Milwaukee, WI.

50

KRESSMAN, Heinrich – I, 88 Illinois, 05/10/1875, Collapse of lungs, Home Cemetery.

LAHY, Kam – C, 41 Wisconsin, lived in Greenfield, WI at time of enlistment, died in *Wisconsin Soldiers' Home ,Milwaukee, WI, 10/30/1864, cause unknown, cemetery unknown.

LANNING, Patrick C. – I, 15 Massachusetts, 03/07/1876, Concussion of brain, died while on leave, Milwaukee, WI cemetery.

LARKIN, Thomas – F, 5 Wisconsin, 04/20/1976, Dropsy, Home Cemetery.

LEAVITT, E. – Company & Regiment unknown, lived in Oshkosh, WI at time of enlistment, died in *Wisconsin Soldiers' Home, Milwaukee, WI, 03/01/1866, Chronic diarrhoea, cemetery unknown.

LEE, Wm. – B, 60 Indiana, 10/16/1870, died while on leave cause unknown, Forest Home Cemetery, Milwaukee, WI.

LEISCHEL, August – E, 98 Pennsylvania, 07/30/1870, Phthisis pulmonalis, Forest Home Cemetery, Milwaukee, WI.

LEMBRICHT, F. – M, 4 Missouri Cav., died in *Wisconsin Soldiers' Home, Milwaukee, WI, 10/31/1866, Apoplexy, cemetery unknown.

LOFTIS, Thomas – G, 82, New York, 05/17/1875, Congestive chill, Home Cemetery.

LUCAS, Joseph – B, 24 Michigan, 01/09/1873, Sequela to erysipelas, Home Cemetery.

LUDECK, Albert – L, 102 New York, 10/27/1871, Apoplexy, Home Cemetery.

LUNZ, John – G, 113 Illinois, 02/11/1870, Chronic dysentery, Forest Home Cemetery, Milwaukee, WI.

LUTZ, Henry – E, 8 Kansas, discharged from Home 09/01/1870, died 05/18/1874, Railroad accident near Milwaukee, WI, cemetery unknown.

LYONS, Jeremiah – L, 14 Illinois Cav., 12/20/1875, Railroad accident while on leave, cemetery unknown.

MAHONEY, Michael – E, 57 New York, 06/23/1876, Consumption, Home Cemetery.

MALONEY, Michael – U. S. Navy, 08/__/1867, Consumption, Calvary Cemetery, Milwaukee, WI.

MANNING, Patrick – Company & Regiment unknown, died in *Wisconsin Soldiers' Home,* Milwaukee, WI, 03/27/1867, Erysipelas, cemetery unknown.

MANNING, Peter – E, 19 Massachusetts, 03/20/1875, Chronic hepatitis, Home Cemetery.

MARQUERINCK, Gerritt – H, 2 Wisconsin Cav., 10/01/1877, Surgical operation, Home Cemetery.

MARSH, Darius – E, 10 Wisconsin, 05/05/1871, died while on leave, cause unknown, Portage, WI cemetery.

MASON, Joseph – K, 31 Wisconsin, 09/19/1972, General debility, Home Cemetery.

MATTHEWS, Patrick H. – D, 61 New York, 12/03/1873, Disease of stomach, Home Cemetery.

MAYERS, John – B, 3 U. S. Reserve Corps, 08/23/1877, Senile decay, Home Cemetery.

MCADAM, James – E, 4 Kentucky, 07/28/1876, Cancer, Home Cemetery.

MCCAIGNE, Michael – I, 2 Wisconsin Cav., 01/14/1872, Frozen, Calvary Cemetery, Milwaukee, WI.

MCCARTHY, Wm. – I, 72 Pennsylvania, 01/05/1873, Heart disease, Home Cemetery.

MCCLELLAN, Charles – I, 8 Michigan Cav., 04/16/1870, Disease of bladder, Forest Home Cemetery, Milwaukee, WI

MCCOY, James – F. 164 New York, 05/29/1868, Chronic diarrhoea, Forest Home Cemetery, Milwaukee, WI.

MCDONALD, Thom. B. – U. S. Navy, 06/10/1874, Marasmus, Home Cemetery.

MCDOUGALL, John – K, 481 New York, 04/28/1874, Constriction of larynx, Home Cemetery.

MCINERNEY, Dennis – H, 23 Illinois, 03/26/1871, Convulsions, Calvary Cemetery, Milwaukee, WI.

MCINTOSH, Thomas – E, 97 Pennsylvania, 05/23/1874, Apoplexy, Home Cemetery.

MCINTYRE, Hugo – C, 12 New Jersey, 07/01/1872, Heart disease, Home Cemetery.

MCLAUGHLIN, Thomas – H, 105 New York, 06/19/1871, Consumption, Home Cemetery.

MCLEAN, Thomas – K, 72 Illinois, 08/05/1874, Scrofula, Home Cemetery.

MEIGHAN, Peter – F, 16 U. S. Infantry, 08/29/1876, died while on leave, cause unknown, Chicago, IL cemetery.

MERCKER, Wm. C. – 1 Ohio Brig. Band, 10/22/1872, Cancer in stomach, Home Cemetery.

MERKEL, Joseph – A, 17 Illinois Cav., 05/06/1873, Inflammation of bowels, Home Cemetery.

METZGER, John – D, 21 Wisconsin, 10/16/1876, Consumption, Home Cemetery.

MEYER, Andrew – K, 15 Missouri, 11/28/1875, Hepatitis, Home Cemetery.

MEYER, Gottlieb – D, 82 Illinois, 05/31/1873, Consumption, Home Cemetery.

MEYER, Henry – A, 142 Illinois, 05/31/1872, Haematuria, Home Cemetery.

MEYERS, Hiram D. – H, 8 New York Heavy.Art., 12/12/1877, Consumption, Home Cemetery.

MILLER, Jacob F. – __, 37 New York, 01/11/1872, Dropsy-heart, Home Cemetery.

MILLER, Michael – B, 1 Maryland Cav., 09/06/1876, Dropsy, Home Cemetery

MILLIGAN, Robert – H, 41 Wisconsin, lived in Milwaukee, WI at time of enlistment, died in *Wisconsin Soldiers' Home, Milwaukee, WI, 10/02/1865, cause of death unknown, cemetery unknown.

MINEHEART, Henry – E, 11 Pennsylvania Cav., 05/03/1876, Heart disease, Home Cemetery.

MINNICK, David – H, 27 Wisconsin, died in *Wisconsin Soldiers' Home, Milwaukee, WI, 11/06/1864, cause of death unknown, cemetery unknown.

MITCHELL, John – C, 8 Michigan Cav., 02/09/1875, Consumption, Home Cemetery.

MOODIE, James – F, 18 New York, 11/18/1876, Heart disease, Home Cemetery.

MOSER, Hugh – I, 93 Illinois, 07/01/1870, Epileptic fit, Forest Home Cemetery.

MULLIGAN, John P. – F, 13 New Hampshire, 03/15/1877, Consumption, Home Cemetery.

MURRAY, John – B, 57 Massachusetts, 03/28/1874, Consumption, Home Cemetery.

MURTHA, Michael – H, 159 New York, 12/26/1873, Dropsy, Home Cemetery.

NAYS, Louis – G, 17 Wisconsin, 10/14/1874, Apoplexy, Home Cemetery.

NICKLES, Thomas – E, 55 Illinois, 08/23/1876, Consumption, Home Cemetery.

NISSAN, James P. – U. S. Marine Corps, 09/22/1870, Consumption, Forest Home Cemetery, Milwaukee, WI.

NUGENT, James – E, 19 Wisconsin, 01/29/1872, Consumption, Home Cemetery.

O'BRIEN, Patrick – C, 48 New York, Phthisis pulmonalis, Calvary Cemetery, Milwaukee, WI.

O'BRIEN, Thomas – F, 6 Missouri, 03/05/1875, Dropsy, Home Cemetery.

O'CONNOR, Dennis – I, 29, Michigan, 10/15/1871, died while on leave, cause unknown, Maple Valley, Michigan cemetery.

O'CONNOR, Michael – M, 6 Kansas Cav., 03/24/1877, Locomotor ataxia, Home Cemetery.

O'CONNOR, Timothy – E, 60 Massachusetts, 08/17/1872, Consumption, Home Cemetery.

O'DELL, Ezekiel – War of 1812, 10/14/1872, Heart disease, died while on leave, Racine, WI cemetery.

O'LEARY, Michael – I, 3 Wisconsin, 07/19/1868, Consumption, Calvary Cemetery, Milwaukee, WI.

O'NEAL, Patrick – I, 1 Wisconsin Heavy Art., 07/24/1874, Meningitis, Home Cemetery.

O'REGAN, Michael – D, 36 New York, 12/19/1869, Phthisis pulmonalis, Calvary Cemetery, Milwaukee, WI.

O'ROURKE, Thomas – G, 14 Michigan, 04/19/1869, Senile debility, Calvary Cemetery, Milwaukee, WI.

ORTELL, George – D, 26 Wisconsin, died in *Wisconsin Soldiers' Home,* Milwaukee, WI, 12/26/1866, Consumption, cemetery unknown.

OTTO, Urban – M, 13 Pennsylvania Cav., 03/12/1871, Bleeding from lungs, Calvary Cemetery, Milwaukee, WI.

OUDIN, Eugene – E, 47 N. Y., 04/27/1871, cause of death unknown, Calvary Cemetery. Milwaukee, WI.

PARKER, William J. – C, 22 New York Cav., 09/22/1872, Consumption, Home Cemetery.

PARUCKER, Nicholas – D, 15 U. S. Infantry, 08/10/1877, Heart disease, Home Cemetery.

PEITSCH, Edmund – D, 14 New York, 09/07/1877, Consumption, Home Cemetery.

PELHAM, Theodore – K, 50 New York, 12/01/1872, Pneumonia, Home Cemetery.

PENDLEBERG, Abraham – A, 2 New York Heavy Art., 10/07/1869, Phthisis pulmonalis, Forest Home Cemetery, Milwaukee, WI.

PERRY, William – F, 10 New York, 01/24/1872, Consumption, Home Cemetery.

PERTHOLD, Lewis – G, 26 Wisconsin, 04/03/1877, Drowned while on leave, Home Cemetery.

PETERSON, William – U. S. Navy, 10/07/1872, Scorbutus, Home Cemetery.

PFEIFFER, John – I, 52 New York, 12/26/1872, Paralysis, Home Cemetery.

PHILIP, Frank – H, 19 Wisconsin, 04/09/1876, Consumption, Home Cemetery.

PIRIE, Robert – D, 6 Wisconsin, 01/08/1877, died while on leave, cause unknown, Milwaukee, WI cemetery.

PLATT, Andrew – K, 2 Wisconsin, 12/31/1875, died while on leave, cause unknown, Baraboo, WI cemetery.

POPP, Martin – E, 55 Illinois, 06/13/1874, Congestion of lungs, Home Cemetery.

POTTS, Samuel K. – H, 7 Wisconsin, 11/26/1871, Chronic diarrhoea, Home Cemetery.

PRITZEHELLY, John – K, 24 Illinois, 04/16/1874, Consumption, Home Cemetery.

PUTT, John – B, 46 Wisconsin, 03/05/1874, Consumption, Home Cemetery.

QUINN, James – C, 73 Pennsylvania, 04/13/1875, Consumption, Home Cemetery.

QUINN, Michael – B, 55 New York, 03/23/1873, Consumption, Home Cemetery.

RAUSH, Adam – F, 62 New York, 06/09/1877, Hemorrhage, Home Cemetery.

REA, Thomas L. – I, 2 Illinois Cav., 09/09/1869, Phthisis pulmonalis, Forest Home Cemetery, Milwaukee, WI,

REED, Thomas M. – B, 1 Michigan Engineers, 09/14/1877, Paralysis, Home Cemetery.

REEDER, George W. – I, 14 Wisconsin, 01/14/1873, Necrosis of skull, Home Cemetery.

REEVES, Albert – I, 35 Wisconsin, 08/23/1870, Phthisis pulmonalis, Forest Home Cemetery, Milwaukee, WI.

REICK, Charles – __, 32 Wisconsin, died in *Wisconsin Soldiers' Home, Milwaukee, WI, 6/20/1865, Chronic diarrhoea, cemetery unknown.

REINER, Elias – D, 74 Pennsylvania, 11/01/1870, Hemorrhage-lungs, Home Cemetery.

RENECKE, Charles – K, 1 Kansas, 121/03/1877, Paralysis, Home Cemetery.

RHODES, James – D, 18 U. S. Infantry, 02/09/1875, Consumption, Home Cemetery.

RICH, Henry – C, 22 Indiana, 04/04/1874, Consumption, Home Cemetery.

RICKER, John S. – C, 5 New Hampshire, 11/04/1874, died while on leave, Drowned, Dunleith, Illinois cemetery.

RING, John G. – H, 148 New York, 08/04/1874, Consumption, Home Cemetery.

RING, Patrick – K, 6 Missouri, 07/16/1873, Diabetes, Home Cemetery.

RIPLEY, J. A. – K, 38 Wisconsin, died in *Wisconsin Soldiers' Home, Milwaukee, WI, 12/10/1866, Consumption, cemetery unknown.

ROBBINS, John D. – G, 5 New York Art., 10/26/1873, Apoplexy, Home Cemetery.

ROBERTS, Sidney – C, 64 Illinois, 11/06/1877, Railroad accident, Home Cemetery.

ROBEY, George – H, 22 Massachusetts, 10/23/1869, Phthisis pulmonalis, Forest Home Cemetery, Milwaukee, WI.

ROOT, Cyrus – War of 1812, 08/19/1876, Old age, Home Cemetery.

ROOT, Elias B. – __, 142 Illinois, 06/05/1873, Apoplexy, Home Cemetery.

ROTH, Frederick – G, 16 Michigan, 03/26/1875, Gastrosis, Home Cemetery.

RUNYON, Samuel – A, 1 New York Cav., 05/21/1875, Apoplexy, Home Cemetery.

RUSSELL, Sidney D. – 6 U. S. Infantry, 07/13/1873, Sunstroke, Home Cemetery.

SANDS, Patrick – A, 4 New York, 12/19/1877, Ulceration of stomach, Home Cemetery

SCHAEFFER, John F. – D, 9 Iowa Cav., 12/25/1867, Paralysis, Forest Home Cemetery, Milwaukee, WI.

SCHILLER, Frederick – K, 7 New York, 07/08/1874, Pneumonia, Home Cemetery.

SCHILLING, Egnas – E, 5 Missouri, 01/13/1871, Chronic diarrhoea, Calvary Cemetery, Milwaukee, WI.

SCHLEISSELBERGER, Edw. – B, 3 Missouri, 05/24/1871, Chronic diarrhoea, Home Cemetery.

SCHLOSSER, Albert – F, 98 Pennsylvania, 10/13/1872, Apoplexy, Home Cemetery.

SCHMIDT, Henry – H, 90 Illinois, 09/11/1870, Hernia, Forest Home Cemetery, Milwaukee, WI.

SCHMIDT, Mathias – K, 12 Illinois Cav., 03/22/1873, Apoplexy, Home Cemetery.

SCHMITZ, Matthias – K, 3 Missouri, 12/30/1875, Heart disease, Home Cemetery.

SCHNEITER, John – F, 9 Wisconsin, 06/18/1877, Diabetes mellitus, Home Cemetery.

SCHNITZLER, William – K, 26 Wisconsin, 08/26/1872, Cancer, Home Cemetery.

SCHOELL, Michael – F, 74 Pennsylvania, 03/22/1874, Consumption, Home Cemetery.

SCHROEDER, Ernest – I, 32 Illinois, 03/21/1875, Apoplexy-cerebral, Home Cemetery.

SCHULE, Frederick – C, 75 Pennsylvania, 05/14/1870, Dropsy-heart, Forest Home Cemetery, Milwaukee, WI.

SCRIBNER, Charles J. – E, 1 Wisconsin, 04/11/1871, Suicide by hanging, Forest Home Cemetery, Milwaukee, WI.

SCULLY, William – D, 12 New York Cav., 09/28/1873, Renal dropsy of chest, Home Cemetery.

SEATON, George G. – K, 1 Wisconsin Cav., 08/02/1876, Cystitis, Home Cemetery.

SELLS, Jacob – A, 15 Iowa, 04/20/1871, Consumption, Forest Home Cemetery, Milwaukee, WI.

SEVEY, Frank W. – A, 1 Wisconsin Cav., 04/30/1875, Consumption, Home Cemetery.

SHARP, Stephen – M, 10 Michigan Cav., 10/23/1871, Old age, Home Cemetery.

SHERRY, John – 8 Wisconsin Battery, died in *Wisconsin Soldiers' Home*, Milwaukee, WI, 01/04/1866, Consumption, cemetery unknown.

SIEFERT, Nicholas – A, 58 Ohio, 04/13/1874, Pleurisy, Home Cemetery.

SILLER, Louis R. G. – 2 Wisconsin Battery, 10/15/1877, Malignant variola, Home Cemetery.

SIMONS, Fletcher – F, 117 New York, 06/09/1874, Congestion of brain, Home Cemetery.

SINGER, Joseph – H, 64 New York, 10/12/1872, Congestion of lungs, Home Cemetery.

SLATTERY, Robert – F, 3 Rhode Island Heavy Art., 02/19/1871, Consumption, Calvery Cemetery, Milwaukee, WI.

SLOAT, Myron – I, 8 New York Cav., 07/31/1874, Typhoid fever, Home Cemetery.

SMALL, Thomas – H, 60 New York, 01/06/1870, died while on leave, cause unknown, cemetery unknown.

SMITH, Charles – B, 63 New York, 04/01/1875, Consumption, Home Cemetery.

SMITH, James – D, 5 Maryland, discharged from home 10/18/1871, died 10/14/1877 of Heart disease in Milwaukee, WI, Home Cemetery.

SMITH, James J. – C, 9 Illinois, 08/08/1876, Hypertrophy of liver, Home Cemetery.

SNYDER, Joseph – I, 16 Michigan, 07/25/1875, Tuberculosis, Home Cemetery.

SPENCER, John C. – H, 3 Indiana Cav., 08/29/1871, Scrofula, Home Cemetery.

SPENCER, Thomas – D, 6 Wisconsin, 11/27/1870, Consumption, Forest Home Cemetery, Milwaukee, WI.

STALSMITH, Eoban – H, 15 New York H. A., 12/19/1877, died while on leave, Liver disease, Home Cemetery.

STENSON, John – K, 122 New York, 05/10/1873, Consumption, Home Cemetery.

STINKEY, John – A, 82 Illinois, 05/23/1867, died while on leave, Rheumatism, cemetery unknown.

STONBROUGH, Thos. M. – G, 56 New York, 03/01/1874, Scrofula, Home Cemetery.

SULLIVAN, David Jr. – I, 35 Massachusetts, 10/20/1872, Railroad accident, Home Cemetery.

SULLIVAN, Humphrey – C, 28 Massachusetts, 09/11/1871, Consumption, Home Cemetery.

SULLIVAN, John – F, 45 Illinois, 06/07/1875, Consumption, Home Cemetery.

SWEENEY, Robert – A, 23 Wisconsin, 08/27/1877, Consumption, Home Cemetery.

TANNER, Charles – Company & Regiment unknown, died in *Wisconsin Soldiers' Home*. Milwaukee, WI, 02/29/1867, Paralysis, cemetery unknown.

TEAL, David H. – D, 3 New York Cav., 02/07/1872, Chorea, Home Cemetery.

TENNEY, David – Company & Regiment unknown, at time of enlistment lived in Wautoma, WI, blind, died in *Wisconsin Soldiers' Home,* Milwaukee, WI, 07/23/1866, Consumption, cemetery unknown.

THIECK, Rudolph – K, 5 Michigan, 02/28/1872, Cancer in stomach, Home Cemetery.

THOMAS, James H. – D, 19 Wisconsin, 01/21/1868, Chronic diarrhoea, Forest Home Cemetery, Milwaukee, WI.

THOMPSON, Frank – F, 1 Connecticut, 11/23/1877, Ulceration of stomach, Home Cemetery.

THOMPSON, Leander – F, 56 New York, 05/02/1869, Phthisis pulmonalis, Forest Home Cemetery, Milwaukee, WI.

THORNBERRY, Edw. – A, 67 New York, 12/26/1874, Senility, Home Cemetery.

TILLMAN, William – D, 10 New York, 07/01/1871, Consumption, Forest Home Cemetery, Milwaukee, WI.

TUCKER, Samuel – A, 31 Wisconsin, 04/16/1870, Phthisis pulmonalis, Forest Home Cemetery, Milwaukee, WI.

TURNER, Daniel – B, 13 Wisconsin, 12/27/1871, Frozen to death, Home Cemetery.

TURNER, Henry A. – C, 16 Wisconsin, 10/12/1868, Chronic diarrhoea, Forest Home Cemetery, Milwaukee, WI.

TURNER, Lyman – A, 4 Michigan Cav., 08/10/1875, Dropsy, Home Cemetery.

TYNE, Zachariah – H, 23 Illinois, 02/08/1874, Pneumonia, Jewish cemetery place unknown.

VAIL, John – K, 2 Massachusetts, 07/17/1877, Consumption, Home Cemetery.

VANDOOZER, William W. – A, 27 Wisconsin, 05/26/1877, Consumption, Home Cemetery.

VANDOVER, James M. – G, 62 Illinois, 04/04/1869, Pulmonary consumption, Forest Home Cemetery, Milwaukee, WI.

VAN WAGENEN, William – A, 18 Wisconsin, 10/30/1877, Fall from embankment, Home Cemetery.

VERDON, James – A, 17 U. S. Infantry, 07/28/1871, died while on leave, cause unknown, Milwaukee, WI cemetery.

WALDO Joseph – H, 39 Wisconsin, lived in Green Bay, WI at time of enlistment, died in *Wisconsin Soldiers' Home*, Milwaukee, WI, 09/21/1864, cause unknown, cemetery unknown.

WALLIS, Ira – H, 47 New York, 11/14/1873, Old age, Home Cemetery.

WALSH, John J. – A, 2 New York Art., 05/26/1871, Pyaemia, Home Cemetery.

WALSH, Roger L. – E, 8 Ohio, 05/06/1876, Remittent fever, Home Cemetery.

WARNER, George R. – K, 9 Ohio, day & month of death unknown, 1868, Drowned, Lake Michigan.

WASHBURN, Henry – F, 11 Illinois, 12/02/1877, Paralysis, Home Cemetery.

WEBER, William – K, 24 Illinois, 01/02/1876, died while on leave, Dropsy, Milwaukee, WI cemetery.

WECK, Otto – A, 46 New York, 04/11/1871, Consumption, Forest Home Cemetery, Milwaukee, WI.

WEIR, William – C, 33 Wisconsin, 07/06/1877, died while on leave, cause unknown, Portage, WI cemetery.

WELSH, Michael – D, 51 N. Y., 01/17/1876, died while on leave, cause unknown, New York City cemetery,

WERTZ, Anthony – F, 14 Michigan, 08/02/1868, Inflammation of bowels, Forest Home Cemetery, Milwaukee, WI.

WHEELER, Frederick – K, 8 New York Cav., 01/18/1877, Pneumonia, Home Cemetery.

WHITE, James – B, 100 Pennsylvania, 09/25/1869, died while on leave, cause unknown, cemetery unknown.

WHITE, James – E, 19 Wisconsin, 11/11/1869, Phthisis pulmonalis, Forest Home Cemetery, Milwaukee, WI.

WHITE, John – B, 111 New York, 02/20/1871, Consumption, Forest Home Cemetery, Milwaukee, WI.

WHITNEY, Joseph – H, 39 Wisconsin, lived in Oconto, WI at time of enlistment, died in *Wisconsin Soldiers' Home, Milwaukee, WI, 09/21/1864, cause unknown, cemetery unknown.

WIGGINS, Eli – A, 18 Wisconsin, 12/30/1874, Consumption, Home Cemetery.

WIGMORE, Joseph F. – __, 1 & 17 Wisconsin, 05/02/1874, Sequela to an acute disease, Home Cemetery.

WILSON, E. H. – I, 8 Kansas, 03/29/1874, Dropsy, Home Cemetery.

WILSON, Mattis. – H, 39 Wisconsin, lived in Green Bay, WI at time of enlistment, died in *Wisconsin Soldiers' Home, Milwaukee, WI, 09/24/1864, cause unknown, cemetery unknown.

WINSLOW, John P. – B, 58 Illinois, 04/28/1875, died while on leave, Consumption, Chicago, IL cemetery.

WOOD, Charles – Company & Regiment unknown, lived in Sheboygan, WI at time of enlistment, died in *Wisconsin Soldiers' Home, Milwaukee, WI, 07/17/1865, Chronic diarrhoea, cemetery unknown.

WOOD, Thomas B. – I, 48 New York, 10/21/1873, Delirium tremens, Home Cemetery.

WOOLEY, John – __, Lt. Col., 8 Indiana, Appointed Deputy Governor of Home 09/14/1870, served until 12/31/1872, died in Milwaukee, WI, 04/06/1873, Home Cemetery.

YOUNG, David – F, 102 Illinois, 06/27/1877, Senile decay, Home Cemetery.

YOUNG, Frederick – E, 16 New York Heavy Art., 04/27/1877, Heart disease, Home Cemetery.

*Wisconsin Soldiers' Home, Milwaukee, WI, founded and maintained by the women of Milwaukee, WI until the establishment of Old Soldiers' Home in Wawautosa, WI.

Sources:

First Annual Report of the Wisconsin Soldiers' Home in Milwaukee for the Year Ending April 15, 1865. Daily Wisconsin Book and JOB Steam Printing House, 1865. Mrs. G. P. Hewitt, Jr., President.

Second Annual Report of the Wisconsin Soldiers' Home Milwaukee. Jermain & Brighton Sentinel Printing House, 1866. Mrs. G. P. Hewitt, Jr., President.

Third Annual Report and Memorial of the Wisconsin Soldiers' Home Milwaukee to the Legislature. Milwaukee Daily Wisconsin Printing House, corner east Water and Huron Streets, 1867. Mrs. C. K. Watkins, President

Annual Report of the Commandant and Treasurer of the Northwestern Branch National Home for Disabled Volunteer Soldiers. 1878. National Home Job Printing Office, near Milwaukee, Wisconsin, Gen. Edward W. Hincks, Commandant and Treasurer.

DEATHS IN 1878

FORMAT: NAME, COMPANY & REGIMENT, DATE OF ADMISSION, PLACE OF BIRTH, AGE, DATE OF DEATH, CAUSE OF DEATH, PLACE OF DEATH.

AIKEY, Samuel – B, 15 Illinois, 03/20/1878, Pennsylvania, 35, 04/14/1878, Accident by railroad car, Davis' Station, Illinois while on leave.

ALLEN, Robert – E, 11 Illinois Cav., 06/291878, New York, 73, 09/22/1878, Hepatitis, Home Hospital.

BOGART, Joseph – G, 17 Wisconsin, 10/06/1868, Belgium, 72, 08/13/1878, Senility, Home Hospital.

BOUCHER, George – A, 76 New York, 07/31/1878, Canada, 40, 08/03/1878, Alcoholism, Home Hospital.

BRAUER, George A. – B, 3 Wisconsin, 07/25/1878, Germany, 60, 09/01/1878, Consumption, Home Hospital.

BUCKLEY, Owen – C, 37 New York, 06/30/1870, Ireland, 45, 10/27/1878, Rheumatism, & Paralysis, Home Hospital.

BURDEN, Michael – H, 37 Iowa, 09/02/1873, Ireland, 59, 02/06/1878, Rupture of heart, Quarters.

CARROLL, Barney – G, 16 New York Heavy Art., 05/01/1873, Ireland, 58, 04/06/1878, Senile decay, Home Hospital.

CARROLL, James – B, 5 New York Heavy Art., 01/03/1876, Ireland, 71, 06/22/1878, Senile decay, Home Hospital.

CHANDLER, Hiram – D, 19 Wisconsin, 01/30/1878, New York, 39, 03/16/1878, Epileptic convulsions, Home Hospital.

CLARKE, Joseph – H, 72 Illinois, 04/29/1873, England, 72, 04/22/1878, Senile decay, Home Hospital.

CLINE, Michael – I, 17 Wisconsin, 01/15/1872, Ireland, 66, 11/18/1878, Accident in Milwaukee, WI, Home Hospital.

COOK, Cornelius – C, 96 New York, 08/28/1877, New York, 38, 03/10/1878, Cardiac disease, died in Evansville, Wisconsin while on leave.

DORN, William – E, 4 Illinois Cav., 9/08/1875, Ireland, 43, 10/04/1878, Cancer, Home Hospital.

ELLIOTT, James F. – B, 5 Wisconsin, 06/20/1878, Maine, 37, 06/21/1878, Consumption, Home Hospital.

FIELDS, George H. – F, 15 U. S. Infantry, 06/30/1873, Vermont, 57, 07/28/1878, Consumption, Home Hospital.

GORDON, George M. – B, 17 Wisconsin, 10/30/1877, Scotland, 55, 08/31/1878, Consumption, Home Hospital.

HAGAN, Andrew – B, 29 Ohio, 09/08/1877, Norway, 58, 07/28/1878, Exposure, found dead near the Home.

HANASE, Jacob – E, 16 Michigan, 12/08/1877, Michigan, 36, 12/29/1878, Cardiac disease, died in Lake County, Michigan while on leave.

HAYS, Patrick – C, 15 Illinois, 08/06/1978, Ireland, 32, 10/03/1878, Consumption, Home Hospital.

HENRY, William – G, 10 U. S. Infantry, 03/24/1869, Ireland, 57, 12/23/1878, Rheumatic carditis, Home Hospital.

HOFFER, Frederick – C, 14 Michigan, 01/08/1868, France, 69, 07/28/1878, Chronic bronchitis, Home Hospital.

HUNDHAUSEN, Fred. W. – __, Q. M. 26 Wisconsin, 07/06/1878, Germany, 51, 07/14/1878, Pulmonary consumption, Home Hospital.

IVES, Henry – G, 23, New York, 12/29/1873, Pennsylvania, 35, 03/24/1878, Alcoholism, Guardhouse.

KEARNEY, Dennis – H, 92 New York, 12/26/1876, Ireland, 52, 04/06/1878, Consumption, Home Hospital.

KEEFER, Logan F. – B, 99 Ohio, 03/08/1877, Pennsylvania, 34, 03/07/1878, Spermatorrhoea, Home Hospital.

KIMBALL, Charles C. – E, 1 Wisconsin, 01/04/1876, New York, 54, 04/29/1878, Consumption, Home Hospital.

KNIGHT, Charles H. – B, 5 New York Art., 11/26/1878, New York, 40, 12/04/1878, Diphtheria, Home Hospital.

LANGTRY, Phillip – A, 17 Wisconsin, 05/23/1867, Ireland, 63, 09/27/1878, Chronic cystitis, Home Hospital.

LINDSEY, James – G, 88 Illinois, 11/27/1877, Wisconsin, 29, 04/14/1878, Consumption, died in Milwaukee, WI while on leave.

MARSH, Alexander – D, 2 Minnesota Cav., 10/16/1877, New York, 43, 08/31/1878, Consumption, Home Hospital.

MEIGHAN, William H. – E, 3 Pennsylvania, 01/23/1878, Ireland, 37, 02/15/1878, Consumption, Home Hospital.

MOLLOY, Patrick – D, 1 Illinois Light Art., 09/16/1878, Ireland, 48, 11/24/1878, Consumption, Home Hospital.

MORTON, William H. – I, 24 Michigan, 01/17/1878, New York, 39, 05/25/1878, Hepatitis & Paralysis, Home Hospital.

MYERS, Henry W. – H, 30 Illinois, 06/01/1876, Germany, 35, 01/22/1878, Syphilis, Home Hospital.

NAUE, Ferdinand – A, 75 Pennsylvania, 03/22/1878, Germany, 67, 12/09/1878, Cancer, Home Hospital.

NORTON, Andrew – E, 19 Massachusetts, 01/21/1873, Ireland, 49, 08/13/1878, Alcoholism, Home Hospital.

OWENS, Phillip – D, 90 Illinois, 11/23/1876, New York, 70, 05/27/1878, Chronic bronchitis, Home Hospital.

PETER, AUGUST – E, 37 Wisconsin, 12/08/1877, Germany, 55, 12/17/1878, cause of death unknown, died in Huron Lake, Minnesota.

PORTER, Charles, - H. 18 New York, 05/08/1876, Connecticut, 72, 03/02/1878, Senility, Home Hospital.

RICH, John – K, 13 Wisconsin, 08/02/1869, Germany, 58, 08/27/1878, Hepatitis, Home Hospital.

RIEBLING, William – C, 9 Wisconsin, 06/01/1878, Germany, 47, 11/20/1978, Cancer, Home Hospital.

STEWART, James – B, 27 Michigan, 04/09/1878, Ireland, 42, 11/07/1878, Consumption, died in Lexington, Michigan while on leave.

STOREY, Morgan – B, 1 Wisconsin Heavy Art., 10/16/1874, New York, 66, 03/09/1878, Senility, Home Hospital.

SWAIN, William – B, 5 Minnesota, 06/19/1877, New York, 47, 04/25/1878, Insanity, Home Hospital.

TESKE, John – I, 3 Pennsylvania Art., 09/16/1876, Germany, 52, 11/10/1878, Consumption, Home Hospital.

TRUDELL, Charles – B, 7 Pennsylvania Cav., 10/16/1877, Canada, 57, 09/___/1878, died while on leave, cause of death unknown, place of death unknown.

VAN VORT, John – I, 61 Illinois, 05/07/1877, New York, 72, 01/20/1878, Senile decay, Home Hospital.

WILSON, Henry – I, 12 New York Cav, 01/28/1876. England, 70, 01/17/1878, Pneumonia, Home Hospital.

Source:
The Annual Report of the Commandant and Treasurer of the Northwestern Branch National Home for Disabled Volunteer Soldiers. 1879. Near Milwaukee, Wisconsin: National Home Job Printing Office. Gen. Edward W. Hincks, Commandant and Treasurer.

DEATHS IN 1879

FORMAT: NAME, COMPANY & REGIMENT, DATE OF ADMISSION, PLACE OF BIRTH, AGE, DATE OF DEATH, CAUSE OF DEATH, PLACE OF DEATH.

ALLEN, Levi – A, 3 Wisconsin Cav., 06/20/1878, New York, 56, 02/08/1879, Phthisis pulmonalis, Home Hospital.

AVERILL, Peter – M, 4 Missouri, 11/27/1877, Germany, 55, 09/12/1879, Phthisis pulmonalis, Home Hospital.

BATTERSON, Horace – K, 28 Illinois, 04/02/1878, Pennsylvania, 50, 01/10/1879, Phthisis pulmonalis, Home Hospital.

BELLOWS, William – G, 6 Kansas, 04/20/1870. Scotland, 68, 09/21/1879, Fall from porch, Home Hospital.

BENTZ, Frederick – E, 19 Wisconsin, 10/09/1870, Germany, 69, 09/29/1879, cause of death unknown, died in Milwaukee, WI while on leave.

BOCK, Louis – H, 24 Illinois, 06/14/1879, Germany, 60, 10/05/1879, Phthisis pulmonalis, Home Hospital.

BOLAND, Michael – E, 53 Illinois, 06/29/1877, New York, 49, 01/03/1879, Phthisis pulmonalis, Home Hospital.

BOWERS, Phillip – D, 149 Pennsylvania, 03/22/1879, Pennsylvania, 33, 11/08/1879, Phthisis pulmonalis, Home Hospital.

BUSHEY, Charles S. – G, 3 Wisconsin, 01/23/1879, Vermont, 43, 12/04/1879, Brain disease, Home Hospital.

CONLON, Michael – A, 117 New York, 10/28/1874, Ireland, 58, 01/22/1879, Bright's disease of kidneys, Home Hospital.

CORCORAN, Thomas – I, 6 Connecticut, 02/12/1878, Ireland, 39, 12/23/1879, Pulmonary hemorrhage, Home Hospital.

DOUGHERTY, Martin – H, 105 New York, 07/20/1878, Ireland, 57, 12/02/1879, Phthisis pulmonalis, Home Hospital.

FARRELL, Peter – B, 1 New York Art., 05/23/1879, Ireland, 52, 07/15/1879, Acute mania, Home Hospital.

FITZGIBBON, William - K, 19 Illinois, 09/05/1878, Illinois, 36, 01/14/1879, Phthisis pulmonalis, Home Hospital.

FITZPATRICK, Richard – F, 42 New York, 06/02/1870, Ireland, 55, 01/06/1879, Paralysis, Main building.

FLYNN, Michael – G, 8 Wisconsin, 01/10/1877, Ireland, 39, 06/23/1879, Phthisis pulmonalis, Home Hospital.

GORDON, Peter – C, 1 Louisiana, 05/06/1879, Scotland, 53, 08/27/1879, Cardiac disease, died in Milwaukee while on leave.

GODFREY, James – D, 5 Maine, 01/14/1878, Ireland, 39, 01/21/1879, Cerebral congestion, Home Hospital.

GROSS, Daniel – F, 58 Illinois, 02/23/1878, Germany, 57, 07/27/1879, Railroad accident near the Home, Home Hospital.

GROTTO, Louis – E, 21 Wisconsin, 09/16/1878, New York, 47, 02/17/1879, cause of death unknown, died in Chilton, WI while on leave.

HAHN, Hubert - __, 13 Wisconsin Battery, 05/05/1878, Germany, 55, 08/04/1879, Brain disease, Home Hospital.

HANLON, Maurice J. – B, 26 Michigan, 11/08/1868, Ireland, 73, 01/24/1879, Chronic hepatitis, Home Hospital.

HUFF, John – E, 184 Ohio, 11/18/1879, Germany, 39, 12/14/1879, Cardiac disease, Home Hospital.

JANNEE, Louis – B, 3 Wisconsin Cav., 07/06/1877, Belgium, 53, 09/20/1879, Cardiac disease, Home Hospital.

JENSEN, John – C, 1 Wisconsin, 10/22/1877, Norway, 38, 02/13/1879, Phthisis pulmonalis, Home Hospital.

JOHNSON, Joseph – B, 1 Michigan Light Art., 07/11/1879, New Jersey, 52, 07/12/1879, Cancer, Home Hospital.

KING, Matthew – Mexican War, 11/19/1878, Germany, 62, 11/02/1879, Chronic dysentery, Home Hospital.

LEE, John – I, 76 Pennsylvania, 08/30/1878, Ireland, 55, 02/26/1879, Phthisis pulmonalis, Home Hospital.

LEIST, Ferdinand - __, 3 New Jersey Light Art., 01/02/1877, Germany, 57, 06/29/1879, Phthisis pulmonalis, Home Hospital.

LYNCH, Timothy W. – A, 1 Illinois Light Art., 11/26/1869, Ireland, 44, 11/14/1879, Alcoholism, died in Wauwatosa, WI, absent without leave.

MCINTYRE, Thomas – I, 24 Wisconsin, 01/09/1877, Ireland, 57, 01/21/1879, Pulmonary hemorrhage, Home Hospital.

MEHL, Edward – A, 1 Wisconsin, 04/05/1878, Massachusetts, 43, 06/05/1879, Phthisis, pulmonalis, Home Hospital.

MENKE, John – C, 7 New York, 12/06/1878, Germany, 49, 10/23/1879, found dead near Home in Wauwatosa, WI, absent without leave.

MEYER, Leonard – A, 132 Pennsylvania, 07/03/1879, Germany, 60, 07/03/1879, Congestive chill, in Quarters.

MURRY, James – A, 1 U. S. Art., 08/30/1876, Ireland, 50, 03/11/1879, Ulcer of stomach, Home Hospital.

OGDEN, Joseph – G, 37 Illinois, 11/11/1874, Scotland, 68, 05/22/1879, Phthisis pulmonalis, Home Hospital.

PATCHIN, David C. – H, 193 New York, 10/11/1877, New York, 63, 09/23/1879, Paralysis of heart, died while on leave in Frankford, Minnesota.

PIERSON, John L. – War of 1812, 12/11/1877, New Jersey, 85, 06/10/1879, Senility, Home Hospital.

QUIGLEY, Thomas – F, 25 Michigan, 10/12/1879, New York, 37, 12/20/1879, Phthisis pulmonalis, Home Hospital.

ROBBINS, Joseph - __, 8 Wisconsin Battery, 06/18/1875, New York, 40, 03/12/1879, Phthisis pulmonalis, Home Hospital.

ROEBRIG, Antony – A, 11 Illinois Cav., 10/08/1878, France, 47, 03/18/1879, Phthisis pulmonalis, Home Hospital.

ROSENAU, John – I, 1 Illinois Light Art., 03/06/1875, Poland, 46, 10/02/1879, Apoplexy, Home Hospital.

SCHOTT, Gustavus – K, 9 Minnesota, 12/29/1876, Germany, 64, 12/29/1879, Tabes, Home Hospital.

STONE, Charles H. – H, 46 Illinois, 11/14/1876, New Jersey, 70, 08/27/1879, Cystitis and Diarrhoea, Home Hospital.

TRIM, Samuel – H, 50 New York, 07/26/1878, New York, 34, 03/17/1879, Phthisis pulmonalis, Home Hospital.

TURNER, Franklin – L, 2 Illinois Cav., 07/21/1876, Maine, 57, 01/06/1879, Phthisis pulmonalis, Home Hospital.

WATSON, George W. – K, 20 Illinois, 12/15/1877, Pennsylvania, 56, 08/21/1879, Railroad accident in Milwaukee while on leave.

WHITE, William P. – G, 19 Illinois, 05/26/1876, New York, 64, 07/06/1879, Phthisis pulmonalis, Home Hospital.

WILSON, William B. – A, 147 Illinois, 12/14/1878, Ireland, 53, 03/14/1879, Cancer of stomach, Home Hospital.

WISEMAN, James – H, 31 Maine, 10/04/1877, Ireland, 54, 03/17/1879, Cirrhosis of liver, died at his house on Home grounds.

WITTENBERGER, Andrew – B, 37 Iowa, 02/22/1878, Germany, 79, 06/16/1879, Cardiac disease, Home Hospital.

ZIMMERMAN, William – I, 9 Wisconsin, 04/01/1879, Germany, 62, 08/08/1879, Chronic cystitis, Home Hospital.

ZWICK, Alois – A, 105 New York, 04/14/1879, Germany, 54, 05/12/1879, Fracture of skull, Home Hospital.

Source:

Annual Report of the Commandant and Treasurer of the Northwestern Branch National Home for Disabled Volunteer Soldiers for the Fiscal Year Ending June 30, 1880. Milwaukee County, Wisconsin: National Home Printing Office.. Gen. Edward W. Hincks, Commandant

DEATHS IN 1880

FORMAT: NAME, COMPANY & REGIMENT, DATE OF ADMISSION, PLACE OF BIRTH, DATE OF DEATH, PLACE OF DEATH.

BUCKLEY, James – K, 53 Illinois, 07/02/1879, New York, 35 04/19/1880, Coxarium morbus, Home Hospital.

CLARK, John – D, 26, Illinois, 04/17/1877, Delaware, 64, 05/06/1880, Cardiac disease, Home Hospital.

CLARK, William – E, 2 Wisconsin Cav., 06/25/1875, England, 48, 03/16/1880, Epilepsy and Paralysis, Home Hospital.

COOK, Moses A. – F, 50 Wisconsin, 11/30/1872, New York, 58, 02/14/1880, Exhaustion from chorea, Home Hospital.

CORTWRIGHT, William – K, 187 Pennsylvania, 10/01/1879, Pennsylvania, 57, 02/01/1880, Paralysis, Home Hospital.

CUSHION, Patrick – C, 17 Wisconsin, 10/19/1876, Ireland, 37, 04/21/1880. Pneumonia, Home Hospital.

DEERY, Henry S. – K, 5 Wisconsin, 07/10/1874, New York, 41, 03/16/1880, Phthisis pulmonalis, Home Hospital.

DOWNING, Lucius – B, 10 Vermont, 07/21/1880, Vermont, 38, Lung disease, 07/25/1880, Home Hospital.

DUPON, Louis – I, 98 Pennsylvania, 08/13/1870, Germany, 53, 01/23/1880, Phthisis pulmonalis, Home Hospital.

EVANS, Griffith O. – Capt. Q. M. Dept., 03/19/1878, On the Sea, 47, 04/09/1880, Nervous exhaustion, Home Hospital.

FERGUSON, James D. – B, 11 Ohio, 09/20/1880, Scotland, 34, 09/27/1880, Concussion of brain, Home Hospital.

FINLIESON, Walter – I, 1 Wisconsin, 04/29/1880, Scotland, 74, 06/22/1880, Gastritis and Cystitis, Home Hospital.

FRANK, Phillip – M, 2 Illinois Art., 10/16/1877, Germany, 49, 01/13/1880, cause unknown, died in Mendota, Illinois while on leave.

GENUNG, Charles – H, 8 Minnesota, 08/16/1874, New Jersey, 72, 08/13/1880, Cancer, Home Hospital.

GOODIN, Amos H. – Mexican War, 12/31/1879, Missouri, 57, 01/11/1880, Phthisis pulmonalis, Home Hospital.

HAY, Henry – __, 13 Wisconsin Battery 06/30/ 1873, Mississippi, 39, 09/17/1880, Chronic myelitis, Home Hospital.

HIGGINS, Michael – I, 13 New York, 07/31/1873, Ireland, 60, 03/19/1880, Senility, Home Hospital.

HOPPE, Francis – G, 16 Iowa, 11/07/1873, Switzerland, 67, 04/20/1880, Apoplexy, Home Hospital.

HUMMEL, John – G, 32 Indiana, 05/15/1880, Germany, 60, 05/27/1880, Phthisis pulmonalis, Home Hospital.

IGRA, Henry – I, 39 Illinois, 10/28/1879, Germany, 47, 12/09/1880, Phthisis pulmonalis, Home Hospital.

KARCHER, Valentine – B, 1 Michigan Light Art., 03/02/1874, Germany, 64, 01/15/1880, Pneumonia, Home Hospital.

KIMBALL, Albert H. – F, 1 Michigan Engineers, 04/23/1879/ New Hampshire, 45, 04/19/1880, Chronic myelitis, Home Hospital.

KLAUDER, Frank – K, 1 Maryland, 02/16/1877, Germany, 44, 11/03/1880, Chronic Cystitis, Home Hospital.

KNAUBER, Michael – G, 12 Ohio, 01/07/1879, Germany, 53, 09/22/1880, Asthma, Home Hospital.

KOCH, John – C, 52 New York, 12/17/1874, Germany, 49, 11/12/1880, Cardiac disease, died in Milwaukee, WI while on leave.

LATERNICHT, John – C, 80 Illinois, 03/05/1880, Germany, 60, 03/20/1880, Heart disease, Home Hospital.

LINDBERG, Paul James – I, 61 Illinois, 12/16/1867, On the Sea, 77, 03/11/1880, Exposure, Home Hospital.

LOCKER, Lorenz – D, 26 Wisconsin, 10/08/1880, Germany, 57, 10/11/1880, Paralysis, Home Hospital.

LUSTOFKA, Wenzel – I, 26 Wisconsin, 10/04/1880, Austria, 36 10/05/1880, Phthisis pulmonalis, Home Hospital.

MAFFETT, Eugene – I, 97 New York, 01/27/1880, New York, 35, 04/01/1880, Phthisis pulmonalis, Home Hospital.

MANGAN, Michael – C, 17 Wisconsin, 07/21/1880, Ireland, 60, 11/01/1880, Cancer, Home Hospital.

MANN, Moritz – F, 9 Wisconsin, 12/21/1875, Germany, 61, 12/23/1880, Phthisis pulmonalis, Home Hospital.

MAYHEW, Martin – F, 1 Wisconsin Cav., 10/08/1878, Connecticut, 44, 10/09/1880, Chronic diarrhoea, Home Hospital.

MULLADY, Patrick – C, 88 New York, 01/24/1880, Ireland, 36, 10/12/1880, Cardiac disease, Home Hospital.

MURPHY, Francis T. – F, 72 Illinois, 01/30/1880, New York, 43, 02/10/1880, Phthisis pulmonalis, Home Hospital.

MURPHY, Thomas C. – I, 4 Illinois, 11/23/1879, New Hampshire, 50, 05/09/1880, Pneumonia, Home Hospital.

O'CONNOR, John – A, 7 Wisconsin, 06/29/1871, Ireland, 69, Phthisis pulmonalis, Home Hospital.

O'DELL, Henry – H, 45 Pennsylvania, 05/15/1880, Pennsylvania, 52, 06/05/1880, Paralysis, Home Hospital.

O'NEIL, John – G, 106 Pennsylvania, 10/29/1874, Ireland, 73, 12/04/1880, Hemoptisis (hemoptysis), Main Building.

PHELPS, George A. – E, 6 Wisconsin, 10/04/1880, Michigan, 38, 11/22/1880, Hemorrhage, died in Milwaukee while on pass.

PITZHOLD, August – A, 12 Pennsylvania Cav., 12/07/1880, Germany, 55, 12/09/1880, Phthisis pulmonalis, Home Hospital.

RACK, Christian – F, 12 Illinois, 07/27/1877, Germany, 66, 09/12/1880, Phthisis pulmonalis, Home Hospital.

RAFFERTY, William A. – L, 21 Pennsylvania Cav., 09/15/1880, Pennsylvania, 33, 11/15/1880, Hemoptisis (hemoptysis), Home Hospital.

ROBINSON, James W. – D, 19 Wisconsin, 10/24/1879, New York, 45, 06/15/1880, Phthisis pulmonalis, Home Hospital.

RONAYNE, Michael – C, 99 New York, 05/08/1877, Ireland, 37, 03/26/1880, Drowned in Big Sioux River, died near Flandreau, D. T. while on leave.

RUSSELL, Robert – C, 14 Illinois Cav., 09/24/1877, Canada, 42, 11/12/1880, Paralysis, Home Hospital.

THOMAS, Henry – G, 104 New York, 11/18/1875, Ireland, 79, 12/15/1880, Senility, Home Hospital.

TOWNSELY, Thomas T. – C, 56 New York, 01/22/1879, New York, 50, 01/17/1880, Asthma, Home Hospital.

VAN ALLEN, Peter – K, 15 New York, 10/13/1880, New York, 46, 10/29/1880, Cardiac disease, Home Hospital.

WALSH, Thomas – G, 18 Missouri, 11/11/1874, Ireland, 65, 08/30/1880, Cardiac disease, Main Building.

WELSH, James – A, 52 New York, 10/17/1875, Ireland, 48, 07/25/1880, Larynegal (laryngeal) Phthisis, Home Hospital.

WERNER, John M. – C, 9 Wisconsin, 01/17/1873, Germany, 42, 05/02/1880, Drowned in Menomonee River, died in Milwaukee while on leave.

WILES, Walter – G, 6 Wisconsin, 08/08/1876, England, 36, 12/04/1880, Exposure, Home Hospital.

WILKINSON, William G. – B, 71 Pennsylvania, 07/24/1874, England, 38, 01/11/1880, Suicide (shot himself), Quarters.

WILSON Samuel W. – __, Surg., 4 Wisconsin Cav., 07/27/1875, Massachusetts, 76, 01/25/1880, Apoplexy, Home Hospital.

WOOLNOUGH, Wm. R. – H, 3 Wisconsin, 09/12/1869, Wales, 63, 09/27/1880, Phthisis pulmonalis, Home Hospital.

YOUNG, Isaac – War of 1812, 03/28/1879, Maine, 87, 02/28/1880, Senility, Home Hospital.

Sources:

Annual Report of the Governor and Treasurer of the Northwestern Branch National Home for Disabled Volunteer Soldiers, for the Fiscal Year Ending June 30, 1880. Milwaukee County, Wisconsin: National Home Job Printing Office. Gen. Edward W. Hincks, Commandant and Treasurer

Annual Report of the Governor and Treasurer of the North-Western Branch National Home for Disabled Volunteer Soldiers for the Fiscal Year Ending June 30, 1881. Milwaukee County, Wisconsin: National Home Printing Office. General Jacob Sharpe, Governor

FORMAT: NAME, COMPANY & REGIMENT, DATE OF ADMISSION, PLACE OF BIRTH, AGE, DATE OF DEATH, CAUSE OF DEATH, PLACE OF DEATH.

ARMSTRONG, William J. – G, 7 Wisconsin, 09/19/1881, Ireland, 59, 12/11/1881, cause of death unknown, died in Marshfield, WI while on leave.

BENNETT, Marinus P. – H, 10 Wisconsin, 09/13/1876, Rhode Island, 68, 03/24/1881, Railroad accident, Home Hospital.

BRYAN, John H. – I, 87 Pennsylvania, 04/07/1881, place of birth unknown, 35, 11/22/1881, cause of death unknown, Milwaukee County Insane Asylum.

CADWELL, Anthony – C, 5 Wisconsin, 08/15/1881, Austria, 35, 10/02/1881, cause of death unknown, died in Manitowoc, WI while on leave.

CLARK, Edward P. – E, 53 Illinois, 03/19/1881, Pennsylvania, 36, 07/29/1881, cause death unknown, died in Milwaukee, WI while on leave.

COOKINBACK, Joshua – C, 4 Delaware, 01/08/1881, Pennsylvania, 61, 05/17/1881, Dysentery, Home Hospital.

CRANFORD, Samuel J. – A, 90 Ohio Cav., 06/14/1880, Pennsylvania, 44, 10/02/1881, cause of death unknown, died in Milwaukee County Insane Asylum.

DELANY, James – K, 115 Pennsylvania, 11/13/1880, Ireland, 47, 05/07/1881, Railroad accident, Home Hospital.

DEVOUGHT, Joseph – G, 15 Missouri, 10/18/1874, Germany, 83, 12/23/1881, Phthisis, Home Hospital.

DOSSER, Ignaz – C, 16 Illinois Cav., 09/09/1871, Germany, 57, 08/31/1881, Exhaustion, Home Hospital.

DOUGLASS, James – A, 15 Kentucky, 04/07/1881, Ireland, 65, 07/29/1881, cause of death unknown, died in Milwaukee County Insane Asylum.

DRYER, William – L, 6 Indiana, 04/07/1881, Indiana, 33, 04/15/1881, Insanity, died in Milwaukee County Insane Asylum.

EVES, Pemberton R. – G, 14 Kansas Cav., 12/03/1879, Canada, 43, 03/12/1881, Phthisis pulmonalis, Home Hospital.

FERRY, George H. – F, 5 Ohio, 02/18/1881, Ohio, 40, 02/28/1881, Cancer, Home Hospital.

FISHER, John – B, 124 Indiana, 11/29/1875, Germany, 58, 12/10/1881, cause of death unknown, died in Milwaukee County Insane Asylum.

FOREMAN, Daniel – War of 1812, 10/29/1878, New York, 93, 10/12/1881, Exhaustion, Home Hospital.

GANGRIN, Louis – A, 19 Indiana, 08/11/1881, Switzerland, 50, 10/17/1881, Apoplexy, Home Hospital.

GIBBONS, James – F, 63 New York, 08/28/1877, Ireland, 53, 11/13/1881, Apoplexy, Home Hospital.

GIBSON, William – D, 35 Ohio, 01/04/1881, District of Columbia, 72, 01/22/1881, Exhaustion, Home Hospital

GILMORE David – A, 79 New York, 11/04/1874, Scotland, 61, 11/22/1881, Congestion of the lungs, Home Hospital.

HENSHEL, Carl F. – E, 18 U. S. Infantry, 10/05/1877, Germany, 71, 12/10/1881, Uraemia, Home Hospital.

HESLIN, Owen – H, 4 Wisconsin Cav., 08/13/1869, Ireland, 65, 09/10/1881, Cancer of stomach, Home Hospital.

JOYCE, William R. – G, 6 Ohio, 10/02/1880, New Jersey, 52, 10/20/1881, Chronic diarrhoea, Home Hospital.

KENDALL, Edwin A. – E, 1 California Cav., 06/20/1877, Massachusetts, 50, 5/11/1881, Opium habit, died in Hot Springs, Arkansas while on leave.

KIRBACH, Frederick – F, 19 Wisconsin, 04/01/1877, Germany, 51, 04/28/1881, Insanity, died in Milwaukee County Insane Asylum.

KITCHEN, Wheeler – D, 27 Wisconsin, 04/26/1879, Pennsylvania, 58, 05/11/1881, Cardiac disease, Main Building.

KUFFENKAM, Carl – I, 24 Wisconsin 07/11/1877, Germany, 62, 04/22/1881, cause of death unknown, died in Milwaukee, WI while on leave.

LANGNER, Samuel – B, 46 New York, 07/21/1879, Germany, 50, 02/12/1881, Asphyxia, Home Hospital.

LEWIS, Elisha - __, 5 Ohio Sharp Shooters, 06/17/1879, Vermont, 70, 01/20/1881, Apoplexy, Home Hospital.

LEWIS, John – K, 8 Kansas, 07/06/1877, England, 54, 21/22/1881, Congestion of lungs, Home Hospital.

LOCKER, Francis – L, 1 Missouri Cav., 08/25/1878, Germany, 58, 11/13/1881, Phthisis, Home Hospital.

MCDEVITT, John C. – C, 71 Pennsylvania, 04/08/1881, Pennsylvania, 38, 10/15/1881, Phthisis pulmonalis, Home Hospital.

MCHUGH, George – E, 36 Illinois, 11/09/1881, England, 61, 12/05/1881, Asthma, Home Hospital.

MCKENZIE, William – I, 15 Illinois, 05/10/1879, England, 60, 12/25/1881, cause of death unknown, died in Milwaukee County Insane Asylum.

MCMACKIN, Henry – D, 47 Illinois, 11/27/1879, Indiana, 38, 02/08/1881, Asphyxia, Old Hospital building.

MCMANUS, Peter, __, 18 New York, 09/14/1876, New York, 37, 04/22/1881, Cardiac disease, Home Hospital.

MCNAMARA, Lawrence – G, 90 Illinois, 09/16/1880, Ireland, 47, 08/29/1881, cause of death unknown, died in Milwaukee, WI while on leave.

MCNUTT, William – B, 83 Ohio, 04/07/1880, Ohio, 40, 05/29/1881, Insanity, Milwaukee County Insane Asylum.

MELCHOR, Freeman – H, 62 Illinois, 11/26/1879, Illinois, 42, 06/13/1881, Injury to brain, Milwaukee County Insane Asylum.

MILLER, John F. W. – G, 9 Wisconsin, 09/21/1880, Germany, 56, 11/27/1881, cause of death unknown, died in Milwaukee, WI while on leave.

O'DELL, Joseph – I, 65 Indiana, 10/16/1880, Indiana, 62, 04/10/1881, Cardiac disease, Home Hospital.

O'DONNELL, Edward – D, Engineer's Regiment West, 08/03/1876, Ireland, 65, 03/18/1881, Cardiac disease, Main Building.

PATCHIN, Edward A. – L, 10 New York Cav., 12/11/1876, New York, 67, 09/04/1881, Exhaustion, Home Hospital.

PIES, John – A, 2 Missouri Res., 10/23/1880, Germany, 50, 04/04/1881, cause of death unknown, died in Washington County, WI while on leave.

POWERS, John – E, 37 Illinois, 07/01/1879, Ireland, 61, 06/26/1881, Hepatitis, Home Hospital.

QUINN, Dennis – D. 16 Illinois, 04/10/1879, Ireland, 60, 07/16/1881, Apoplexy, Home Hospital.

ROGERS, Alfred B. – F, 26 Iowa, 02/26/1881, Iowa, 42, 09/27/1881, Softening of brain, Home Hospital.

ROSBOURNE, Theodore – G, 82 Illinois, 02/24/1875, Belgium, 81, 11/13/1881, Phthisis, Home Hospital.

ROWLEY, William – C, 90 Illinois, 03/17/1876, Ireland, 59, 04/02/1881, cause of death unknown, died in Belvidere, Illinois while on leave.

RYAN, John S. – G, 5 Wisconsin, 03/29/1881, New York, 41, 04/03/1881, Phthisis pulmonalis, Home Hospital.

SCANLON, Robert – I, 77 Illinois, 02/07/1880, Ireland, 61, 05/06/1881, Phthisis pulmonalis, Home Hospital.

SCHEURIG, Nicholas – D, 17 Wisconsin, 12/21/1875, Germany, 55, 12/10/1881, Chronic dysentery, Home Hospital.

SCHWEISTAHL, Nicholas – K, 6 Wisconsin, 02/10/1875, Germany, 59, 06/07/1881, Dropsy, Home Hospital.

SCHWEIZER, Frank – E, 60 Illinois, 06/14/1880, Germany, 61, 09/29/1881, Apoplexy, Home Hospital.

SHAW, Thomas – D, 20 Wisconsin, 09/12/1879, Ireland, 61, 01/28/1881, Senility, Home Hospital.

SONNEMAN, Ernest – H, 75 Ohio, 06/24/1881,Germany, 61, 06/25/1881, Cardiac disease, Home Hospital.

STEVENS, Byron – E, 49 Wisconsin, 08/05/1881, New York, 43, 09/11/1881, Phthisis, Home Hospital.

VENABLES, George – A, 65 New York, 06/07/1881, England, 42, 10/15/1881, Chronic diarrhoea, Home Hospital.

WALDSMITH, Albert – B, 4 Missouri Cav., 04/16/1878, Germany, 53, 06/01/1881, Disease of bladder, Home Hospital.

WEST, Ezckiel – War of 1812, 04/07/1879, New York, 89, 05/06/1881, Senility, Home Hospital.

ZACHARIAS, Conrad – G, 39 New York, 02/10/1881, Germany, 55, 03/01/1881, Phthisis pulmonalis, Home Hospital.

ZANTNER, Charles – K, 7 Wisconsin, 12/24/1873, Germany, 47, 08/15/1881, cause of death unknown, died in Milwaukee, WI while on leave.

Sources:

Annual Report of the Governor and Treasurer of the Northwestern Branch National Home for Disabled Volunteer Soldiers for the Fiscal Year Ending June 30, 1881. Milwaukee County, Wisconsin: National Home Job Printing Press. Gen. Edward W. Hincks, Commandant and Treasurer

Annual Report of the Governor and Treasurer of the North-Western Branch National Home for Disabled Volunteer Soldiers for the Fiscal Year Ending June 30, 1882. Milwaukee County, Wisconsin: National Home Printing Office. General Jacob Sharpe, Governor.

FORMAT: NAME, COMPANY & REGIMENT, DATE OF ADMISSION, PLACE OF
BIRTH, AGE, DATE OF DEATH, CAUSE OF DEATH, PLACE OF DEATH.

ABLE, James – B, 4 Iowa, 01/18/1882, Virginia, 58, 05/04/1882,
   Fatty degeneration of the heart, Home.
ASPEN, Thomas – G, 3 Pennsylvania Cav., 10/03/1876, England,
   58, 03/22/1882, Abscess of liver, Home Hospital.
BAKER, Henry – H, 18 Wisconsin, 07/19/1882, Germany, 45,
   09/28/1882, Paralysis, Home Hospital.
BARKER, Edward R. – G, 148 New York, 05/07/1880, New York,
   50, 10/02/1882, Insanity, Milwaukee County Insane Asy-
   lum.
BECKER, Theodore – G, 9 Wisconsin, 09/01/1881, Germany, 57,
   07/22/1882, Abscess in brain, Home Hospital.
BISHOP, Henry C. – I, 137 New York, 10/19/1875, Illinois, 79,
   09/21/1882, Paralysis, Home Hospital.
BLUM, David – A, 15 Missouri, 07/08/1875, Germany, 52,
   11/10/1882, Valvular disease of the heart, Home Hospital.
BOYLE, Patrick – G, 72 New York, 05/12/1874, Ireland, 75,
   04/24/1882, Heart disease & Senility, Home Hospital.
BRATTON, James – E, 96 Ohio, 04/07/1881, Ohio, 40, 02/10/1882,
   cause of death unknown, died in Milwaukee County Insane
   Asylum.
BURGWARD, William – B, 6 Illinois Cav., 07/10/1877, Germany,
   59, 05/28/1882, Paralysis, Home Hospital.
BURNS, Andrew – C, 13 New York, 08/24/1881, Virginia, 41,
   04/09/1882, Heart disease, died in Milwaukee, WI while on
   leave.
BUSH, William H. – A, 1 Michigan Art., 08/19/1882, New York,
   52, 09/30/1882, Paralysis, Home Hospital.
CALLAHAN, John – E, 2 Wisconsin, 03/09/1882, Delaware, 45,
   03/11/1882, Heart disease-valvular, Home Hospital.
CALLIGAN, James – I, 27, Michigan, 01/06/1882, Ireland, 72,
   03/14/1882, Senile debility, Milwaukee County Insane
   Asylum.
CLARK, John – B, 1 Louisiana, 12/08/1870, England, 62,
   05/26/1882, Inflammatory rheumatism, Home Hospital.

CRIPPS, William – B, 28 Illinois, 10/10/1878, Germany, 52, 06/17/1882, Apoplexy, Home Hospital.

DIEFENBACHER, John – E, 52 New York, 12/20/1881, Germany, 44, 10/29/1882, Pneumonia, Home Hospital.

DOERING, John – F, 37 Iowa, 07/22/1882, Germany, 72, 10/22/1882, Exhaustion of old age, Home Hospital.

DOLAN, Patrick – I, 77 New York, 11/04/1879, Ireland, 70, 03/13/1882, Exhaustion of old age, Home Hospital.

DUNLOP, James – F, 34 Wisconsin, 07/17/1877, Ireland, 49, 04/29/1882, Phthisis, Home Hospital.

ENGLISH, James – B, 23 Illinois 10/02/1881, Ireland, 43, 11/29/1882, Railroad accident, Home Hospital.

FITZPATRICK, James – E, 51 Illinois, 08/10/1881, Ireland, 65, 10/03/1882, Chronic diarrhoea, Home Hospital

FLANNERY, Michael – D, 11 Illinois, 09/24/1881, Ireland, 45, 02/05/1882, Phthisis, Home Hospital.

FOX, Edwin – E, 1 Wisconsin, 11/09/1881, Wisconsin, 42, 07/06/1882, cause of death unknown, died in Bannack, Montana, while on leave.

GALLAGHER, John – A, 39 Illinois, 10/17/1877, Ireland, 65, 04/01/1882, Phthisis, Home Hospital.

GANNAN, Michael – F, 177 New York, 01/12/1882, Ireland, 46, 01/30/1882, Pneumonia, Home Hospital.

GEEN, Thomas – G, 82 Indiana, 07/16/1882, England, 45, 10/11/1882, Cerebral hemorrhage, Home Hospital.

GERBER, Henry – E, 12 Missouri, 10/16/1879, Switzerland, 42, 02/09/1882, Railroad accident, near the Home grounds.

GOEDEN, Max – A, 15 Missouri, 06/20/1879, Germany, 46, 03/05/1882, Railroad accident, died in Milwaukee, WI while on leave.

GOLDSTEIN, Henry – Mexican War, 12/17/1879, Germany, 57, 08/11/1882, Hemorrhage, Home grounds.

GRELL, Frederick – H, 9 Wisconsin, 06/19/1875, Germany, 57, 06/20/1882, Enlargement of the heart, Home Hospital.

HAWKINS, Charles - __, 14 Michigan Battery, 01/11/1874, England, 68, 04/14/1882, Exhaustion from senile gangrene, Home Hospital.

HAYS, Samuel – B, 45 Illinois, 07/30/1880, Pennsylvania, 75, 12/12/1882, Old age, Home Hospital.

HERRMAN, Hyronimus – C, 4 Missouri Cav., 07/10/1875, Germany, 70, 10/28/1882, Paralysis, Home Hospital.

HEWITT, John R. – B, 50 New York, 09/19/1879, Arkansas, 35, 03/27/1882, cause of death unknown, died in Los Angeles, California while on leave.

HOENER, Henry – F, 3 Missouri, 07/25/1882, Germany, 53, 09/04/1882, Chronic diarrhoea, Home Hospital.

HOFFARTH, Anton – I, 37 Iowa, 04/20/1870, France, 61, 01/23/1992, cause of death unknown, died in New Berlin, WI while on leave.

JOHNSON, William – H, 32 Illinois, 07/20/1882, England, 61, 11/26/1882, Chronic diarrhoea, Home Hospital.

KANE, John H. – B, 26 Illinois, 12/09/1880, New York, 65, 07/30/1882, Paralysis, Home Hospital.

KEHOE, Patrick – C, 23 Illinois, 04/03/1880, Ireland, 56, 09/03/1882, Drowned, died in Chicago IL while on leave.

LARKIN, Michael – B, 12 Michigan, 07/03/1967, Ireland, 38, 02/03/1882, Pyaemia, Home Hospital.

LYON, James – F, 21 Wisconsin, 09/29/1882, Massachusetts, 62, 10/11/1882, Phthisis, Home Hospital.

MAHER, Dennis – G, 23 Illinois, 04/04/1879, Ireland, 46, 03/27/1882, Exhaustion from paralysis, Home Hospital.

MASHA, Eli – D, 5 Wisconsin, 06/01/1881, France, 44, 12/09/1882, Asthma, Home Hospital.

MCFAY, William – G, 17 Wisconsin, 08/12/1879, Scotland, 74, 06/23/1882, Phthisis, Home Hospital.

MCKEON, Michael – K, 53 Illinois, 04/16/1877 Ireland, 63, 07/02/1882, Railroad accident, near the Home.

MCLAUGHLIN, Thomas – __, U. S. Marine Corps, 02/26/1868, Pennsylvania, 77, 12/08/1882, Phthisis, Home Hospital.

MULVIHILL, Jeremiah – C, 51 Wisconsin, 01/09/1880, Ireland, 33, 07/13/1882, Phthisis, Home Hospital.

MURPHY, William – H, 10 Missouri, 05/17/1880, Ireland, 74, 07/07/1882, Phthisis pulmonalis, Home Hospital.

POOS, William – K, 2 Missouri Art., 07/27/1882, Germany, 71, 09/13/1882, Insanity, Milwaukee County Insane Asylum.

PORTER, William – F, 47 Illinois, 04/20/1880, New York, 36, 05/19/1882, cause of death unknown, died in Chicago, IL while on leave.

RALSTON, David R. – H, 119 Illinois, 10/20/1881, Virginia, 44, 03/23/1882, Phthisis, Home Hospital.

ROEHRIG, Adam – A, 17 New York, 12/13/1877, Germany, 50, 04/22/1882, Progressive paralysis, Home Hospital.

RUNCIMAN, Francis – H, 27 Michigan, 04/07/1881, Scotland, 58, 08/02/1882, Erysipelas, Milwaukee County Insane Asylum.

SCULLY, Martin – I, 69 New York, 01/01/1881, Ireland, 47, 05/05/1882, cause of death unknown, died in Chicago, Illinois while on leave.

SHAW, Leonard O. – K, 14 Wisconsin, 09/18/1880, Ohio, 44, 01/31/1882, Chronic diarrhoea, Home Hospital.

SHEPPARD, William – I, 90 Illinois, 02/19/1878, Ireland, 67, 09/02/1882, Phthisis, Home Hospital.

SHIELDS, Andrew – G, 69 Illinois, 02/23/1869, Wisconsin, 38, 07/12/1882, cause of death unknown, died in Monges, WI while on leave.

SIMPSON, Stephen D. – C, 33 Wisconsin, 08/01/1992, Wisconsin, 47, 08/22/1882, cause of death unknown, died in Madison, WI while on leave.

SMITH Joseph L. – F, 4 Michigan, 04/07/1881, New Hampshire, 51, 05/30/1882, General paralysis of the insane, Milwaukee County Insane Asylum.

SMITH, Patrick P. – C, 1 New York Maryland Rifles, 06/27/1876, Ireland, 42, 04/04/1882, Phthisis, Home Hospital.

STAMNITZ, Henry – E, 44 Illinois, 08/06/1880, Germany, 61, 04/23/1882, Paralysis & Locomotor Atoxia (Ataxia), Home Hospital.

SULLIVAN, Michael – K, 93 Illinois, 07/10/1882, Ireland, 66, 08/23/1882, Apoplexy, Home Hospital.

THOMPSON, George W. – D, 1 Missouri Light Art., 11/11/1881, Virginia, 69, 04/20/1882, Pneumonia, Home Hospital.

THURSTON, Leander F. – C, 13 Maine, 12/20/1881, Maine, 37, 06/06/1882, Phthisis pulmonalis, Home Hospital.

TOBIN, Thomas – C, 23 Kentucky, 03/29/1879, Ireland, 66, 02/16/1882, Exhaustion, Home Hospital.

USINGER, John – E, 19 Wisconsin, 12/16/1879, Germany, 77, 04/22/1882, Congestion of brain, Home Hospital.

VOIGTLANDER, Herrman – K, 13 New York Heavy Art., 06/13/1870, Germany, 60, 05/09/1882, Apoplexy, Home Hospital.

WEBER, John – C, 105 Illinois, 08/08/1878, Germany, 65, 04/22/1882, Pneumonia, Home Hospital.

WEIS, Dominique – C, 26 Wisconsin, 12/22/1875, Germany, 51, 10/21/1882, Abscess of liver, Home Hospital.

WEST, William – U. S. Navy, 08/11/1871, Pennsylvania, 49, 01/03/1882, Pneumonia, died in Aminas City, Colorado while on leave.

WYMAN, Charles F. – H, 5 Wisconsin, 08/09/1881, New York, 45, 01/01/1882, Nervous exhaustion, Home Hospital.

ZIESACK, Michael – A, 9 Wisconsin, 01/20/1880, Germany, 62, 10/02/1882, Drowned, in Wauwatosa, WI while absent without leave.

Sources:

Annual Report of the Governor and Treasurer of the North-Western Branch, National Home for Disabled Volunteer Soldiers, for the Fiscal Year ending June 30, 1882. Milwaukee County, Wisconsin: National Home Printing Office. General Jacob Sharpe, Governor and Treasurer.

Annual Report of the Governor of the North-Western Branch, National Home for Disabled Volunteer Soldiers, for the Fiscal Year Ending June 30, 1883. Milwaukee County, Wisconsin: National Home Printing Office. General Jacob Sharpe, Governor.

DEATHS IN 1883

FORMAT: NAME, COMPANY & REGIMENT, PLACE OF BIRTH, AGE, DATE OF DEATH, CAUSE OF DEATH, PLACE OF DEATH.

ABBEY, Samuel – War of 1812, 06/28/1878, Vermont, 88, 04/16/1883, Old age, Home Hospital.

BAGG, John – I, 3 Iowa, 06/18/1877, Germany, 58, 09/10/1883, Softening of the brain, Home Hospital.

BAKER, Torralbia M. – E, 17 Illinois, 12/15/1882, Illinois, 40, 07/21/1883, Syphilis-tertiary, Home Hospital.

BARRIGAN, John – H, 90 Illinois, 07/15/1878, Ireland, 71, 05/15/1883, Old age-Dementia, Home Hospital.

BEACH, James B. – A, 35 Wisconsin, Never arrived, Germany, 60, 09/21/1883, cause of death unknown, died in Baldwin, WI before actual admission to the Home.

BENNETT, Daniel – F, 7 Ohio, 10/10/1882, New York, 66, 10/03/1883, Fatty degeneration of the heart, Home Hospital.

BLOOMER, Arthur – A, 2 Nebraska, 07/10/1880, Ireland, 42, 09/10/1883, Paralysis, Home Hospital.

BOWMAN, John – K, 39 Indiana, 09/17/1883, Ireland, 46, 12/24/1883, Railroad accident, died in Milwaukee, WI.

BUETNER, John H. – I, 33 Indiana, 11/21/1882, North Carolina, 56, 10/13/1883, Heart disease, died in Winston, North Carolina.

CASE, Horace – I, 1 Michigan, 11/26/1875, New York, 72, 04/18/1883, Old age, Home Hospital.

CLEVELAND, Alonzo J. – C, 7 Maryland, 10/13/1882, Massachusetts, 68, 04/11/1883, Paralysis, Home Hospital.

CONNOR, Francis – C, 37 Illinois, 04/12/1876, Ireland, 76, 03/16/1883, Old age, Home Hospital.

CROSBY, James – E, 9 Illinois, 07/24/1880, Ireland, 65, 09/09/1883, Phthisis, Home Hospital.

DALLER, John – D, 11 Indiana, 11/01/1882, Germany, 44, 05/14/1883, found dead near the Home.

DOOSE, Casper N. – A, 39 Illinois, 11/28/1869, Germany, 60, 09/25/1883, Chronic inflammation of the bowels, Home Hospital.

DOUGLAS, Merrill – E, 4 Illinois Cav., 11/22/1882, New York, 63, 10/02/1883, Phthisis, Home Hospital.

DUENK, Gerrett H. – I, 24 Wisconsin, 06/01/1883, Holland, 58, 08/15/1883, Drowned in Milwaukee, WI.

DUSO, Joseph – E, 12 Illinois Cav., 12/01/1882, France, 75, 02/03/1883, Old age & Epilepsy, Home Hospital.

ENGELBERT, John – C, 24 Wisconsin, 07/22/1871, Switzerland, 72, 10/15/1883, found dead outside the Home grounds.

FILL, George – G, 75 Illinois, 10/03/1882,Germany, 50, 05/13/1883, Cancer of stomach, Home Hospital.

FRAENZEL, Joseph – E, 27 Wisconsin, 03/11/1881, Germany, 61, 09/18/1883, Heart disease, Main building.

FUZZARD, John – K, 12 Wisconsin, 09/28/1882, England, 63, 06/13/1883, Chronic bronchitis, Home Hospital.

GARRITY, John – I, 13 Wisconsin, 03/05/1878, Ireland, 73, 05/14/1883, Old age, Home Hospital

GLASSIE, William – I, 29 Illinois, 11/29/1882, New York, 71, 04/23/1883, Phthisis, Home Hospital.

GOBLE, Aaron L. – D, 52 Indiana, 03/30/1883, New York, 76, 10/20/1883, Debility senile, Milwaukee County Insane Asylum.

GRAFF, John – F, 16 Illinois Cav., 08/26/1880, Ireland, 76, 07/01/1883, Old age, Home Hospital.

HASE, Adolph – C, 6 Kentucky, 05/09/1879, Germany, 61, 06/29/1883, Drowned, found in lake on Home grounds.

HAUSER, John F. – Major, 6 Wisconsin, 05/20/1880, Switzerland, 59, 06/08/1883, Chronic diarrhoea, Home Hospital.

HEISEL, John N. – K, 11 Illinois, 08/10/1883, France, 44, 11/25/1883, Phthisis, Home Hospital.

HERRMAN, Joseph – G, 16 Illinois Cav., 08/17/1874, Germany, 59, 05/02/1883, Progressive Paralysis, Home Hospital.

HUBBARD, James E. – A, 31 Massachusetts, 09/17/1882, Massachusetts, 39, 05/06/1883, Phthisis, Home Hospital.

HUNNEYBURN, Thomas – G, 18 Wisconsin, 11/09/1881, England, 76, 07/02/1883, Old age, Home Hospital.

KAYES, Robert – K, 57 Illinois, 08/22/1883, Pennsylvania, 67, 11/25/1883, Dropsy of chest, Home Hospital.

KING, Patrick – B, 69 Pennsylvania, 10/16/1876, Ireland, 48, 11/11/1883, Congestion of the lungs, Home Hospital.

KNIGHT, John P. – G, 13 Illinois, 10/09/1883, New York, 57, 12/24/1883, Heart disease, found dead on Home grounds.

KNOLL, Leopold – E, 2 Missouri Heavy Art., 05/17/1883, Ger many, 70, 12/23/1883, Paralysis, Home Hospital.

KOENEMAN, Henry – E, 82 Illinois, 12/10/1877, Germany, 76, 06/07/1883, Abscess of the brain, Home Hospital.

LEMP, William – D, 37 Iowa, 01/21/1877, Germany, 64, 07/04/1883, Heart disease, found dead on Home grounds.

LYONS, John – G, 23 Illinois, 02/16/1873, Ireland, 82, 02/15/1883, found dead near the Home.

MADDEN, Richard E. – C, 3 Minnesota, 03/13/1883, Massachu- setts, 55, 03/24/1883, Phthisis, Home Hospital.

MCCARTHY, Michael – B, 50 New York, 06/11/1870, Ireland, 80, 09/26/1883, Old age, Home Hospital.

MCCAULIFF, Timothy – A, 35 Indiana, 09/14/1883, Ireland, 42, 11/12/1883, Phthisis, Home Hospital.

METZLER, George – A, 33 New York, 06/01/1881, Germany, 66, 08/14/1883, Apoplexy, died in Main building.

MEYER, Adolph – G, 14 Indiana, 04/30/1879, Germany, 45, 09/20/1883, Acute mania, Home Hospital.

MILLER, George W. – F, 16 Wisconsin, 06/07/1875, New York, 54, 01/26/1883, Phthisis, Home Hospital.

MILLS, Adam – G, 36 Illinois, 04/04/1882, England, 47, 01/31/1883, Phthisis, Home Hospital.

MITCHELL, Joseph – I, 179 Ohio, 05/30/1883, Ohio, 36, 10/20/1883, Railroad accident on Home grounds.

MOSELY, Henry – A, 13 Illinois, 03/29/1877, Germany, 66, 05/30/1883, Railroad accident on Home grounds.

NEILLIE, Robert – I, 6 Pennsylvania, 12/14/1882, Pennsylvania, 38, 12/01/1883, cause of death unknown, died while on leave.

NELLE, Augustus H. – G, 7 New York, 07/13/1879, Germany, 56, 12/25/1883, cause of death unknown, died while on leave.

O'SULLIVAN, Philip – G, 8 Delaware, 10/28/1868, Ireland, 78, 04/10/1883, Old age, Home Hospital.

OLSON, Solfast – B, 1 Illinois Light Art., 12/22/1871, Norway, 33, 05/19/1883, Exhaustion, Home Hospital.

PHILLIPS, Simon – D, 40 Iowa, 10/04/1882, Pennsylvania, 86, 05/05/1883, Old age, Home Hospital.

PHILLIPSON, Gerhard – B, 9 Wisconsin, 10/01/1875, Germany, 63, 09/23/1883, Phthisis, Home Hospital.

PORTER, Thadeus P. – D, 7 Wisconsin, 01/10/1877, New York, 47, 08/25/1883, Congestive chills, Home Hospital.

REUSCH, Frederick – A, 2 Missouri, 09/28/1882, Germany, 60, 04/03/1883, Phthisis, Home Hospital.

ROACH, John – F, 24 Wisconsin, 04/24/1882, New York, 52, 09/05/1883, Paralysis, Home Hospital.

SMITH, CLARK F. – B, 15 Ohio, 09/19/1882, Ohio, 36, 02/20/1883, Phthisis-Hemorrhage, Home Hospital.

SPARLING, George – I, 20 New York, 12/23/1871, New York, 75, 06/26/1883, Valvular disease of the heart, Home Hospital.

SPURR, Rufus – A, 147 Illinois, 05/19/1881, Pennsylvania, 71, 03/31/1883, Paralysis & Old age, Home Hospital.

TAYLOR, John – I, 95 New York, 10/28/1882, Ireland, 63, 02/02/1883, Phthisis, Home Hospital.

TIMMONS, James – A, 2 U. S. Cav., 12/19/1882, Illinois, 53, 01/31/1883, Chronic diarrhoea, Home Hospital.

TOMPKINS, Samuel J. – B, 153 Illinois, 10/04/1883, New York, 59, 11/17/1883, Hemorrhage of the lungs, Home Hospital.

VAN GENT, John – E, 58 Illinois, 04/06/1878, Holland, 50, 09/01/1883, Delirium tremens, Home Hospital.

WAGNER, Casper – L, 14 Illinois Cav., 06/07/1874, Germany, 74, 09/06/1883, Old age, Home Hospital.

WARRENS, John B. – C, New York Engineers, 03/10/1882, Netherlands, 47, 09/20/1883, Paralysis, Home Hospital.

WELSH, Thomas – G, 13 Illinois, 03/19/1873, Ireland, 65, 12/18/1883, Paralysis, Home Hospital.

WHITE, Eugene G. – A, 65 Illinois, 11/30/1882, New York, 52, 09/26/1883, Syphilis-tertiary, Home Hospital.

WING, Philip – C, 3 New York Cav., 03/17/1878, Germany, 43, 05/07/1883, Paralysis, Home Hospital.

ZIMMERMAN, Henry – K, 46 New York, 02/28/1871, Germany, 65, 06/11/1883, cause of death unknown, died in Wauwatosa, WI while on leave.

ZUMSTEG, Jacob – A, 3 Missouri, 09/20/1881, Switzerland, 43, 04/29/1883, found dead in Wauwatosa, WI.

Sources:

Annual Report of the Governor of the North-Western Branch, National Home for Disabled Volunteer Soldiers, for the Fiscal Year Ending June 30, 1883. Milwaukee County, Wisconsin: National Home Printing Office. General Jacob Sharpe, Governor.

Annual Report of the Governor of the North-Western Branch, National Home for Disabled Volunteer Soldiers, for the Fiscal Year Ending June 30, 1884. Milwaukee County, Wisconsin: National Home Printing Office. General Jacob Sharpe, Governor.

DEATHS IN 1884

FORMAT: NAME, COMPANY & REGIMENT, DATE OF ADMLISSION, PLACE OF BIRTH, DATE OF DEATH, CAUSE OF DEATH, PLACE OF DEATH.

AMES, George W. – E, 2 Wisconsin Cav., 04/03/1884, Vermont, 43, 12/10/1884, cause of death unknown, died while on leave.

BAILEY, Abraham – War of 1812, 02/16/1882, Pennsylvania, 88, 05/31/1884, Old age, Home Hospital.

BIESENBACH, John – C, 16, New York Cav., 01/03/1879, Germany, 66, 10/16/1884, Apoplexy, Home Hospital

BLACK, Robert – K, 1 Wisconsin Heavy Art., 05/13/1884, Wisconsin, 41, 11/18/1884, Phthisis, Home Hospital.

BLECKSCHMIDT, Leopold – B, 2 California, 09/26/1877, Germany, 60, 01/24/1884, Pneumonia, Home Hospital.

BRADY, Edward – L, 6 Iowa Cav., 09/07/1877, Ireland, 60, 10/22/1884, Phthisis, Home Hospital.

BREECHER, John – A, 14 Wisconsin, 06/12/1883, Germany, 70, 01/29/1884, Paralysis, Home Hospital.

BRETZKE, Ernst – B, 1 New York Eng., 11/12/1878, Germany, 65, 01/01/1884, Phthisis, Home Hospital.

BRITTON, Ebenezer – War of 1812, 01/08/1876, Vermont, 96, 05/23/1884, Old age, Home Hospital.

BUNKER, Isaiah W. – D, 84 Pennsylvania, 03/19/1881, Pennsylvania, 68, 11/18/1884, Internal injury from fall, Home Hospital.

CHADEAYNE, Samuel – I, 26 Michigan, 08/21/184, New Brunswick, 73, 12/31/1884, found dead near Home grounds.

CILLEN, James W. - __, 2 Illinois Light Art., 07/18/1884, Ireland, 75, 08/19/1884, Haematemesis, Home Hospital.

CLARK, John – F, 13 Illinois, 03/25/1875, England, 76, 02/01/1884, Suicide, Home Hospital.

COLLINS, James – B, 1 New York Art., 08/28/1883, Ireland, 78, 08/05/1884, Old age, Home Hospital.

COMES, Peter – A, 15 Missouri, 09/14/1882, Germany, 57, 01/21/1884, Insanity, Home Hospital.

CONNELLEE, Henry – G, 23 Illinois, 01/16/1881, Pennsylvania, 66, 02/17/1884, Alcoholism, Home Hospital.

CUTLER, Benoni H. – A, 9 Michigan Cav., 08/01/1883, Vermont, 84, 07/01/1884, Old age, Home Hospital.

DEENEY, Cornelius – B, 12 Iowa, 05/23/1879, Ireland, 40, 04/12/1884, Phthisis, Home Hospital.

DODGE, Cyrus J. – F, 1 Michigan, 11/14/1869, New York, 82, 03/06/1884, Old age, Home Hospital.

DOUGHERTY, Archibald – B, 6 Pennsylvania Heavy Art., 04/16/1884, Ireland, 70, 08/17/1884, Cholera morbus, Home Hospital.

DRESCHER, Ernest – A, 1 Minnesota, 03/04/1884, Germany, 54, 12/16/1884, Exhaustion from debauch, Home Hospital.

ELLENWOOD, Almon M. – C, 8 Michigan Cav., 02/29/1884, New York, 54, 09/25/1884, Cancer, Home Hospital.

FLEMMING, Frederick – E, 5 Minnesota, 05/10/1880, Germany, 54, 12/23/1884, Suicide, Main building.

FLENTJEN, Victor C. J. – E, 30 Massachusetts, 10/29/1871, France, 48, 04/13/1884, cause of death unknown, died in Milwaukee, WI while on leave.

FLYNN, Patrick – E, 16 Kansas, 10/15/1884, Ohio, 44, 12/29/1884, Phthisis, Home Hospital.

FRANK, Mathias – E, 8 Minnesota, 06/10/1884, Germany, 49, 09/15/1884, Chronic gastritis, Home Hospital.

FRENCH, James – F, 3 New Hampshire, 12/02/1882, New York, 62, 06/05/1884, Maramus tabes, Home Hospital.

FRITCHE, Joseph – A, 44 Illinois, 05/06/1884, Bohemia, 59, 07/08/1884, Phthisis, Home Hospital.

FRITZ, Adolph – H, 52 New York, 10/11/1880. Germany, 68, 12/21/1884, Cancer of face, Home Hospital.

FROWLEY, John – M, 1 Missouri Light Art., 10/15/1881, Ireland, 48, 08/11/1884, Phthisis, Home Hospital.

GALLAGAN, Patrick – E, 1 Connecticut Art., 07/03/1883, Ireland, 44, 12/20/1884. Phthisis, Home Hospital.

GEISTBECK, Ignatz – L, 5 :Kansas Cav., 04/13/1883, Germany, 60, 11/10/1884, Intermittent fever, Home Hospital.

GROAT, Robert Y. – F, 1 Michigan, Mexican War, 09/04/1884, New York, 56, 10/07/1884, Pneumonia, Home Hospital died while *Temporary at Post.*

GROSS, Leopold – M, 4 Missouri Cav., 08/06/1884, Germany, 45, 08/24/1884, Phthisis, Home Hospital.

HANNAH, George W. – I, 123 Indiana, 07/22/1881, Indiana, 62, 12/28/1884, Chronic diarrhoea, Home Hospital.

HARRIS, George S – K, 8 Michigan, 05/05/1882, England, 78, 05/05/1884, Old age, Home Hospital.

HENDERSON, Charles – G, 2 Michigan, 06/26/1882, Michigan, 47, 01/17/1884, Syphilis-tertiary, Home Hospital.

HESS, Frederick – Band, 99 New York, 08/22/1877, Germany, 65, 08/15/1884, Cardiac disease, Home Hospital.

JAEGER, William – I, 6 Ohio, 01/13/1881, Germany, 59, 04/27/1884, Paralysis, Home Hospital.

JARVIS, Robert – M, 5 New York Cav., 01/23/1884, England, 55, 02/09/1884, Pneumonia, Home Hospital.

JENNINGS, Isaac - __, 7 Wisconsin Light Art., 03/09/1881, New York, 61, Chronic diarrhoea, Home Hospital.

KAUSEN, Henry – L, 3 New York Cav., 10/07/1870, Germany, 56, 03/08/1884, Frozen- outside Home grounds.

KLEGLE, John - D, 8 Illinois Cav., 06/09/1882, Germany, 58, 07/23/1884, Paralysis, Home Hospital.

KRAHL, Joseph - __, 29 New York Battery, 05/12/1884,Germany, 54, 07/17/1884, Paralysis, Home Hospital, died while *Temporary at Post.*

KRIES, James C. – I, 6 Missouri, 06/13/1879, Germany, 64, 01/06/1884, Epilepsy, died in Quarters.

LESTER, Milo A. – C, 10 New York Art., 01/13/1884, Illinois, 51, 11/15/1884, Phthisis, Home Hospital.

LOCKHART, Christian – H, 9 Wisconsin, 03/26/1879, Germany, 58, 01/20/1884, Pneumonia, Home Hospital.

LONG, Henry – B, 119 Pennsylvania, 11/03/1883, Pennsylvania, 60, 01/20/1884, Insanity, Home Hospital.

LOYD, Giles – F, 6 Indiana, 11/16/1882, Kentucky, 63, 03/06/1884, cause of death unknown, died while on leave.

LUBY, William – K, 131 New York, 07/08/1883, Ireland, 46, 11/12/1884, Chronic diarrhoea, Home Hospital.

MACKEY, David – K, 44 Wisconsin, 07/17/1882, Ireland, 57, 04/01/1884, Phthisis, Home Hospital

MARKGRAF, Louis - __, 8 Ohio Battery, 04/22/1884, Germany, 70, 11/26/1884, Chronic Hepatitis, Home Hospital.

MARSH, Nathan – A, 2 Minnesota, 12/18/1875, Vermont, 75, 03/20/1884, Old age, Home Hospital.

MARTZLOFF, Valentine – E, 67 Illinois, 06/13/1875, France, 71, 05/28/1884, Railroad accident near Home grounds.

MCCABE, Edward – M, 3 Pennsylvania Cav., 08/21/1884, Ireland, 46, 09/13/1884, Pneumonia, Home Hospital.

MCCARTEN, John – D, 26 Massachusetts, 07/28/1872, Ireland, 74, 03/26/1884, Phthisis, Home Hospital.

MCCARTHY, Bryan – K, 26 Illinois, 09/24/1877, Ireland, 51, 06/13/1884, Paralysis, Home Hospital.

MCGREGOR, William – B, 147 Illinois, 12/03/1883, Scotland, 67, 06/23/1884, Phthisis, Home Hospital.

MCGUIRE, Patrick – D, 5 New York, 07/10/1871, Ireland, 60, 01/12/1884, Phthisis, Home Hospital.

MCKEOWN, John – A, 42 Nebraska, 09/30/1876, Ireland, 65, 04/29/1884, Softening of the brain, Home Hospital.

MCLAUGHLIN, Dennis – F, 53 Illinois, 09/04/1884, Illinois, 44, 11/08/1884, Chronic gastritis, Home Hospital.

MCLAUGHLIN, Henry – C, 3 New York, 12/14/1881, New York, 63, 06/10/1884, Concussion of the brain, Home Hospital.

MCLAUGHLIN, John – E, 19 Illinois, 12/13/1883, Illinois, 43, 03/12/1884, Pneumonia, Home Hospital.

MEYER, Joseph – C, 24 Wisconsin, 02/08/1871, Germany, 56, 11/02/1884, Phthisis, died while on leave.

MONNETT, George – F, 2 West Virginia, 07/26/1883, Switzerland, 43, 01/05/1884, cause of death unknown, died while on leave.

MOULTON, Isaac R. - __, 5 Wisconsin Battery, 07/08/1880, Canada, 54, 12/21/1884, Paralysis, Home Hospital.

O'DELL, Jacob – E, 19 Wisconsin, 07/13/1870, Vermont, 74, 04/24/1884, Paralysis, died in Quarters.

PENT, Henry – F, 58 Illinois, 06/14/1880, Germany, 78, 10/16/1884, Old age, Home Hospital.

PUTMAN, Union – G, 111 Pennsylvania, 10/12/1883, New York, 75, 01/06/1884, Old age, Home Hospital.

RHODES, Richard – B, 10 Wisconsin, 01/05/1870, New York, 73, 08/20/1884, Old age, Home Hospital.

RILEY, Malachi – C, 17 Wisconsin, 12/09/1875, Ireland, 64, 02/26/1884, Erysipelas, Home Hospital.

RIVERS, Stephen – H, 57 Illinois, 05/09/1874, Canada, 55, 06/26/1884, Phthisis, Home Hospital.

ROSS, Cornelius – H, 90 Pennsylvania, 03/17/1871, Pennsylvania, 36, 04/03/1884, Typhoid fever, Home Hospital.

RYAN, Michael C. - __, 12 U. S. Infantry, 01/23/1884, Ireland, 65, 04/23/1884, Pneumonia, Home Hospital.

SANNER, Frederick – F, 64 Illinois, 1/25/1880, Germany, 53, 12/02/1884, Pneumonia, Home Hospital.

SAWYER, Charles – E, 118 Pennsylvania, 08/21/1884, Wisconsin, 41, 11/18/1884, Haemoptysis, Home Hospital.

SMITH, Henry – K, 3 Wisconsin, Died while *Temporary at Post.* Found dead near the Home grounds, 06/04/1884.

SMITH, John – B, 20 New York, 11/29/1883, Germany, 42, 07/02/1884, Phthisis, Home Hospital.

SMITH, John – F, 16 Indiana, 09/09/1881, Scotland, 57, 03/13/1884, Phthisis, Home Hospital.

SPOORS, Robert – D, 4 Michigan, 03/06/1884, Ohio, 49, 05/14/1884, Chronic mania, Home Hospital.

STADMAN, Bernhard – C, 1 Missouri, 02/22/1881, Switzerland, 55, 05/10/1884, Phthisis, Home Hospital.

STRAUB, Adam – E, 9 Wisconsin, 09/10/1884, Germany, 53, 12/18/1884, Chronic gastritis, Home Hospital.

THOMPSON, Francis – L, 6 Ohio Cav., 06/08/18778, New York, 43, 02/11/1884, Paralysis, Home Hospital.

TREEHOUSE, Edward – B, 56 New York, 09/19/1884, New York, 42, 09/29/1884, Heart disease, Home Hospital.

WAGNER, John – H, 9 Wisconsin, 10/06/1882, Germany, 65, 07/26/1884, cause of death unknown, died while on leave.

WATSON, Robert – I, 5 Wisconsin, 06/03/1883, England, 78, 05/10/1884, Phthisis, Home Hospital.

WELSH, Lawrence – A, 141 Illinois, 06/15/1882, Ireland, 72, 06/03/1884, Old age, Home Hospital.

WESTON, Newcomb J. – K, Lt., 6 New York Cav., 10/12/1884, New York, 60, 11/21/1884, cause of death unknown, died before reaching Home for admission.

WIDMER, Samuel – G, 116 New York, 01/20/1880, Switzerland, 59, 06/09/1884, Phthisis, Home Hospital.

Sources:

Annual Report of the Governor of the North-Western Branch, National Home for Disabled Volunteer Soldiers, for the Fiscal Year Ending June 30, 1884. Milwaukee County, Wisconsin: National Home Printing Office. General Jacob Sharpe, Governor.

Annual Report of the Governor of the North-Western Branch, National Home for Disabled Volunteer Soldiers, for the Fiscal Year Ending June 30, 1885. Milwaukee County, Wisconsin: National Home Printing Office. General, Jacob Sharpe, Governor.

DEATHS IN 1885
*First six months, ending June 30

FORMAT: NAME, COMPANY & REGIMENT, DATE OF ADMISSION, PLACE OF BIRTH, AGE, DATE OF DEATH, CAUSE OF DEATH, PLACE OF DEATH.

ASHURST, Perry – H, 2 Illinois Light Art., 03/26/1884, Illinois, 41, 04/09/1885, Phthisis, Home Hospital.

BENDT, Frederick A. – B, 1 Wisconsin, 12/06/1879, Germany, 58, 03/30/1885, Paralysis, Home Hospital.

BEATTY, Samuel – F, 16 Kentucky, 07/12/1881, Pennsylvania, 67, 02/07/1885, cause of death unknown, died near Home grounds.

BIGELOW, Wm. E. – K, 105 Ohio, 09/04/1884, Ohio, 69, 01/11/1885, cause of death unknown, died while on leave.

BLEICHMAN, Joseph – C, 15 Missouri, 01/18/1885, Switzerland, 66, 03/21/1885, Abscess of liver, Home Hospital.

BURSEN, Ole O. – K, 6 Minnesota, 08/27/1884, Norway, 42, 01/25/1885, Phthisis, Home Hospital.

EMERICH, August – A, 45 New York, 01/21/1885, Germany, 64, 03/31/1885, died suddenly on Home grounds.

ELSBURG, Frederick – K, 1 Ohio, 09/15/1883, Ohio, 51, 06/14/1885, cause of death unknown, died while on leave.

ENDEMILLER, Jacob – H, 21 Wisconsin, 03/25/1884, Germany, 45, 04/29/1885, cause of death unknown, died while on leave.

FITZGERALD, John – B, 1 Wisconsin, 08/20/1878, Massachusetts, 42, 03/25/1885, Paralysis, Home Hospital.

FLOCKER, Joseph – G, 38 New York, 04/10/1885, New York, 70, 04/24/1885, cause of death unknown, died before admission to the Home.

FOGARTY, John – B, 17 Wisconsin, 01/18/1882, Ireland, 65, 02/25/1885, Carbuncle, Home Hospital.

FOGLE, George – A, 77 Pennsylvania, 06/29/1884, Germany, 68, 02/19/1885, Facial erysipelas, Home Hospital.

FOLMER, Henry – E, 12 Pennsylvania Cav., 12/20/1876, Germany, 86, 04/07/1885, Old age, Home Hospital.

GARN, Gustavus – E, 82 Illinois, 10/26/1881, Poland, 64, 05/23/1885, Disease of heart, Home Hospital.

GLASS, John – G, 3 Vermont, 03/21/1884, Canada, 44, 02/07/1885, Chronic diarrhoea, Home Hospital.

GRIMES, James – L, 10 Illinois Cav., 10/02/1883, New York, 46, 04/29/1885, Phthisis, Home Hospital.

GUELLER, Peter – A, 52 New York, 12/21/1881, Germany, 67, 02/14/1885, Phthisis, Home Hospital.

HARKNER, Christian – F, 2 Missouri, 10/12/1880, Germany, 62, 02/07/1885, Railroad accident near Home grounds.

HICKEY, Michael – G, 14 Michigan, 10/22/1878, Ireland, 67, 05/22/1885, Drowned while on leave in Chicago, Illinois.

HOSLEY, Frederick P. – E, 3 Massachusetts Cav., 08/12/1884, Vermont, 40, 05/06/1885, Heart disease, died while on leave.

HUGHES, Thomas – C, 45 Illinois Cav., 03/08/1885, Ireland, 62, 05/14/1885, Congestion of brain, Home Hospital.

JONES, James E. – A, 10 Ohio, 08/12/1884, Ireland, 61, 06/01/1885, Paralysis, Home Hospital.

KOPKE, Jacob – D, 24 Illinois, 10/13/1882, Germany, 46, 01/07/1885, Exhaustion from debauch, Home Hospital.

MADERSPACHER, Joseph – D, 16 Illinois Cav., 05/17/1882, Germany, 73, 05/04/1885, Old age, Home Hospital.

MARSH, Sanford B. – D, 3 Wisconsin Cav., 12/31/1883, New York, 41, 01/09/1885, Exhaustion from debauch, Home Hospital.

MCCURDY, Chandler – H, 37 Wisconsin, 07/19/1883, Maine, 75, 04/22/1885, Old age, Home Hospital.

MCDONOUGH, Michael – F, 38 Wisconsin, 03/25/1880, Ireland, 60, 05/11/1885, Pneumonia, Home Hospital.

MCMAN, Frederick – E, 81, Pennsylvania, 07/14/1873, Ireland, 75, 06/17/1885, Exhaustion from debauch, Home Hospital.

MCMILLAN, Wm. J., Jr. – E, Battery, Pennsylvania Art., 01/08/1885, Pennsylvania, 42, 02/17/1885, Insanity, Home Hospital.

MCREA, John – K, 70 New York, 01/29/1884, Canada, 53, 03/05/1885, cause of death unknown, died while on leave,

METTLER, Robert – E, 15 Wisconsin, 05/28/1885, Switzerland, 55, 06/07/1885, Phthisis, Home Hospital.

MURPHY, James – H, 162 New York, 03/25/1871, Ireland, 48, 02/27/1885, cause of death unknown, died while on leave.

MOELLER, Ernst – G, 5 Missouri Cav., 02/26/1885, Germany, 62, 03/02/1885, Facial erysipelas, Home Hospital.

MOLITOR, Jacob – A, 3 Missouri, 09/15/1881, France, 67, 04/14/1885, found dead on National Avenue, near Home grounds.

NOXON, Smith M. – C, 10 Wisconsin, 11/29/1883, New York, 45, 03/29/1885, Paralysis, Home Hospital.

O'BIERNE, James – C, 1 U. S. Art., 08/18/1879, Ireland, 66, 03/24/1885, Pneumonia, Home Hospital.

O'BRIEN, Cornelius – C, 11 Vermont, 01/06/1885, Ireland, 41, 04/03/1885, Phthisis, Home Hospital.

PINE, Samuel – War of 1812, 02/09/1876, Vermont, 93, 03/02/1885, Old age, Home Hospital.

POLLATH, Frank – B, 32 Illinois, 10/03/1879, Germany, 65, 02/04/1885, cause of death unknown, died while on leave.

REINER, Louis C. – G, 14 Illinois, 09/03/1884, Germany, 59, 05/28/1885, cause of death unknown, Milwaukee County Insane Asylum.

ROBERTS, Daniel – K, 53 U. S. Colored Troop, 10/17/1884, Louisiana, 76, 05/11/1885, Pneumonia, Home Hospital.

ROSENBURG, Samuel - F, 14 Michigan, 09/07/1884, Maryland, 41, 05/03/1885, Apoplexy, Home Hospital.

SATTLER, John – E, 28 Ohio, 12/24/1881, Germany, 77, 02/18/1885, Old age, Home Hospital.

SHEPARD, Alonzo C. – D, 44 New York, 03/20/1884, New York, 46, 05/28/1885, Phthisis pulmonalis, Home Hospital.

SHERIDAN, Patrick – K, 90 Illinois, 10/07/1881, Ireland, 70, 02/15/1885, cause of death unknown, died while on leave.

SKINNER, John – I, 55 Illinois, 03/12/1878, New York, 62, 01/31/1885, cause of death unknown, died while on leave.

SNYDER, Phillip – H, 45 Illinois, 09/01/1879, Germany, 72, 06/08/1885, cause of death unknown, died in a National Avenue saloon near Home grounds.

STEVENS, Augustus – K, 103 New York, 09/28/1881, New York, 69, 04/26/1885, Chronic rheumatism, Home Hospital.

TAYLOR, Luke – I, 13 Wisconsin, 02/07/1885, New York, 75, 06/11/1885, Typhoid pneumonia, died while on leave.

TOTTEN, Wesley, - F, 72 Pennsylvania, 08/29/1884, Pennsylvania, 56, 01/02/1885, Phthisis, Home Hospital.

WALTER, George – B, 51 Pennsylvania, 01/04/1885, Pennsylvania, 59, 03/06/1885, Heart disease, Home Hospital.

WHITE, James D. – E, 73 New York, 09/13/1881 England, 89, 04/29/1995, Old age, Home Hospital.

WILLIS, Samuel A. – G, 53 Pennsylvania, 08/27/1884, Pennsylvania, 68, 01/05/1885, Exhaustion from debauch, Home Hospital.

WILLMAN, Julius F. C. – A, 4 Maryland, 01/15/1885, Maryland, 46, 04/20/1885, Suicide, Home, Company F Quarters.

WOLFGRAM, Frederick – I, 26 Wisconsin, 12/19/1882, Germany, 55, 05/15/1885, Phthisis pulmonalis, died while on leave from hospital.

Source:

Annual Report of the Governor of the North-Western Branch, National Home for Disabled Volunteer Soldiers, for the Fiscal Year Ending June 30 1885. Milwaukee County, Wisconsin: National Home Printing Office. General Jacob Sharpe, Governor.

DEATHS IN 1885
*After June 30

FORMAT: NAME, COMPANY & REGIMENT, DATE OF ADMISSION, PLACE OF
BIRTH, AGE, DISABILITY, DATE OF DEATH.

CHENEY, William F. – E, 2 Massachusetts Cav., 01/11/1885,
Maine, 47, Cystitis, 09/01/1885.

COAKLEY, Nathan B. – A, 12 Missouri Cav., 08/21/1885, Ohio,
47, Hemorrhoids, 11/05/1885.

CYPHERS, Emanuel – E, 127 New York, 06/10/1883, New York,
50, Diarrhoea, 10/22/1885.

DELANEY, William – H, 16 Kansas, 08/30/1883, Ireland, 75,
Rheumatism, 11/27/1885.

DEVINE, William R. – A, 145 Pennsylvania, 09/15/1876, France,
61, Wound-right arm, 09/02/1885.

FLOREY, Jacob – D, Cpl., 155 Pennsylvania, 03/06/1882, Pennsylvania, 52, Hernia, 11/19/1885.

GARRAHAN, William – H, 7 New York Heavy Art.04/04/1870,
New Jersey, 36, Loss-right leg, 12/06/1885.

HANDY, Edward H. – G, Lt., 31 Iowa, 12/27/1884, New York, 68,
Rheumatism, 10/01/1885.

HARRIS, Henry – F, 14 Indiana, 07/07/1885, Pennsylvania, 43,
Heart disease, 10/31/1885.

HARTWELL, Alexander – F, 3 Wisconsin, 04/26/1885, Connecticut, 67, Heart disease, 09/01/1885.

HIBBS, Thomas – G, 2 New York Heavy Art., 02/11/1873, England, 40, Loss-left leg, 10/06/1885.

KELLY, Cornelius A. – Unassigned, Mexican War, 09/12/1883,
Pennsylvania, 60, Lung disease, 11/01/1885.

LINGENBERG, Fred. L. – K, 7 Pennsylvania, 09/16/1884, Germany, 48, Rheumatism, 10/11/1885.

MCCREADY, Thomas – A, 14 Wisconsin, 01`/21/1871, Ireland,
48, Injury-left side, 11/03/1885.

MITCHELL, Farral – G, 8 Illinois Cav., 05/29/1877, Ireland, 63,
General debility, 12/28/1885.

MUNSON, John – C, 66 New York, 03/30/1885, New Jersey, 55,
Wound-right thigh, 09/11/1885.

PERRY, John – D, 32 Wisconsin, 05/17/1880, New York, 55,
Phthisis, 12/29/1885.

PYNE, Thomas – D, 29 Indiana, 02/04/1884, Ireland, 52, Rheumatism, 09/02/1885.

ROHR, Herman – __, Rhode Island Hospital Guards, 01/07/1885, Switzerland, 52, Deaf, 09/11/1885.

RUEL, George – H, 14 Michigan, 10/06/1883, New York, 55, Wound-left leg, 09/04/1885.

STARKEY, Thomas – K, 1 Wisconsin Heavy Art., 06/21/1880, Massachusetts, 55, Rheumatism, 11/09/1885.

TREWELLEGER, Joseph – F, Sgt., 2 West Virginia, 02/27/1885, Ohio, 63, Hemorrhoids, 09/07/1885.

TOLAS, Charles – A, 2 Michigan, 09/27/1882, Michigan, 45, Paralysis, 12/04/1885.

VROMAN, Peter – I, 2 U. S. Inf. Florida War, 07/15/1885, New York, 71, Heart disease, 08/19/1885.

ZEHREN, Peter – F, 9 Wisconsin, 08/05/1880, Germany, 69, Hernia, 08/11/1885.

*Beginning 07/01/1885, national documents are used as the source of soldier's records. . Information regarding CAUSE OF DEATH & PLACE OF DEATH were deleted and DISABILITY was added in those records. Therefore, there is a change in *format* in the continuing data collection.

Source:
The Miscellaneous Documents of the House of Representatives for the Second Session of the 49th Congress, 1886-87. Record of Disabled Volunteer Soldiers Who Now Are And Have Been Members of the National Home for Disabled Volunteer Soldiers, from July 1, 1885, to July 1, 1886. #2488. Washington: Government Printing Office, 1888. (Extracted from Annual Reports - National Homes for Disabled Volunteer Soldiers.)

FORMAT: NAME, COMPANY & REGIMENT, DATE OF ADMISSION, AGE, PLACE
OF BIRTH, DISABILITY, DATE OF DEATH.

ALLISON, Thomas S. – I, 26 Indiana, 07/15/1886, Indiana, 41,
Rheumatism, 08/14/1886.

ARNOLD, Andrew – M, 3 Pennsylvania Art., 07/02/1885,
Germany, 51, Fracture-patella, 04/13/1886.

ATWOOD, Amos C. – E, 1 Illinois Cav., 12/23/1879, Ireland, 47,
Wound-left leg, 04/03/1886.

BAKER, Justus P. – I, 5 Vermont, 01/28/1879, Vermont, 34,
Wound-right leg, 12/03/1886.

BARBER, George W. – E, 9 New Hampshire, 01/01/1876,
Massachusetts, 39, Loss-left arm, 09/26/1886.

BARNES, Michael – E, 11 Wisconsin, 02/24/1886, Ireland, 42,
Phthisis, 04/07/1886.

BARRY, William – Seaman, U. S. Navy, 01/08/1885, Pennsylvania,
65, Hernia, 12/22/1886.

BECK, John – D, Independent Battalion, Minnesota Cav.,
06/07/1885, Connecticut, 39, Heart disease, 02/02/1886.

BIGELOW, Henry M. – I, 1 California, 06/29/1886, Ohio, 53,
Diarrhoea, 08/28/1886.

BENTILL, Christian - __, 4 Wisconsin Battery, 08/25/1872,
Germany, 37, Rheumatism, 02/11/1886.

BONE, Edward – B, 9 Wisconsin, 08/25/1880, Germany, 32,
Hemorrhoids, 04/16/1886.

BOYLE, Henry – H, 58, Illinois, 11/09/1883, Ireland, 55, Wound-
right arm, 05/01/1886.

BRETT, Charles, F. – B, 11 U. S. Veteran Reserve Corps,
10/21/1882, England, 56, Rheumatism, 05/17/1886.

CAMPBELL, Isaac T. – B, 7 Pennsylvania Cav., 03/25/1881, Pennsylvania, 45, Injury- right leg, 09/11/1886.

CAMPBELL, John – A, 152 Indiana, 09/18/172, Ireland, 62, Rheumatism, 04/15/1886.

CHETWIN, Ephraim – I, 37 Iowa, 06/24/1883, England, Wound-
right hand, 02/01/1886.

CHRISTOPHER, John – C, 16 Kansas Cav., 07/11/1867, Denver,
49, Wound-left hand & arm, 08/21/1886.

COLE, Alonzo – B, 21 Iowa, 09/23/1884, New York, 72, Injury-right knee, 04/26/1886.

COLEMAN, John – C, 38 Illinois, 04/01/1884, Ireland, 52, Rheumatism, 06/25/1886.

COLEN, John H. – D, Sgt., 3 Delaware, 06/28/1880, Pennsylvania, 36, Wound-right arm, 07/16/1886.

CONN, George F. – B, Capt., 1 Ohio Cav., 10/17/1883, Ohio, 47, Wound-left hand, 10/14/1886.

COTTER, Michael – E, 2 Michigan, 07/28/1884, Ireland, 68, Wound-left hip, 09/15/1886.

CRASSEY, Irwin K. - __, Sgt., 1 Kansas Battery, 09/07/1884, Kentucky, 47, Phthisis, 03/13/1886.

DERMODY, Timothy – I, 19 New York, 12/16/1879, Ireland, 45, Disease-eyes, 04/07/1886.

DOWNEY, Barth – Fireman, U. S. Navy, 07/27/1886, Ireland, 46, Paralysis, 12/12/1886.

DUCOTA, C. C. – A, 1 Nebraska Cav., 05/10/1885, France, 72, Diarrhoea, 12/19/1886.

FAYS, Peter – H. 10 Missouri, 08/21/1884, Belgium, 54, Rheumatism, 02/23/1886.

FORBES, Joseph B. – A, 8 Kansas, 07/17/1884, New York, 53, Rheumatism, 03/01/1886.

FORSTEL, Philip – H, 50 Wisconsin, 11/06/1885, Ireland, 37, Loss-both feet, 02/08/1886.

FRAKES, Oliver P. – D, 6 Michigan, 09/29/1883, Ohio, 60, Diarrhoea, 10/15/1886,

GAFNEY, William – C, 107 Pennsylvania, 01/05/1885, Maryland, 61, Varicose veins, 07/26/1886.

GEISEL, John – K, 119 Illinois, 11/11/1879, Germany, 63, Ophthalmia, 06/14/1886.

GIRTY, Thomas – 1st Asst. Engineer, U. S. Navy, 06/15/1886, Pennsylvania, 69, Wound- head, 10/02/1886.

GORPE, Charles – B. 3 Missouri, 07/15/1879, Germany, 63, Varicose veins, 06/27/1886.

GOULD, Charles – H, 24 New York, 09/02/1880, New York, 61, Wound-right leg, 05/19/1886.

GOWSAN, Christopher – F, 39 Illinois, 08/05/1884, Germany, 80, Epilepsy, 03/05/1886.

GRANELS, John – B, 100 Illinois, 06/27/1883, Ireland, 56, Dropsy, 06/23/1886.

GREEN, Timothy – K, 10 U. S. Veteran Reserve Corps, 04/12/1868, Ireland, 38, Loss- left leg, 06/14/1886.

HARNEY Dennis – H, 2 Rhode Island, 04/22/1885, Ireland, 38, Epilepsy, 08/21/1886.

HARPER, James – I, 102 New York, 06/24/1881, Ireland, 58, Hernia, 08/29/1886.

HARTMAN, Louis, - I, 13 Missouri, 09/16/1880, Germany, 64, Rheumatism, 05/19/1886.

HILL, Alexander – H, 2 Iowa Cav., 06/07/1885, Pennsylvania, 60, Paralysis, 04/15/1886.

HINES, Albert – E, 10 New York Heavy Art., 06/03/1886, New York, 55, Heart disease, 12/07/1886.

HOECK, Sebastian – K, 26 Wisconsin, 09/13/1872, Germany, 48, Asthma, 07/06/1886.

HORNBURG, Julius - I, Cpl., 12 U. S. Veteran Reserve Corps, 04/29/1879, Germany, 60, Rheumatism, 03/07/1886.

HUNT, Norman V. – Illinois Cogswell's Battery, 06/23/1881, New York, 38, Asthma, 07/11/1886.

HUNTHOUSEN, William – C, 16 Wisconsin, 07/28/1886, Germany, 52, Heart disease, 08/06/1886.

KEEGAN, John – F, 51 Illinois, 05/19/1885, Ireland, 64, Wound-left thigh, 05/12/1886.

KEENAN, Owen – F, 133 New York, 09/14/1886, Ireland, 43, Bronchitis, 12/28/1886.

KELLY, Michael – G, 14 Wisconsin, 07/28/1886, Ireland, 70, Bronchitis, 09/28/1886.

KETCHLEDGE, James. – F, 7 Michigan, 09/27/1878, Pennsylvania, 52, Disease-lungs, 12/12/1886.

KNICKERBOCKER, C. – K, 18 Wisconsin, 06/03/1886, New York, 55, Rheumatism, 07/25/1886.

LAHAN, Patrick – B, 3 New York Light Art., 05/05/1886, Canada, 44, Rheumatism, 08/10/1886.

LEINDECKER, Gottfreid – I, 9 Wisconsin, 02/28/1879, Germany, 64, Rheumatism, 05/21/1886.

LONGENOLL, Joseph - ___, 9 Wisconsin Battery, 01/17/1884, Germany, 67, Hernia, 08/02/1886.

MACK, Thomas – I, 150 New York, 06/15/1886, Ireland, 47, Lung disease, 10/14/1886.

MAHONY, Patrick – B, 9 U. S. Veteran Reserve Corps, 11/28/1883, Ireland, 67, Varicose veins, 01/17/1886.

MANGAN Eugene – H, 17 Wisconsin, 12/09/1881, Wisconsin, 37, Wound-left leg, 09/16/1886.

MANN, Frank – E, 46 Illinois, 02/25/1885, Germany, 64, Lumbago, 01/14/1886.

MARTIN, Lawrence – K, 99 Pennsylvania, 08/22/1871, Ireland, 36, Wound-right leg, 05/30/1886.

MCCALL, Sanford – E, 13 Wisconsin, 07/08/1885, New York, 62, Wound-neck, 05/21/1886.

MCKENZIE, Duke – K, Sgt., 3 Michigan, 11/16/1882, Ireland, 61, Piles, 12/14/1886.

MCLEAN, John – B, 7 Kansas Cav., 05/13/1882, Maryland, 39, Rheumatism, 07/17/1886.

MCMAHON, Patrick - ___, 8 Wisconsin Battery, 05/03/1881, Ireland, 55, Hernia, 09/12/1886.

MEYER, Fritz – I, 27 Wisconsin 08/26/1879, Germany, 60, Rheumatism, 10/08/1886.

MEYER, Jacob – F, 74 Pennsylvania, 08/18/1881, Switzerland, 58, Hernia, 01/01/1886.

MEYER, John – C, 33 Illinois, 10/03/1874, Germany, 37, Wound-back, 05/22/1886.

MILLER, Joseph – C, 113 Illinois, 07/05/1884, Missouri, 39, Lung disease, 12/22/1886.

MILLER, Peter – C, 14 Pennsylvania Cav., 09/02/1886, Bavaria, 49, Lung disease, 09/26/1886.

MONTMAN, Charles. F. - D, 2 Wisconsin Cav., 04/24/1880, Germany, 47, Rheumatism, 12/30/1886.

MURPHY, Michael – A, 10 Illinois, Cav., 09/07/1883, Ireland, 50, Paralysis, 11/28/1886.

NONGASSER, Louis – Band, 32 Indiana, 09/24/1884, Germany, 65, Disease-lungs, 12/28/1886.

OBERDICK, Charles – D, 61 Illinois, 07/19/1873, Germany, 57, Dropsy, 04/02/1886.

PARROW, Charles – K, 24 Illinois, 04/06/1870, Germany, 54, Rheumatism, 08/16/1886.

PFEIFFER, Frank – I, 1 Kansas, 10/28/1882, France, 50, Varicose veins, 08/03/1886.

PLATZLER, John – F, 74 Pennsylvania, 07/15/1885, Germany, 60, Rheumatism, 07/10/1886.

PRINDLE, Timothy H. – A, 1 Dakota Cav., 06/07/1885, New York, 69, Injury-right hip, 12/25/1886.

PRINN, Adam – A, 2 New York Mounted Rifles, 01/01/1871, Germany, 30, Loss-left arm, 03/01/1886.

QUICK, Moses C. – D, Sgt., 2 U. S. Colored Troop Light Art., 07/21/1886, California, 51, Disease-bladder, 11/26/1886.

REA, John – F, 37 Iowa, 04/26/1871, Ireland, 55, Loss-left eye, 10/08/86.

REYNOLDS, Robert – Unassigned, Mexican War, 03/24/1885, Ireland, 71, Frozen feet, 06/06/1886.

RIGGS, Charles – K, 16 New York Heavy Art., 08/18/1885, New York, 37, Phthisis, 06/09/1886.

ROWELL, John – E, 6 Wisconsin, 03/15/1884, England, 56, Rheumatism, 10/18/1886.

RUDDY, Patrick – D, 14 Wisconsin, 07/18/1883, Ireland, 62, Hernia, 07/29/1886.

SANFORD, T. C. – G, 11 New York Cav., 09/24/1884, England, 51, Epilepsy, 08/25/1886.

SCHACHMEIER, John – E, 45 Wisconsin, 05/12/1886, Germany, 63, Rheumatism, 06/25/1886.

SCHMIDT, Michael – M, 2 Wisconsin Cav., 10/08/1880, Germany, 66, Wound-legs, 10/08/1886.

SCHNEIDER, John – B, 39 New York, 09/09/1885, Germany, 55, Hernia, 01/15/1886.

SCHWAB, Andrew – A, 127 Illinois, 11/23/1883, Germany, 65, Rheumatism, 11/15/1886.

SCHWEDER, Charles – B, 41 New York, 09/02/1880, Germany, 60, General debility, 08/01/1886.

SCHWINGLER, Jacob – I, 8 Minnesota, 12/23/1884, Germany 72, Asthma, 02/20/1886.

SEAVER, William – A, 40 Wisconsin, 11/14/1886, New York, 43, Paralysis, 1/23/1886.

SEIFERT, Charles M. – I, 31 Wisconsin, 06/09/1885, Ohio, 60, General.debility, 3/15/1886.

SISSON, Alanson – I, 9 Illinois Cav., 05/19/1885, New York, 65, Injury-shoulder, 03/19/1886.

STAVES, John H. – C, 3 Wisconsin Cav., 09/10/1878, England, 45, Epilepsy, 5/17/1886.

STEITLING, Gustavus – Seaman, U. S. Marine Corps, 07/29/1885, Germany, 66, General debility, 10/30/1886.

STONE, John – E, 90 Illinois, 07/24/1875, Ireland, 62, Epilepsy, 03/13/1886.

STRATTON, Harman – E, 31 Ohio, 10/09/1884, Ohio, 38, Kidney disease, 02/06/1886.

STUBBS, Henry – K, 90 New York, 09/12/1883, Maine, 71, Rheumatism, 05/23/1886.

SYVERSON, Ole – A, 15 Wisconsin, 09/30/1882, Norway, 60, Varicose ulcers, 08/21/1886.

VOGT, Anton – C, 5 Missouri Cav., 04/20/1870, Germany 57, Injury-back, 01/15/1886.

WERNER, Frank - __, 2 Wisconsin Battery, 07/27/1880, Germany, 64, Rheumatism, 05/16/1886.

WOLF, William – K, 1 Michigan Light Art., 01/22/1884, Germany, 59, Rheumatism, 112/12/1886.

WOLFITT, William – G, 27 Wisconsin, 07/21/1886, England, 61, Rheumatism, 09/11/1886.

WONDERS, Joseph - B, 33 Illinois, 01/24/1884,England, 39, Sciatica, 10/14/1886.

WOODMANSEE, H. S. – F, 15 Iowa, 03/18/1884, New York, 56, Lung disease, 01/06/1886.

WRENN, Joseph – M, 9 New York Cav., 05/06/1869, Ireland, 50, Loss-left arm, 01/21/1886.

Sources:

The Miscellaneous Documents of the House of Representatives for the Second Session of the 49th Congress, 1886-87. Record of Disabled Volunteer Soldiers Who Now Are and Have Been Members of the National Home for Disabled Volunteer Soldiers, from July 1, 1885, to July 1, 1886. #2488.* Washington: Government Printing Office, 1887. (Extracted from Annual Reports – National Homes for Disabled Volunteer Soldiers.).

The Miscellaneous Documents of the House of Representatives for the First Session of the 50th Congress, 1887-88. Record of Disabled Volunteer Soldiers Who Now Are and Have Been Members of the National Home for Disabled Volunteer Soldiers, from July 1, 1886 to July 1, 1887. #2565. Washington: Government Printing Office, 1888. (Extracted from Annual Reports – National Homes for Disabled Volunteer Soldiers.)

DEATHS IN 1887

FORMAT: NAME, COMPANY & REGIMENT, DATE OF ADMISSION, PLACE OF BIRTH, AGE, DISABILITY, DATE OF DEATH.

ACKERMAN, George H. – K, Sgt., 18 Wisconsin, 01/21/1884, Germany, 55, Rheumatism, 05/30/1887.

ANDERSON, John – G, 24 Wisconsin, 12/23/1884, Ireland, 64, Rheumatism, 05/22/1887.

ATKINSON, Jacob – 3 Engineer, U. S. Navy, 06/08/1887, New York, 61, Rheumatism, 08/08/1887.

ALTHAMMER, William – H, Lt., 187 Ohio, 09/11/1883, Germany, 59, Rheumatism, 05/01/1887.

AULD, John – C, 37 Iowa, 08/03/1887, Ireland, 77, General debility, 08/27/1887.

BAKER, William – A, 1 Massachusetts Cav., 11/29/1887, Massachusetts, 48, Rheumatism, 08/01/1887.

BARNEY, Z. T. – H, 49 Wisconsin, 11/05/186, New York, 45, Disease-lungs, 02/21/1887.

BARRE, George – E, 16 Michigan, 05/13/1885, France, 60, Wound-left hip, 01/20/1887.

BAST, John W. – G, 40 New Jersey, 11/26/1884, Pennsylvania, 62, Disease-liver, 03/01/1887.

BELLIS, Jacob S. - F, 16 Illinois, 12/22/1884, New Jersey, 51, Frozen-feet, 01/04/1887.

BENSON, Peter – A, 3 West Virginia Cav., 01/13/1876, Ireland, 66, Piles, 08/28/1887.

BERGER, Alex. W. - __, 83 Ohio, H. S., 07/16/1885, Sweden, 62, Paralysis, 5/28/1887.

BUCKER, Joseph – A, 82 Illinois, 11/19/1880, Germany, 48, Heart disease, 12/26/1887.

BUEL, James T. – I, Capt., 1 Missouri Light Art., 01/01/1880, New York, 63, Rheumatism, 08/20/1887.

BUTCHER, Theodore – E, 183 Pennsylvania, 03/13/1887, Pennsylvania, 42, Heart disease, 07/26/1887.

CARROLL, John – I, 23 Illinois, 07/21/1883, Ireland, 50, Heart disease, 08/26/1887.

CLAPP, James G. – B, Cpl., 18 Wisconsin, 08/27/1886, Connecticut, 47, Paralysis, 09/26/1887.

CLARKE, George B. – A, 1 Minnesota, 12/26/1886, Pennsylvania, 44, Paralysis, 03/16/1887.

CODE, William – C, 1 U. S. Army Art., 10/05/1886, Ireland, 53, Disease-lungs, __/25/1887.

CONNELLY, Morris – G, 24 Wisconsin, 01/12/1882, Ireland, 60, Bronchitis, 03/19/1887.

COSGROVE, M. G. – H, 46 Illinois, 06/07/1883, Ireland, 49, Diarrhoea, 12/03/1887.

COSTIGAN, John – K, 1 New York, 01/11/1870, Ireland, 48, Varicose veins, 11/16/1887.

CUNEEN, John – A, 7 Illinois Cav., 02/06/1887, Ireland, 40, Diabetes, 03/26/1887.

DALEY, Michael – B, 11 Wisconsin, 11/28/1883, Ireland, 52, Disease-spine, 12/04/1887.

DALTON, Mathew – E, 35 Wisconsin, 02/06/1887, New York, 39, Injury-jaw, 08/16/1887.

DANE, Thomas – Seaman, U. S. Navy, 05/07/1870, Ireland, 50, Wound-head, 06/09/1887.

DELANEY, Joseph – B, 61 Ohio, 05/ 22/1887, Ireland, 47, Wound-head, 06/08/1887.

DENKER, Peter – I, 2 Wisconsin Cav., 04/06/1887, Germany, 51, Dropsy, 05/01/1887.

DENTON, Charles – E, Cpl., 3 Iowa, 10/24/1878, Iowa, 36, Wound-left hip, 06/26/1887.

DICKINSON, John – G, 4 Michigan, 11/28/1886, New York, 46, Dropsy, 06/24/1887.

DILLON, Henry – F, 168 New York, 01/05/1887, Ireland, 60, Disease-lungs, 01/05/1887.

DUGAN, John - __, Sgt., 22 U. S, Veteran Reserve Corps, 05/20/1880, New York, 38, Wound-left thigh, 12/13/1887.

ECKHART, George - __, Major, 9 Wisconsin, 05/22/1883, Germany, 47, Disease-lungs, 04/16/1887.

EPPENBERGER, A. – B, 1 Minnesota, 05/28/1879, Switzerland, 59, Hernia, 11/23/1887.

FEILMEIER, Joseph - __, 2 Wisconsin Battery, 08/16/1884, Germany, 72, Rheumatism, 03/16/1887.

FERGUSON, S. E. – C, 4 Minnesota, 08/25/1885, Virginia, 55, Rheumatism, 08/25/1887.

FITZGIBBON, Edward – C, 90 Illinois, 06/21/1973, Ireland, 75, Wound-left leg, 03/24/1887.

FITZPATRICK, M. – K, 16 New York, 03/03/1887, New York, 44, Rheumatism, 03/18/1887.

FOSS, Stephen - H, 2 Wisconsin, 07/09/1887, New Hampshire, 58, Wound-face, 11/02/1887.

GARVIG, John – A, 113 Illinois, 04/27/1887, Ireland, 54, Deaf, 09/27/1887.

GAUS, Michael – C, 29 New York, 08/25/1881, Germany, 61, Wound-right thigh, 05/01/1887.

GEER, William E. – E, 68 Illinois, 10/05/1885, Connecticut, 71, Lung disease, 10/27/1887.

GREGORY, Robert – L, 9 Michigan Cav., 10/14/1875, Ireland, 65, Deaf, 08/24/1887.

GROGAN, Michael – G, 24 Wisconsin, 08/28/1870, Ireland, 53, Rheumatism, 06/16/1887.

GRUBBS, Jacob J. – C, Sgt., 112 Pennsylvania, 01/12/1881, Pennsylvania, 49, Wound-right thigh, 02/15/1887.

HALE, Joel – G, Sgt., Wisconsin Cav., 05/20/1887, New York, 52, Injury-left hip, 07/13/1887.

HANLEY, Morris – I, 11 Illinois, 08/18/1885, Ireland, 45, Lung disease, 03/09/1887.

HANSLER, Herman - __, 30 New York Battery, 07/17/1877, Germany, 50, Ulcer-right leg, 04/15/188

HARRIS, James B. – B, 7 U. S., Mexican War, 04/21/1886, Kentucky, 67, Disease-eyes, 02/18/1887.

HAYDEN, Frederick – C, 7 New York, 08/10/1887, Germany, 52, Hernia, 12/25/1887.

HEBLE, Christian – C, 13 Illinois, 05/05/1887, Germany, 50, Pneumonia, 05/05/1887.

HEBRINGER, Michael – Unassigned, Mexican War, 12/21/1882, Maine, 67, Disease-eyes, 05/25/1887.

HOEFT, Charles – C, Sgt., 7 New York, 07/08/1887, Germany 62, Asthma, 11/30/1887.

JACOBS, Mathias – I, 52 New York, 06/19/1883, Germany, 50, Wound-left wrist, 06/04/1887.

KELLY, Andrew B. – D, 23 New York, 12/30/1885, New York, 43, Disease-lungs, 02/12/1887.

KNITTEL, Louis – E, 9 Illinois Cav., 04/14/1885, France, 54, Rheumatism, 11/21/1887.

KOLLBERG, John – I, 26 Wisconsin, 12/11/1876, Germany, 60, Disease-spine, 04/21/1887.

KUNZE, Frederick – I, 1 Missouri Engineers, 11/03/1882, Germany, 60, Rheumatism, 08/02/1887,

LA PRAIRIE, Bahice –Unassigned, War of 1812, 06/02/1884, California, 106, General debility, 01/08/1887.

LAWLER, Thomas – B, 7 Ohio Cav., 04/14/1886, Ireland, 52, Rheumatism, 10/14/1887.

LEDEBAUGH, Christian – G, 4 Pennsylvania Cav., 01/20/1887, Germany, 74, General debility, 08/03/1887.

LEEDOM, Frank – A, 7 U. S. Veteran Volunteers, 10/27/185, Pennsylvania, 53, Rheumatism, 11/26/1887.

LORING, Isaiah – H, 9 Maine, 01/05/1885, Maine, 65, General debility, 05/16/1887.

LOVELY, Thomas – I, 58 Illinois, 05/26/1886, England, 72, Injury-left shoulder, 01/03/1887.

LUDIN, John – G, 14 New York Cav., 10/25/1872, Switzerland, 53, Wound-right leg, 09/01/1887.

MAYNARD, James – Seaman, U. S. Navy, 03/04/1887, New York, 46, Hydrocele, 09/02/1887.

MCCARTHY, William – C, 22 U. S. Army, 03/09/1887, Ireland, 50, Lumbago, 03/10/1887.

MCMILLAN, Neil – H, 72 Illinois, 01/08/1885, Scotland, 54, Lung disease, 10/06/1887.

MIFFLIN, Henry J. – A, 23 U. S. Veteran Reserve Corps, 02/15/1870. Pennsylvania, 44, Diarrhoea, 05/21/1887.

MURRAY, Hugh – D, 2 Wisconsin, 09/08/1873, Ireland, 53, Wound-left shoulder, 01/11/1887.

NERTZ, John – D, 1 Wisconsin, 10/27/1883, Germany, 69, Hernia, 07/30/1887.

NICHOLS, Aura – L, Sgt., 8 Michigan Cav., 07/08/1885, Michigan, 46, Paralysis, 11/28/1887.

O'BRIEN, Cornelius – D, 102 Pennsylvania, 07/14/1885, Ireland, 70, General debility, 03/20/1887.

OCHS, Ferdinand – H, 24 Illinois, 07/09/1884, Germany, 47, Rheumatism, 09/28/1887.

O'CONNER, Patrick – G, 17 Massachusetts, 09/23/1881, Ireland, 42, Rheumatism, 10/24/1887.

O'NEIL, Terrence - F, 36 Wisconsin, 04/27/1870, Ireland, 47, Wound-head, 12/24/1887.

PEDERSON, Charles E. – F, 14 U. S. Veteran Reserve Corps, 11/01/1881, Russia, 48, Paralysis, 06/02/1887.

PHILLIPS, Louis H. – G, 43 Wisconsin, 08/09/1887, Wisconsin, 55, Asthma, 12/15/1887.

PICKERT, Charles – G, 1 Michigan Sharpshooters, 02/12/1874, Germany, 50, Fracture- right leg, 08/08/1887.

RANSOM, Benjamin – E, 145 New York, 12/18/1876, New York, 56, Hernia, 08/03/1887.

REED, Jerry – K, 2 Wisconsin Cav., 07/15/1872, Wisconsin, 30, Epilepsy, 05/17/1887.

REIK, Constance – C, Capt., 4 Missouri Reserve Corps, 07/08/1887, Germany, 61, Hernia, 10/01/1887.

RISS, Frank – G, 1 Illinois Light Art., 12/17/1878, Germany, 58, Wound-left hand, 11/25/1887.

ROMMELFAUGERZ, Jacob – G, 46 Illinois, 02/08/1884, Germany, 60, Asthma, 10/19/1887.

RUBENDALL, D. R. – A, Cpl., 46 Illinois, 05/05/1886, Pennsylvania, 40, Wound-right thigh, 01/06/1887.

RUEBACH, William – D, 21 Wisconsin, 06/05/1880, Germany, 56, Rheumatism, 08/13/1887.

RUTHER, Frank – C, 35 Wisconsin, 12/02/1886, Germany, 70, Rheumatism, 07/09/1887.

RYAN, Patrick G. – F, 14 Wisconsin, 10/03/1885, Massachusetts, 45, Rheumatism, 06/29/1887.

SANDERS, William – I, 13 Ohio Cav., 09/24/1884, Ireland, 63, Rheumatism, 06/22/1887.

SANFORD, Josiah B. - E, 4 Ohio, 07/21/1885, New York, 47, Hernia, 04/27/1887.

SCHAFFER, George – E, 7 New York, 08/29/1887, Germany, 61, Injury-leg, 11/27/1887.

SCHREADER, Gottfr'd. – H, 2 Michigan Cav., 12/17/1883, Germany, 60, Hernia, 06/13/1887.

SCHULTZ, George – E, 9 Missouri Cav., 03/27/1877, Germany, 37, Paralysis, 05/21/1887.

SELBY, Charles M. – B, 11 U. S. Veteran Reserve Corps, 02/03/1887, New York, 70, Wound-left hand, 12/08/1887.

SHARKEY, Nicholas - Unassigned, Mexican War, 12/24/1879, Germany, 59, Varicose veins, 10/31/1887.

SHURTER, William H. – B, 36 New York, 10/01/1885, New York, 56, Wound- right leg, 05/25/1887.

SPRING, Frederick – F, 9 Wisconsin, 08/31/1881, Germany, 62, Varicose veins, 06/27/1887.

STARK, John – E, 26 Wisconsin, 10/02/187, Germany, 43, General debility, 11/23/1887.

STEWART, James J. – C, 7 New York Heavy Art., Ireland, 55, Piles, 10/14/1887.

STODDARD, John – C, Cpl., 17 Wisconsin, 04/17/1879, Scotland, 47, Piles, 09/01/1887.

WADSWORTH, A. H. - __, Musician, 6 Wisconsin, 08/09/1887, New York 73, Paralysis, 12/24/1887.

WALKER, John G. – E, 82 Illinois, 03/10/1871, Germany, 50, General debility, 01/26/1887.

WETTENDORF, William. – A, 29 Missouri, 07/26/1973, Germany, 53, Rheumatism, 02/04/1887.

WHITEHEAD, J. W. – New York Independent Battery, 09/16/1873, England, 37, Wound-right hand, 01/21/1887.

WOODWORTH, E. – E, 2 Connecticut Heavy Art., 05/201879, Connecticut, 60, Wound-left thigh, 01/08/1887.

WRIGHT, John Q. – B, 14 Illinois, 11/20/1882, Kentucky, 43, Bronchitis, 06/07/1887.

VOIGHT, William – A, 1 Wisconsin Cav., 10/21/1887, Germany, 66, Diarrhoea, 11/01/1887.

ZIMMER, Nicholas – G, 61 New York, 12/07/1869, Germany, 47, Wound-side, 09/01/1887.

Sources:

The Miscellaneous Documents of the House of Representatives for the First Session of the 50th Congress, 1887-88. Record of Disabled Volunteer Soldiers Who Now Are And Have Been Members of the

National Home for Disabled Volunteer Soldiers, from July 1,1886 to July 1, 1887. #2565. Washington: Government Printing Office, 1888. (Extracted from Annual Reports – National Homes for Disabled Volunteer Soldiers.)

The Miscellaneous Documents of the House Of representatives for the Second Session of the 50th Congress, 1888-89. Record of Disabled Volunteer Soldiers Who Now Are And Have Been Members of the National Home for Disabled Volunteer Soldiers, from July 1. 1887 to July 1, 1888. #2654. Washington: Government Printing Office, 1889. (Extracted from Annual Reports – National Homes for Disabled Volunteer Soldiers.)

FORMAT: NAME, COMPANY & REGIMENT, DATE OF ADMISSION, PLACE OF BIRTH, AGE, DISABILITY, DATE OF DEATH.

AMBROSE, Michael – D, 6 Wisconsin, 06/23/1886, Ireland, 56, Hernia, 07/08/1888.

ANGST, John – F, 39 Ohio, 08/12/1886, Switzerland, 70, Rheuma tism, 11/11/1888.

ASH, John – C, 3 U. S Army Corps, 3 Cav., 01/29/1887, Ireland, 54, Heart disease, 02/27/1888.

BEHRENS, Charles – I, 82 Illinois, 09/03/1885, Germany, 72, Ulcer-right leg, 04/19/1888.

BENDER, Charles – I, 98 Pennsylvania, 08/04/1874, Germany, 56, Rheumatism, 06/12/1888.

BLAIR, William – A. 90 New York, 07/01/1870, Scotland, 48, Paralysis, 12/28/1888.

BLAKELEY, Joseph C. – H, 18 Wisconsin, 05/12/1886, New York, 67, Wound-right foot, 01/08/1888.

BOBEL, Thomas – C, 167 Ohio, 12/12/1887, Germany, 62, Rheumatism, 05/29/1888.

BOTSET, Henry – C, 20 Indiana, 03/27/1875, Germany, 43, Paralysis, 11/22/1888.

BRESNEHAN, John – E, 19 Illinois, 12/17/1883, Ireland, 54, Wound-head, 05/22/1888.

BROWN, Simon H. – C, 50 New York Engineers, 02/26/1888, New York, 57, Disease- eyes, 07/12/1888.

BROWN, Thomas – K, 33 Wisconsin, 01/01/1888, Ireland, 46, Wound-right leg, 03/22/1888.

BROWN, William – G, 46 Illinois, 01/16/1885, Pennsylvania, 75, Wound-left hip, 04/21/1888.

COLT, Stephen S. – K, 13 Wisconsin, 05/08/1888, New York, 67, Lung disease, 09/12/1888.

COOPER, Silas – G, 1 New York Engineers, 07/09/1887, 43, Asthma, 09/06/1888.

CROWE, John – H, 89 New York, 12/22/1884, Ireland, 73, Rheumatism, 04/01/188

DAY, Daniel O. – M, 2 New York Heavy Art., 10/21/1887, New York, 46, Wound-left shoulder, 07/27/1888.

DENTON, Sidney – F, 13 Wisconsin, 07/30/1880, New York, 64, Asthma, 08/24/1888.

DOELLE, William – G, 3 Wisconsin Cav., 10/04/1875, Germany, 33, Gun shot wound-arm, 10/04/1888.

DONNELLY, John – L, 5 Iowa Cav., 03/09/1875, New York, 65, Asthma, 01/07/1888.

DOUGHERTY, James – H, 2 New Jersey Cav., 01/06/1888, New York, 56, Asthma, 08/03/1888.

DUNN, Michael - E, 5 Wisconsin, 11/11/1874, Connecticut, 38, Injury-left arm, 03/22/1888.

DWYER, Philip – B, 2 U. S. Army, 12/16/1887, Ireland, 52, Heart disease, 08/24/1888.

EDDY, Cassius – C, Cpl., 3 Wisconsin Cav., 09/01/1888, New York, 43, Liver disease, 11/18/1888.

EMERY, Richard – C, Cpl., 27 Illinois, 07/01/1888, Illinois, 55, Wound-right arm, 11/10/1888.

FARRELL, William – G, 74 New York, 03/16/1875, New York, 41, Wound-left hip, 02/10/1888.

FENERSTEIN, John – A, 16 Illinois Cav., 01/02/1878, Germany, 66, Deaf, 05/30/1888.

FOGAL, Joseph – B, 6 U. S., Mexican War, 10/06/1886, Germany, 68, Rheumatism, 04/30/1888.

FOWLER, Patrick – 117, 2 U. S. Veteran Reserve Corps, 05.08/1888, Ireland, 68, Varicose veins, 08/12/1888.

GADIENT, Casper – C, 2 Wisconsin, 10/21/1875, Germany, 41, Injury-hand, 11/06/1888.

GALLAGHER, Eugene – D, Lt., 1 West Virginia Cav., 09/07/1884, New York, 47, Wound-both shoulders, 03/08/1888.

GAMACH, Lewis – A, 9 Minnesota, 10/07/1885, California, 67, Hernia, 05/01/1888.

GARRICK, John – F, 5 Kentucky, 11/19/1873, Switzerland, 55, Wound-left arm, 08/28/1888.

GARSIDE, John – D, 1 Nebraska Cav., 05/27/1885, England, 70, General debility, 04/03/1888.

GIFFORD, Alonzo – E, 6 Wisconsin, 08/03/1888, Massachusetts 51, Partial paralysis, 11/23/1888.

GOWENS, William W. – G, 8 Wisconsin, 07/12/1887, Kansas, 42, Lung disease, 07/12/1888.

HALL, Henry C. – B, 7 Vermont, 08/14/1888, Vermont, 47, Rheumatism, 08/29/1888.

HAMILTON, George – C, 65 New York, 06/12/1886, New York, 43, Wound-right arm, 05/21/1888.

HARDING, Robert – E, 47 Wisconsin, 12/16/1887, England, 45, Diarrhoea, 01/25/1888.

HASSON, John – E, 90 Illinois, 10/14/1872, Ireland, 45, Heart disease, 06/01/1888.

HAWKINS, William – E, 25 Missouri, 07/10/1880, England, 79, Hernia, 01/05/1888.

HEALEY, William – L, 2 Illinois Light Art., 03/24/1887, Ireland, 67, Diarrhoea, 05/19/1888.

HEITMILLER, William – Fireman, U. S. Navy, 07/21/1888, Germany, 61, Rheumatism, 07/23/1888.

HENRY, William - __, 164 New York, 02/24/1881, California, 65, Rheumatism, 09/05/1888.

HINCHMAN, E. A. – B, Lt., 131 New York, 03/13/1887, New York, 55, Wound-left leg, 03/06/1888.

HINES, James – G, Cpl., 16 Wisconsin, 05/18/1885, Ireland, 48, Deaf, 09/25/1888.

HORAN, Michael – M, 1 Michigan Light Art., 06/07/1883, Ireland, 52, Malaria, 05/11/1888.

HUPEL, Julius – B, Cpl., 37 Ohio, 09/13/1881, Germany, 42, Wound-left arm, 05/26/1888.

JOHNSON, John - D, 6 Wisconsin, 11/08/1882, Denmark, 65, Rheumatism, 04/28/1888.

JOHNSON, John O. – K, 3 Wisconsin, 05/01/1883, Norway, 61 Wound-right foot, 09/22/1888.

JONES, William – C, 1 Kentucky, 10/17/1875, New York, 41, Injury-left leg, 03/19/1888.

KEISER, Frederick – C, Cpl., 56 Pennsylvania, 10/02/1887, Germany, 59, Heart disease, 7/23/1888.

KIEL, William A. – C, 67 Ohio, 09/22/1876, Norway, 76, Rheumatism, 03/19/1888.

KIRCHNER, Clemens – G, 24 Illinois, 07/06/1881, Germany, 44, Diarrhea, 03/11/1888.

KLEIN, Christian - ___, 19 U. S. Veteran Reserve Corps, 09/18/1874, Germany, 39, Wound-right shoulder, 11/01/1888.

KLEIN, William B. – G, Sgt., 203 Pennsylvania, 05/03/1888, Germany, 65, General debility, 09/27/1888.

KOHN, Franz - ___, 2 Wisconsin Battery, 11/05/1886, France, 68, Paralysis, 09/22/1888.

KOMBRINK, E. - H, 2 Missouri, 06/22/1881. Germany, 50, Wound-right arm, 01/11/1888.

LAMB, John S. – B, 1 New Jersey, 07/06/1887, New Jersey, 50, Wound-left hand, 01/22/1888.

LOVELL, William G. – D, Cpl., 27 Wisconsin, 10/11/1887, Connecticut, 46, Bronchitis, 02/02/1888.

LOWRY, James – A, 1 Maine, 03/18/1888, Ireland, 67, Rheumatism, 06/011888.

MANLEY, Thomas – ___, 2 Indiana Battery/Light Art., 01/13/1874, Ireland, 48, Wound-ankle, 01/21/1888.

MARKHAM, Amos – D, 6 Wisconsin, 06/23/1886, New York, 66, Injury-spine, 02/03/1888.

MATHIAS, Charles – F, 15 Missouri, 10/01/1874, Germany, 62, Wound-right arm, 06/08/1888.

MCCOLLIFF, John – B, 2 Illinois Cav., 05/09/1868, Ireland, 33, Wound-left arm, 05/19/1888.

MCGALLOWAY, James – D, 6 Wisconsin, 12/16/1887, Ireland, 66, Rheumatism, 06/22/1888.

MCKNIGHT, George – G, Sgt., 14 Michigan, 09/05/1873, Ohio, 36, General debility, 05/19/1888

MEYER, John – E, 46 New York, 11/18/1877, Germany, 51, Wound-left hand, 04/28/1888.

MILLER, Christian – F, 77 Pennsylvania, 10/23/1884, Pennsylvania, 58, Rheumatism, 03/08/1888.

MONGER, Emery W. – C, 11 Michigan, 01/14/1882, Vermont, 54, Rheumatism, 03/10/1888.

MONNIER, Joseph – B, 21 Wisconsin, 07/23/1887, France, 62, Chronic diarrhoea, 12/27/1888.

MONTAIGNE, Victor – F, 4 Missouri Reserve Corps, 01/12/1885, France, 62, Wound- right side, 05/01/1888.

MORAN, Thomas – D, Cpl., 6 Wisconsin, 10/02/1887, Ireland, 67, Wound-left leg, 03/21/1888.

MORSE, C. C. – K., Sgt., 47 Wisconsin, 03/13/1883, New York, 62, Bronchitis, 09/14/1888.

MUELLER, August – K, 13 Wisconsin, 04/01/1884, Germany, 58, Deaf-right ear, 07/28/1888.

MURPHY, Daniel – K, 7 Michigan Cav., 09/05/1888, California, 45, Wound-right arm, 12/14/1888.

NICHOL, William – M, 1 Illinois Light Art., 05/26/1880, Scotland, 62, Eye disease, 06/29/1888.

NIEDERHAUSER, L. – F, 15 Missouri, 12/25/1881, Switzerland, 66, Rheumatism, 07/17/1888.

O'BRIEN, John – M, 2 California Cav., 02/14/1886, Ireland, 45, Rheumatism, 11/18/1888.

O'MALEY, J. – B, 6 Iowa Cav., 09/12/1876, Ireland, 46, Kidney disease, 06/10/1888.

O'TOOLE, Thomas – K, 19 Wisconsin, 08/28/1872, Ireland, 62, Injury-right arm, 06/25/1888.

PRITCHARD, William H. - __, 10 Ohio Battery, 10/27/1884, Ohio, 44, Rheumatism, 11/07/1888.

REAMHOLD, Philip – G, 115 Pennsylvania, 11/11/1883, Germany, 62, Loss-left eye, 05/14/1888.

REED, Joseph – K, 4 Minnesota, 05/02/1883, Ohio, 65, Sunstroke, 08/21/1888.

REINER, Martin – I, 24 Wisconsin, 02/03/1887, Germany, 57, Rheumatism, 05/03/1888.

RISDON, Edward H. – L, 1 Wisconsin Heavy Art., 11/22/1882, England, 46, Rheumatism, 10/23/1888.

ROHWLES, Adolph – B, 12 Illinois Cav., 12/08/1876, Germany, 56, Lung disease, 03/01/1888.

ROSENBUSH, Paul – H, 17 Missouri, 11/28/1869, Germany, 34, Loss-right arm, 03/13/1888.

SANDROCK, William – E. 16 Wisconsin, 06/29/1882, Germany, 52, Rheumatism, 11/23/1888.

SCHAUVEN, John – K, 5 Wisconsin, 12/10/1884, Germany, 48, Rheumatism, 03/23/1888.

SCHLICKER, Xavier – A, 2 Michigan, 08/24/1883, Germany, 53, Rheumatism, 02/12/1888.

SCHULTEIS, Charles – A, 24 Illinois, 03/24/1885, Germany, 53, Rheumatism, 03/06/1888.

SCHUMAN, Joseph - 74, 2 U. S. Veteran Reserve Corps, 04/23/1880, Germany, 76, Injury-back, 03/11/1888.

SMITH, Charles – E, 2 Rhode Island Cav., 03/09/1871, Germany, 49, Hernia, 08/28/1888.

STOKES, Clayton – F, 9 Indiana, 12/11/1883, Pennsylvania, 67, Scurvy, 10/05/1888.

STREHAN, Henry – I, 61 Illinois, 02/26/1884, Germany, 48, Injury-left hip, 10/03/1888.

STURMAN, Samuel S. – D, 2 Minnesota Cav., 10/12/1884, Ohio, 70, Injury-head, 04/29/1888.

SULLIVAN, Daniel – D, 1 Louisiana, 06/21/1882, Ireland, 59, Loss-left eye, 08/24/1888.

THOMPSON, M. D. – E, 19 Wisconsin, 04/27/1887, New York, 41, Paralysis, 07/02/1888.

TOLAND, George W. – F, 3 Wisconsin, 02/25/1887, Pennsylvania, 65, Catarrh, 08/15/1888.

TURNBULL, Joseph S. – B, Lt., 22 Iowa, 02/26/1887, Ohio, 58, Wound-left side, 07/17/1888.

TROUT, Amos – A, 12 Missouri Cav., 08/19/1885, Pennsylvania, 60, Heart disease, 12/24/1888.

VINCENT, Robert – B, 67 Illinois, 03/20/1873, Ireland, 63, Rheumatism, 02/01/1888.

WEINHEIMER, George – D, 43 Illinois, 07/27/1883, Germany, 58, Rheumatism, 08/22/1888.

WELSH, Michael – F, 11 New York Cav., 05/08/1887, New York, 48, Kidney disease, 01/20/1888.

WHITE, William – E, Lt., 58 U. S. Colored Troop, 01/02/1885, England, 62, Rheumatism, 04/09/1888.

WIEDEMAN, David – C, 14 Ohio, 10/02/1887, Germany, 66, Wound-right arm, 04/04/1888.

WILLIAMS, James E. – __, Major, 1 New York Cav., 10/22/1887, New York, 53, Kidney disease, 11/24/1888.

WILSON, A. J. - __, 3 Iowa Battery, 07/21/1886, Pennsylvania, 49, Varicose veins, 12/23/1888.

WINKLER, George – A, Cpl., 3 Missouri Reserve Corps, 10/14/1887, Germany, 67, Wound-right shoulder, 06/24/1888.

ZIPF, John M. – F, 1 Missouri Light Art., 11/17/1882, Germany, 62, Rheumatism, 11/11/1888.

Sources:

The Miscellaneous Documents of the House of Representatives for the Second Session of the 50ᵗʰ Congress, 1888-89. #2654. Record of Disabled Volunteer Soldiers, Who Now Are and Have Been Members of the National Home for Disabled Volunteer Soldiers, from July 1, 1887 to July 1, 1888. Washington: Government Printing Press, 1889. (Extracted from Annual report – National Homes for Disabled Volunteer Soldiers.)

The Miscellaneous Documents of the House of Representatives for the First Session of the 51ˢᵗ Congress, 1889-90. #2768. Record of Disabled Volunteer Soldiers, Who Now Are and Have Been Members of the National Home for Disabled Volunteer Soldiers, from July 1, 1888 to July 1, 1889. Washington: Government Printing Office, 1890 (Extracted from Annual Report – National Homes for Disabled Volunteer Soldiers.)

DEATHS IN 1889

FORMAT: NAME, COMPANY & REGIMENT, DATE OF ADMISSION, PLACE OF BIRTH, AGE, DISABILITY, DATE OF DEATH.

ALLEY, William – E, 7 Pennsylvania Cav., 07/28/1886, New York, 44, Fistula, 02/17/1889.

ANDERSON, John – C, 1 Michigan Sharpshooters, 04/13/1877, Denmark, 68, Rheumatism, 04/09/1889.

ANGLE, Lyndes – A, 1 Mexican War, 07/29/1884, New York, 67, Infirmity, 03/25/1889.

BARRETT, John H. – L, 10 Illinois Cav., 03/06/1884, Kentucky, 49, Rheumatism, 04/25/1889.

BISSELL, Nelson – A, 16 Missouri Cav., 06/16/1878, Vermont, 42, Paralysis, 05/18/1889.

BOAS, Edward – C, Lt., 119 New York, 04/22/1877, Germany, 66, Asthma, 10/23/1889.

BOLL, Gerhard – A, 1 Wisconsin Heavy Art., 05/22/1877, Germany, 55, Wound-left knee, 10/23/1889.

BOXER, Jacob – L, 5 U. S. Army Art., 11/03/1882, Switzerland, 51, Rheumatism, 01/04/1889.

BOYLE, Patrick – H, 2 U. S. Army, 11/28/1870. Ireland, 50, Wound-breast, 12/16/1889.

BROWN, August – F, 20 Illinois, 12/11/1888, Germany, 59, Rheumatism, 08/02/1889.

BROWN, Fred – Seaman, U. S. Navy, 04/07/1886, Germany, 61, Injury-arm, 08/05/1889.

BUCKNELL, Uriah – B, 12 Michigan, 05/03/1889, Michigan, 42, Lung disease, 05/25/1889.

CAMPBELL, William – C, 32 Massachusetts, 09/29/1876, Ireland, 53, Gunshot wound-leg, 09/07/1889.

CLARK, Levi – A, 1 Minnesota, 03/24/1885, New Brunswick, 55, Bladder disease, 03/09/1889.

CLARK, Thomas E. – G, 1 Wisconsin, 04/01/1887, Massachusetts, 62, Rheumatism, 08/16/1889.

CONNELL, Patrick – H, 17 Wisconsin, 02/26/1887, Ireland, 55, Rheumatism, 08/28/1889.

CRISPELL, Martin – D, 15 New York Engineers, 02/09/1889, New York, 57, Paralysis, 12/02/1889.

DEMPSEY, F. – F, 10 New York, 03/02/1889, Ireland, 46, Partial paralysis, 09/27/1889.

DOWLING, Nicholas – K, 15 New York Heavy Art., 01/04/1886, Ireland, 47, Lung disease, 11/07/1889.

D_____SKY, Chas. – C, 41 New York, 12/22/1887, New York, 59, Wound-left knee, 02/04/1889.

EAGER, Alfred L. – B, Sgt., 3 Wisconsin, 10/31/1888, New York, 57, Heart disease, 06/19/1889.

EDDIE, Alex – H, 14 U. S. Veteran Reserve Corps, 12/10/1878, Norway, 54, Diarrhoea, 08/27/1889.

EHRMAN, Florence – I, 147 Illinois, 10/28/1879, France, 68, Rheumatism, 09/27/1889.

FAHEY, Michael – A, 23 U. S. Veteran Reserve Corps, 12/19/1884, Ireland, 73, Rheumatism, 02/15/1889.

FOLTZ, George – G, 2 Minnesota, 03/21/1884, Germany, 63, Gunshot wound-knee, 09/04/1889.

FRAZIER, Don W. – B, 18 Kentucky Cav., 05/03/1884, Ireland, 57, Loss-right leg, 04/17/1889.

FROELICH, Laurent – K, 9 Wisconsin, 09/11/1874, France, 61, Rheumatism, 05/11/1889.

FULLER, Alfred – G, 23 Wisconsin, 07/02/1889, New York, 60, Varicose veins, 11/11/1889.

GRENELL, Thomas W. – G, 5 U. S. Veteran Reserve Corps, 10/07/1879, New York, 60, General debility, 10/29/1889.

HARTZUNG, L. – K, 9 Wisconsin, 12/31/1883, Germany, 67, Rheumatism, 04/24/1889.

HASKINS, John W. – H, 16 Wisconsin, 03/24/1883, New York, 50, Wound-left leg, 03/27/1889.

HEAD, James – G, 142 New York, 08/20/1879, England, 72, Ulcers, 12/02/1889.

HECKER, Francis – H, 52 Illinois, 01/19/1882, Germany, 52, Hernia, 09/19/1889.

HENNEBERG, Adolph – B, Cpl., 27 Michigan, 08/02/1883, Germany, 55, Injury-right leg, 01/11/1889.

HICKOX, Benj. - __, C. S., 24 Wisconsin, 01/16/1889, New York, 48, Dyspepsia, 02/09/1889.

HILDRETH, Daniel – H, 59, Indiana, 04/27/1887, Ohio, 66, Blind, 08/11/1889.

HILL, Jenkins W. – H, 1 Wisconsin Cav., 10/29/1875, Vermont, 56, Rheumatism, 11/21/1889.

HILL, Louis – D, 116 New York, 12/24/1881, New York, 35, Wound-right hand, 06/18/1889.

HOCK, William – C, 73 Pennsylvania, 11/01/1883, Germany, 59, Rheumatism, 03/10/1889.

HOEFER, Peter – F, 26 Wisconsin, 04/02/1885, Germany, 75, Rheumatism, 03/01/1889.

HOFFMAN, Frank – A, 1 Colorado, 12/12/1889, Switzerland, 51, Chronic ulcers, 05/06/1889. (Date of admission after date of death.)

HOLMES, Fred – Landsman, U. S. Navy, 10/21/1885, New York, 65, Hernia, 12/11/1889.

HUBER, JOSEPH - ___, 2 U. S. Veteran Reserve Corps, 3/31/1880, Germany, 56, Hernia, 02/17/1889.

HUNTER, Thomas – Seaman, U. S. Navy, 12/26/1877, New York, 40, Wound-left leg, 04/17/1889.

H___FRITZ, C. - ___, Missouri, Backof's Battery, 04/15/1881, Germany, 54, Ulcers, 06/01/1889.

JOHANNET, August – G, 17 Wisconsin, 07/19/1883, France, 67, Diarrhoea, 06/03/1889.

JOHNSTON, Alex. S. – G, Capt., 116 U. S. Colored Troops, 06/13/1886, Scotland, 57, Rheumatism, 07/06/1889.

KELLET, Michael – C, 61 Illinois, 10/25/1888, Ireland, 52, General debility, 02/18/1889.

KELLOGG, Jason – K, 75 New York, 03/25/1881, New York, 62, Paralysis, 01/06/1889.

KENNEDY, Rodger – C, 17 Wisconsin, 06/12/1886, Ireland, 55, Wound-right shoulder, 02/26/1889.

KEUP, Joseph – B, 14 Illinois Cav., 03/03/1887, Germany, 64, Asthma, 04/21/1889.

KITSON, James – A, 1 Minnesota Heavy Art., 05/01/1887, Ireland, 76, Hernia, 07/08/1889.

KLEINSHRODT, J. M. – G, 4 U. S. Veteran Reserve Corps, 07/16/1870, Germany, 44, Bronchitis, 10/12/1889.

KNIGHT, Joseph – I, 117 New York, 05/08/1888, Wisconsin, 46, Injury-left hip, 07/02/1889.

LEWIS, John – D, 90 Illinois, 12/28/1869, New York, 36, Injury-right arm, 06/17/1889.

LOBES, John – F, 58 Illinois, 10/19/1871, Germany, 52, Wound-right leg, 06/22/1889,

LOVE, Stephen B. – D, Sgt., 92, Illinois, 11/11/1888, Maryland, 61, Hemiplegia, 05/18/1889.

MADDEN, Bernard – A, 40 New York, 10/21/1885, Ireland, 65, Rheumatism, 11/24/1889.

MADISON, George D, - E, 27 Michigan, 10/13/1881, Michigan, 40, Diarrhoea, 11/11/1889.

MALVIN, Joseph C. – H, 7 Iowa Cav., 12/11/1888, Pennsylvania, 56, Rheumatism, 08/14/1889.

MARSHALL, M. M. – F, 13 New York, 04/18/1876, New York, 37, Hernia, 04/01/1889.

MATTHEWS, Alfred - B, 10 Pennsylvania Reserves, 03/01/1884, Ohio, 42, Wound-breast, 09/14/1889.

MCCARTHY, Thomas – G, 10 Illinois Cav., 07/07/1886, Ireland, 50, Rheumatism, 12/09/1889.

MCCONNELL, William – B, 20 Iowa, 07/21/1886, New York, 46, Sunstroke, 03/17/1889.

MCDONNELL, Alex – C, 26 Michigan, 04/23/1884, Maine, 69, Hernia, 08/17/1889.

MCEVOY, Keeran – E, 73 Indiana, 12/16/1884, Ireland, 54, Phthisis, 06/12/1889.

MERRELL, M. R. – I, Lt., 10 Minnesota, 04/04/1882, New York, 53, Disease-eyes, 06/25/1889.

MESOW, Frederick – H, Sgt., 2 Wisconsin Cav., 10/12/1883, Germany, 50, Rheumatism, 07/21/1889.

MILLER, Henry C. – C, 11 Illinois Cav., 01/21/1884, New Jersey, 53, Injury-back, 07/27/1889.

MORSELOW, Charles – K, 21 New York, 07/28/1888, France, 44, Injury-left leg, 05/15/1889.

O'NEIL, Thomas – B, 51 New York, 08/01/1887, Ireland, 57, Wound-left leg, 03/18/1889.

PAULADN, Ludwig - H, 5 Rhode Island Heavy Art., 03/09/1871, Germany, 49, General debility, 05/14/1889.

PELTIER, John – D, 27 Michigan, 03/02/1889, Michigan, 42, Wound-right arm, 10/18/1889.

PERSONS, D. F. - ___, 13 Wisconsin Battery, 05/08/1887, Wisconsin, 39, Rheumatism, 03/08/1889.

POND, Chauncey G. – F, 1 Oregon Cav., 07/23/1880, Pennsylvania, 44, Chorea, 03/16/1889.

QUINN, Joshua – B, 5 New York Cav., 02/10/1877, Ireland, 53, Injury-left leg, 05/11/1889.

QUOSS, Edward – A, 1 Illinois Cav., 09/04/1873, Germany, 64, Hernia, 02/04/1889.

RIDLEY, Joseph – F, 8 U. S. Colored Troops Heavy Art., 01/070/1879, Virginia, __, Wound-right hip, 09/28/1889.

ROHM, August – B, Sgt., 58 New York, 02/13/1888, Germany, 64, Malaria, 12/13/1889.

RUDER, William F. – C, 7 New York, 10/12/1886, Germany, 46, Hernia, 01/01/1889.

RYAN, Patrick – C, 17 Wisconsin, 05/13/1884, Ireland, 40, Asthma, 11/27/1889.

SALSBURY, Daniel – K, 24 Wisconsin, 02/04/1884, New York, 49, Wound-left leg, 11/22/1889.

SCANLON, John – H, 18 New York Cav., 10/02/1887, Ireland, 43, Pneumonia, 02/01/1889.

SCHURTZ, William – L, 3 Wisconsin Cav., 06/08/1887, Germany, 77, Disease-eyes, 09/27/1889.

SCOFIELD, James – K, Cpl., 26 Pennsylvania, 07/19/1887, England, 59, Diarrhoea, 06/11/1889.

SHEA, Daniel – F, 23, Illinois, 10/03/1877, Ireland, 45, Wound-right hand, 09/24/1889.

SHONOUR, John – B, 88 Pennsylvania, 07/02/18879, Pennsylvania, 52, Heart disease, 10/22/1889.

SHURR, Ferdinand – B, 24 Wisconsin, 07/02/1889, Ohio, 50, Brain disease, 10/02/1889.

SMELTZ, August - D, Sgt., 9 Pennsylvania Reserves, 05/28/1889, Germany, 50, Wound-right shoulder, 08/30/1889.

SMITH, Peter – I, 69 New York, 12/01/1888, Ireland, 54, Paralysis, 09/18/1889.

SMITH, Stephen A. – 8 Wisconsin, 07/28/1889, New York, 54, General debility, 09/01/1889.

STERNARD, Martin – E, 14 Michigan, 01/12/1885, Austria, 72, Rheumatism, 12/21/1889.

STEVENS, Allen – A, 193 New York, 11/12/1889, New York, 75, Piles, 12/12/1889.

STOKER, John – I, 6 Ohio, 03/11/1871, Switzerland, 36, Loss-right arm, 05/18/1889.

TAYLOR, William D, 18 Illinois, 11/17/1886, England, 67, Paralysis, 06/09/1889.

THOMAS, John – E, 4 New York Heavy Art., 03/21/1887, England, 62, Injury-shoulder, 11/26/1889.

THOMPSON, Isaac D. – D, 8 Minnesota, 06/05/1883, New York, 59, Rheumatism, 06/01/1889.

TOBIN, John – K, 5 Minnesota, 05/04/1881, Ireland, 60, Rheumatism, 06/09/1889.

TRIBLE, Eberhard – G, 9 U. S. Army, 12/31/1874, Germany, 54, Rheumatism, 10/14/1889.

VON UNRUH, Max – E, Lt., 5 Missouri Cav., 01/17/1889, Germany, 57, Wound-right leg, 09/03/1889.

VREELAND, HENRY – D, 7 Ohio, 04/13/1889, New York, 65, General debility, 08/16/1889.

WARNER, Norton – Landsman, U. S. Navy, 05/08/1889, New York, 56, Asthma, 09/11/1889.

WENTWORTH, Jonas – C, 18 Connecticut, 10/16/1883, New York, 64, Wound-right hip, 02/13/1889.

WINTERS, James G – B, 1 Wisconsin Heavy Art., 05/02/1872, California, 46, Injury-left side, 01/13/1889.

WRIGHT, Milton – A, Sgt., 3 Indiana Cav., 04/13/1889, Indiana, 80, Bladder disease, 10/16/1889.

Sources:

The Miscellaneous Documents of the House of Representatives for the First Session of the 51ˢᵗ Congress, 1889-90. #2768. Record of Disabled Volunteer Soldiers, Who Now Are And Have Been Members of the National Home for Disabled Volunteer Soldiers, from July 1, 1888 to July 1, 1889. Washington: Government Printing Office, 1890. (Extracted from Annual Report – National Homes for Disabled Volunteer Soldiers.)

The Miscellaneous Documents of the House of Representatives for the Second Session of the 51st Congress, 1990-91. #2869. Record of Disabled Volunteer Soldiers, Who Now Are And Have Been Members of the National Home for Disabled Volunteer Soldiers, from July 1, 1889 to July 1, 1890. Washington: Government Printing Office, 1891. (Extracted from Annual Report – National Homes for Disabled Volunteer Soldiers.)

DEATHS IN 1890

FORMAT: NAME, COMPANY & REGIMENT, DATE OF ADMISSION, PLACE OF BIRTH, AGE, DISABILITY, DATE OF DEATH.

ALEXANDER, Obd. T. - __, 13 Wisconsin Battery, 05/17/1881, New York, 60, General debility, 12/26/1890.

AUBLE, Peter – E, 161 New York, 03/11/1887, New York, 50, Bronchitis, 01/24/1890.

AULFUS, Henry – K, 28 Ohio, 07/13/1882, Germany, 57, Rheumatism, 05/11/1890.

BACHOF, Edward – E, 52 New York, 03/13/1887, Germany, 61, Rheumatism, 8/15/1890.

BEESE, Frederick – G, 65 Illinois, 06/15/1878, Germany, 60, Injury-shoulder, 02/04/1890.

BLESSING, G. – G, 72 Illinois, 09/29/1879, Germany, 52, Fracture-thigh, 11/10/1890.

BONER, George – G, 10 Ohio Cav., 09/02/1875, Germany, 48, Wound-head, 2/31/1890.

BONIGAN, Peter D. – D, 34 Iowa, 06/07/1885, Ireland, 65, Injury-hand, 06/03/1890.

BRACKER, Francis – D, 2 Missouri Light Art., 06/24/1885, Germany, 54, Fracture-ribs, 03/25/1890.

BURKE, Michael – F, 4 Massachusetts Heavy Artillery, 07/26/1882, Ireland, 41, Rheumatism, 08/17/1890.

BURROWS, James – G, 114 U.S. Colored Troop, 08/26/1890, Kentucky, 52, Phthisis, 12/27/1890.

BUSSACK, Charles – C, 9 Veteran Volunteers, U. S. Army, 02/06/1887, Germany, 70, Rheumatism, 09/08/1890.

COLLINS, John – D, 19 U. S. Army, 07/20/1887, Ireland, 48, Cystitis, 01/02/1890.

COLSTON, David – G, Maryland Home Guard, 09/28/1877, England, 64, Hernia, 04/17/1890.

CONNORS, Lawrence – H, 3 New York Prov. Cav., 10/20/1888, Ireland, 41, Loss-right leg, 22/01/1890 (Month of date of death recorded as "22" in records, collected in last six months of 1890).

COSTELLO, Carlos – Seaman, U. S. Navy, 11/07/1886, South America, 54, Bronchitis, 03/08/1890,

COTTY, John – D, 4 Ohio Cav., 09/16/1884, Ohio, 57, Neuralgia, 10/03/1890.

CUNNINGHAM, M. – G, 188 Pennsylvania, 03/13/1887, New York, 54, Rheumatism, 02/16/1890.

DESMOND, Patrick – E, 65 Illinois, 11/26/1873, California, 43, Rheumatism, 2/17/1890.

DILLER, Abraham – B, 44 Indiana, 07/19/1883, Pennsylvania, 72, Disease-eyes, 03/23/1890.

DONOHUE, Frank – B, Corporal, 14 New York Cav., 09/22/1889, New York, 45, Epilepsy, 01/03/1890.

EVERETT, Charles – C, 90 Illinois, 11/21/1888, Ireland, 61, Wound-right hand, 10/12/1890.

EVERSON, Richard – F, 6 U. S. Army Cav., 06/29/1886, England, 67, Hernia, 02/03/1890.

FAHEY, James – B, 9 Illinois Cav., 04/28/1886, New York, 44, Rheumatism, 08/15/1890.

FAY, Philip – K, 43 Wisconsin, 10/05/1877, Ireland, 61, Injury-ankle, 05/11/1890.

FOOT, Frederick – B, 14 Illinois Cav., 10/21/1879, Ireland, 73, Diarrhoea, 01/08/1890.

GAGE, J. B. – B, 67 Minnesota, 12/12/1887, Maine, 54, Hernia, 02/01/1890.

GROSH, Jacob – H, 7 Illinois, 07/22/1879, Germany, 56, Chronic rheumatism, 04/30/1890.

GROSS, John L. – E, 58 Illinois, 10/21/1887, Germany, 76, General debility, 02/08/1890.

HALBERSTADT, Joseph – D, 72 Pennsylvania, 09/07/1890, Pennsylvania, 46, Paralysis, 12/06/1890.

HALL, John – B, 8 Indiana, 12/09/1886, Canada, 50, Rheumatism, 02/11/1890.

HANEY, Milton M. – A, 11 Wisconsin, 10/19/1886, Alabama, 47, Loss-left foot, 09/23/1890.

HANKES, Josh. W. – C, Cpl., 31 Massachusetts, 06/06/1885, 46. Diarrhoea, 11/23/1890.

HARTNEY, Mort. – E, 23 Illinois, 04/27/1887, Ireland, 56, Heart disease, 01/24/1890.

HARVEY, Moses – B, 38 Wisconsin, 04/04/1883, England, 70, Wound-foot, 08/25/1890.

HASTINGS, Thomas – H, 107 Illinois, 05/07/1885, Ohio, 55, Wound-right foot, 02/13/1890.

HAVEMAN, August – K, 2 Veteran Volunteers, U. S. Army, 06/24/1878, Germany, 63, Rheumatism, 10/24/1890.

HUGHES, Thomas – C, 65 New York, 09/20/1878, Ireland, 55, Hemorrhoids, 5/18/1890.

HYDE, Rich. K. – Landsman, U. S. Navy, 02/23/1887, Connecticut, 63, Lumbago, 03/27/1890.

IMMEL, Martin J. – B, 30 Wisconsin, 01/10/1884, Germany, 61, Rheumatism, /31/1890.

ISBELL, Alfred – F. 46 Wisconsin, 02/03/1887, Wisconsin, 36, Disease-lungs, 07/03/1890.

JUNG, Gottfried – D, 9 Wisconsin, 03/20/1883, Germany, 57, Rheumatism, 01/18/1890.

KEEHN, Franklin P. – I, 43 Indiana, 06/12/1886, Pennsylvania, 59, Hemorrhoids, 02/05/1890.

KELLY, Joseph – I, 10 Massachusetts, 07/09/1887, Ireland, 60, Wound-right arm, 05/21/1890.

KELLY, Joseph – F, 7 U. S. Army, 07/19/1887, Ireland, 52, Wound-left arm, 2/07/1890.

KEENAN, James – D, 13 Illinois, 10/30/1888, Ireland, 52, Rheumatism, 12/27/1890.

KING, Thomas - __, A., 1 Delaware, 12/08/1887, Ireland, 50, Wound-right leg, 09/05/1890.

LUCKETT, Frank – M, 2 Wisconsin Cav., 06/17/1885, England, 55 Hernia, 02/01/1890.

LYNCH, Edward – C, 10 Tennessee, 11/29/1871, Ireland, 64, 11/29/71, Rheumatism, 09/18/1890.

MCCALL, Alex – C, 32 Iowa, 11/13/1877, New York, 52, Diarrhoea, 03/09/1890.

MCCARTY, Morris – Engineer, U. S. Navy, 07/28/1888, New York, 51, Asthma, 03/04/1890.

MCKALLOR, Arthur – H, 12 Wisconsin, 12/05/1890, New York, 72, Old age, 12/20/1890.

MCMANNIS, Hugh – A, 5 West Virginia Cav., 01/14/1888, Ireland, 48, Gunshot wound-hand, 02/21/1890.

MEIER, Joseph – C, 6 Kentucky, 08/23/1883, Germany, 83, Old age, 10/17/1890.

131

MENTZEL, Mathias – A, 3 Wisconsin, 11/27/1880, Germany, 54, Varicose veins, 11/11/1890.

MURPHY, Edward – E, 27 Wisconsin, 11/08/1889, Ireland, 51, Rheumatism, 11/11/1890.

MURPHY, James – A, 36 New York, 08/23/1870, Ireland, 60, Bronchitis, 01/29/1890.

NISBIT, Arch'd – B, 5 Mexican War, 05/24/1882, Scotland, 63, Rheumatism, 03/30/1890.

NICHOL, Frank C. – E, 1 New Jersey Artillery, 06/25/1890, Gerany, 52, Heart disease, 10/16/1890.

PERCY, Morgan – G, 40 New York, 10/23/1890, Ireland, 50, Rheumatism, 05/20/1890. (Date of death preceded date of admission.)

PHILLIPS, Francis – C, 64 Illinois, 09/03/1884, Ireland, 61, Varicose veins, 11/05/1890.

PIKE, John – H, 48 New York, 10/07/1879, England, 40, Heart disease, 01/05/1890.

PRATT, Thomas – F, 5 New York, 05/19/1884, England, 71, Asthma, 12/24/1890.

RADFORD, Samuel H. – T, 1 Pennsylvania Prov. Cav., 10/27/1885, Pennsylvania, 38, Epilepsy, 12/04/1890.

RAPP, Samuel A. – E, 1 West Virginia Light Artillery, 04/27/1877, West Virginia, 23, Diarrhoea, 11/03/1890.

REICHTER, August – F, 12 Illinois, 07/15/1885, Germany, 76, General debility, 4/17/1890.

RENDLER, John – F, 19 Wisconsin, 01/10/1882, Germany, 57, Diarrhoea, 02/03/1890.

ROHR, Rudolph – H, 97 New York, 08/05/1887, Switzerland, 66, Hernia, 01/04/1890.

ROTH, Ernest H. – I, 37 Illinois, 07/24/1890, Germany, 47, Rheumatism, 11/21/1890.

RUSHMAN, Joseph – K, 4 New York Heavy Artillery, 11/05/1887, Germany, 64, Wound-right hand, 12/01/1890.

RYAN, John – A, 24 U. S. Veteran Reserve Corps, 01/17/1874, Maine, 52, Rheumatism, 02/05/1890.

SAVAGE, Henry J. – G, 1 Maryland, 11/26/1868, Maryland, 28. Wound-left hip, 12/03/1890.

SCHARBACH, William – C, Corporal, 1 New Jersey, 04/23/1884, Germany, 51, Sunstroke, 09/07/1890.

SCHARFENBERG, William – H, H., 45 Wisconsin, 12/21/1888, Germany, 65, Paralysis, 08/16/1890.

SCHMIDT, John - A, 1 New Jersey Light Art., 03/05/1887, Germany, 49, Rheumatism, 03/05/1890.

SCHNEIDER, Charles - __, U. S. Marine Corps, 05/19/1886, Germany, _8, Asthma, 06/01/1890.

SCHNEIDER, Chris. – B, 27 Iowa, 12/02/1880, Germany, 55, Lumbago, 02/01/1890.

SCOTT, Patrick – E, 116 Pennsylvania, 08/13/1889, Ireland, 47, Injury-right ankle, 01/08/1890.

SEVERSON, S. L. – B, 3 Wisconsin, 03/07/1887, Norway, 42, Disease-spine, 01/07/189

SHERR, Louis – H, 5 New York, 08/09/1889, Germany, 54, Wound-left thigh, 08/17/1890.

SINCE, Clement – C, 15 U. S. Army, 06/28/1887, France, 66, Rheumatism, 07/21/1890.

SMITH, Zebedee – C, 13 U. S. Army, 05/08/1888, Maine, 54, Heart disease, 08/21/1890.

SORENSEN, Peter N. – A, 11 Connecticut, 11/13/1889, Denmark, 61, Hernia, 01/21/1890.

STADER, John – I, D., 1 New York Light Art., 11/09/1874, Germany, 56, Wound-left leg, 04/25/1890.

STEINKE, Henry – F, 2 New York Mounted Rifle, 12/14/1887, Germany, 61, General debility, 11/12/1890.

STOCKMAN, John - __, 31 New York Independent Battery, 03/04/1890, Germany, 60, Heart disease, 11/04/1890.

STOCKWELL, H. B. – B, 1 Iowa Cav., 01/27/1881, Ohio, 53, Disease-eyes, 11/06/1890.

STOKES, Samuel F. –B, 41 U. S. Colored Troops, 05/24/1888, Pennsylvania, 43, Lung disease, 06/04/1890.

THEAS, Frederick – H, 7 Wisconsin, 01/02/1990, Germany, 69, Wound-right arm, 06/26/1890.

TOPPING Henry – F, 137 New York, 12/10/1874, New York, 28, Loss-right arm, 06/21/1890.

WALLACE, Edwin E. – E, 56 Illinois, 05/14/1887, Connecticut, 57, Rheumatism, 11/23/1890.

WALLACE, James – F, 4 Massachusetts Heavy Art., 08/02/1889, Ireland, 43, Rheumatism, 02/21/1890.

WARRICK, George – K, 20 Wisconsin, 06/28/1871, England, 33, Disease-eyes, 07/15/1890.

WEBBER, John – K, 27 Wisconsin, 11/08/1889, Germany, 52, Disease-liver, 11/09/1890.

WILSON, George – K, Lt., 15 Kentucky, 01/17/1884, New York, 62, Varicose veins, 02/08/1890.

WRIGHT, Peter J. – M, Sgt., 2 New York Cav., 06/08/1882, New York, 56, Hernia, 05/24/1890.

Sources:

The Miscellaneous Documents of the House of Representatives for the Second Session of the 51st Congress, 1890-91. Record of Disabled Volunteer Soldiers, Who Now Are And Have Been Members of the National Home for Disabled Volunteer Soldiers, from July 1, 1889 to July 1, 1890. #2869. Washington: Government Printing Office, 1891. (Extracted from Annual Reports – National Homes for Disabled Volunteer Soldiers.)

Report of the Board of Managers of the National Home for Disabled Volunteer Soldiers, for the Year Ending June 30, 1891. Record of Disabled Volunteer Soldiers, Who Now Are And Have Been Members of the National Home for Disabled Volunteer Soldiers from July 1, 1890 to June 30, 1891. Washington: Government Printing Office, 1892. (Extracted from Annual Reports – National Homes for Disabled Volunteer Soldiers.)

DEATHS IN 1891

FORMAT: NAME, COMPANY & REGIMENT, DATE OF ADMISSION, PLACE OF BIRTH, DISABILITY, DATE OF DEATH.

AMBLER, Henry C. – F, 4 Wisconsin, 10/03/1890, Vermont, 50, Rheumatism, 07/23/1891.

AMAN, Joseph – B, 37 Wisconsin, 01/01/1888, Bavaria, 72, General debility, 04/27/1891.

ANDERSON, Joseph – I, C., 17 Wisconsin, 12/26/1878, Ireland, 50, Heart disease, 09/19/1891.

ATWOOD, Darwin F. – F, 1 Wisconsin, Heavy Art., 10/06/1886, Vermont, 59, Piles, 11/17/1891.

BAGLEY, George B. – F, 1 New York Engineers, 01/16/1889, Ireland, 44, Rheumatism, 04/12/1891.

BAIER, Casper – A, 10 U. S. Army, 02/13/1890, Germany, 59, Injury-knee, 11/09/1891.

BAKER, George A. – C, 71 Ohio, 12/21/1888, Vermont, 64, Rheumatism, 04/01/1891.

BALLOU, Erastus – G, Cpl., 2 Vermont, 06/04/1884, Vermont, 50, Wound-lung, 05/23/1891.

BARON, Jacob – A, 158 New York, 01/02/1885, England, 50, Rheumatism, 08/30/1891.

BENZINGER, Her'n. – F, 54 New York, 01/24/1878, Switzerland, 50, Rheumatism, 08/22/1891.

BERNHARDT, Bas. – H, Pennsylvania, Heavy Art., 10/06/1883, Germany, 48, Rheumatism, 08/23/1891.

BEYER, Chris. – E, Sgt., 2 New Jersey, 10/13/1883, Germany, 59, Wound-right hip, 04/25/1891.

BISSING, Franz – A, 26 Wisconsin, 06/28/1889, Germany, 62, Deafness, 03/24/1891.

BOLL, William – D, 16 U. S. Army, 10/27/1890, Germany, 70, Hernia, 04/07/1891.

BRADY, CHARLES – E, 5 New York, 02/07/1888, Ireland, 67, Wound-arm, 08/14/1891.

BREMAN, Patrick W. – G, 69 New York, 06/15/1877, Ireland, 45, Gunshot wound-abdomen, 06/24/1891.

BRIGHT, John – D, 176 Ohio, 05/20/1890, Germany, 58, General debility, 03/17/1901.

BROWN, Jas. – E, Massachusetts Heavy Art., 04/19/1889, Massachusetts, 65, Wound-left hand, 09/12/1891.

BRUIRE, Frank – A, 41 Missouri, 06/10/1887, Germany, 65, General debility, 02/21/1891.

BURKHARD, Math. – A, 15 Missouri, 09/19/1886, Germany, 52, Hernia, 03/24/1891.

CAREY, John – D, 53 Illinois, 09/23/1873, New York, 26, Wound-right arm, __/15/1891.

CARPENTER, John – B, 28 Wisconsin, 10/06/1884, England, 63, Hernia, 09/14/1891.

CHARLTON, John G. – H, 6 Wisconsin, 12/01/1888, England, 42, Fracture-arm, 03/28/1891.

CHASE, Luther M. – C, 5 New Hampshire,, 06/29/1881, New Hampshire, 40, Gunshot wounds-legs, 06/17/1891.

CILL, Wm. – K, 10 U. S. Army, 12/09/1890, Germany, 57, Fracture-ankle, 11/02/1891.

CLARK, PATRICK - Quartermaster, U. S. Navy, 11/11/1887, New York, 50, Fracture-thigh, 05/21/1891.

COLLINS, Philip H. – F, S., 1 Massachusetts, Mexican War, 09/22/1889, Massachusetts, 75, Wound-knee, 12/27/1891.

COURTER, Wm. H. – C, 26 New Jersey, 11/05/1887, New Jersey, 57, Rheumatism, 08/29/1891.

CULVER, Charles D. – H, 2 Wisconsin, 07/09/1887, Connecticut, 55, Paralysis, 09/13/1891.

DALEY, JOHN – A, 8 U. S. Veteran Reserve Corps, 11/15/1868, Ireland, 51, Fracture-thigh, 09/27/1891.

DELANEY, John J. – E, 165 New York,, 12/11/1890, 49, New York, Gunshot wound-thigh, 09/12/1891.

DICKER, James – I, 1 Indiana, Cav., 12/17/1884, New Jersey, 44, Injury-testicle, 01/09/1891.

DIDRA, Chris. – M, Lt., 1 Minnesota, Heavy Art., 10/09/1884, Germany, 57, Rheumatism, 04/24/1891.

DITTMARS, Chas. – H, 3 Wisconsin Cav., 12/08/1890, Wisconsin, 45, Diabetes, 10/16/1891.

ELSNER, Constantine – B, 20 Massachusetts, 01/13/1873, Germany, 35, Loss-left leg, 01/11/1891.

ERB, Abraham – F, 129 Indiana, 01/03/1883, Ohio, Heart disease, 11/17/1891.

EVANS, Henry – M. Mate, U. S. Navy, 01/05/1891, Missouri, 51 Rheumatism, 03/02/1891.

FARLEY, William E. – I, 4 Wisconsin, 12/30/1875, New York, 55, Disease-liver, 04/02/1891.

FARRELLY, Owen - D, 177 New York, 07/21/1888, Ireland, 60, Hernia, 09/12/1891.

FERNAN, John – K, 74 Pennsylvania, 10/02/1885, Germany, 53, Hernia, 03/30/1891.

FEIGEL, Conrad – K, 62 New York, 07/08/1880, Germany, 65, Hernia, 01/02/1891.

FINK, Joseph – I, 1 Illinois, Light Art., 06/11/1877, Germany, 53, Gunshot wound-ankle, 06/03/1891.

FLOYD, (see SLOYD).

FLYNN, Peter - B, 12 Michigan 10/17/1874, Ireland, 59, Gunshot wound-leg, 06/17/1891.

FOLEY, Owen - __, U. S. Marine Corps, 02/03/1885, Ireland, 44, Asthma, 03/17/1891.

GALLINGHAM, Alex. – 75, 2 Bat. U. S. Veteran Reserve Corps, 12/19/1888, Ireland, 62, Varicose veins, 11/26/1891.

GEHRICH, Heinrich – B, 20 Illinois, 10/12/1877, Germany, 60, Rheumatism, 02/06/1891.

GOUDY, Jacob E. – G, 201 Pennsylvania, 09/29/1888, Pennsylvania, 59, Rheumatism, 04/10/1891.

GRAHAM, Mathias – D, 27 Wisconsin, 03/03/1882, Germany, 50, Rheumatism, 08/24/1891.

HAHLY, Adam – C, 15 Missouri, 07/01/1884, Germany, 56, Ulcer-leg, 04/1_/__. (Data in 91 record.)

HARTMAN, Chris. – B, 53 Wisconsin, 05/08/1888, Germany, 73, Hemorrhoids, 06/08/1891.

HENDERSON, Joseph – G, 92 Illinois, 11/19/1884, Ireland, 60, Chronic diarrhoea, 08/08/1891.

HENNESSEY, Par'k. – F, 17 Wisconsin, 06/08/1887, Ireland, 68, Diarrhoea, 10/20/1891.

HERRMAN, Gottlieb – A, 5 Wisconsin, 07/16/1874, Germany, 42, Wound-hip, 05/02/1891.

HERMES, Martin – K, 58 New York, 06/01/1887, Germany, 61, Hernia, 04/01/1891.

HOFINS, George – E, 5 Pennsylvania Cav., 10/23/1876, Germany, 50, Ulcer-leg, 01/12/1891.

HOOPER, Joseph J. – Seaman, U. S. Navy, 04/11/1890, Massachusetts, 46, Injury-hand, 11/07/1891.

HUTCHINSON, D. L. – G, 2 Indiana, 10/21/1887, Kentucky, 67, General debility, 07/02/1891.

JAEGER, John - I, 8 Illinois, 09/19/1876, Germany, 62, Gunshot wound-thigh, 06/27/1891.

JONES, Perry – Gunner, U. S. Navy, 10/05/1890, New York, 55, Sunstroke, 12/23/1891.

JONES, Richard – I, 24 Wisconsin, 03/04/1890, England, 47, Rheumatism, 03/21/1981.

KANE, John – A, 38 Wisconsin, 01/14/1884, New York, 39, Heart disease, 12/08/1891.

KASTNER, Frederick – G, 47 Ohio, 12/13/1872, Germany, 57, Wound-arm, 04/18/1891.

KEENAN, Michael – B, 140 Illinois, 12/26/1883, Ireland, 60, General debility, 03/15/1891.

KEENAN, Robert - Landsman, U. S. Navy, 10/25/1888, Ireland, 60, Rheumatism, __/24/1891.

KEIN, Frederick – D, 41 New York, 10/13/1886, Germany, 65, Rheumatism, 04/02/1891.

KELLNER, Andrew – I, 37 Wisconsin, 06/15/1889, Germany, 66, Wound-head, 01/09/1891.

KLEIN, Chris. – G, 1 Pennsylvania Art., 09/03/1887, Germany, 63, Hernia, 01/05/1891.

KNYROM, Francis – B, 10 Ohio, 10/04/1879, Germany, 45, Lung disease, 02/27/1891.

KOHN, Lewis – H, 134 New York, 1-/02/1887, Germany, 59, Rheumatism, 05/31/1891.

KREBS, Dan'l. – Landsman, U. S. Navy, 12/22/1890, New York, 50, Lumbago, 10/19/1891.

LAWSON, William H. – 1ˢᵗ Cabin Boy, U. S. Navy, 10/05/1890, California, 42, Phthisis, 01/10/1891.

LEWIS, Henry - __, Sgt., U. S. Marine Corps, 09/25/1889, Pennsylvania, 82, Old age, 02/18/1891.

LOTZ, Peter – H, 16 Veteran Reserve Volunteers, 01/11/1873, Germany, 45, Hernia, 03/21/1891.

MCCREA, John – H, 126, New York, 09/28/1883, Ireland, 51, Varicose veins, 09/20/1891.

MCGILL, Patrick – C, 4 Iowa Cav., 11/28/1883, Ireland, 62, Gunshot wound-left arm, 03/01/1891.

MCGUIRE, Daniel – 129, 2 Bat., U. S. Veteran Reserve Corps, 07/26/1891, Ireland, 62, Gunshot wound-hand, 01/02/1891. (Date of death before date of admission.)

MENTOR, Russell W. – B, 15 U. S. Army, 06/03/1884, Connecticut, 59, Rheumatism, 01/02/1891.

MEYERKLINKER, John – F, 16 Illinois Cav., 03/26/1878, Germany, 53, Rheumatism, 09/26/1891.

MINK, Henry – G, 7 Wisconsin, 11/12/1878, Germany, 68, Rheumatism, 06/01/1891.

MITCHELL, Thomas – B, S., 131 New York, 08/21/1884, Scotland, 58, Lung disease, 08/23/1891.

NYE, Harrison – H, 11 Michigan Cav., 05/12/1881, New York, 66, Rheumatism, 08/13/1891.

O'BRIEN, William - A, 3 Wisconsin, 03/08/1874, Ireland, 46, Wound-hand, 04/20/1891.

O'BRIEN, William – H, 83 New York, 04/03/1884, Ireland, 67, Gunshot wound-hip, 06/25/1891.

OLES, Oscar J. – I, 17 Illinois Cav., 03/11/1891, New York, 57, Piles, 07/08/1891.

O'SULLIVAN, Patrick – A, 1 Nebraska Cav., 02/28/1876, Ireland, 55, Hernia, 02/26/1891.

PARKS, Anthony - __, 6 Wisconsin Battery, 07/15/1885, Georgia, 65, Paralysis, 08/23/1891.

PEABODY, Steph. V. – A, Musician, 128 Indiana, 06/24/1885, New York, 39, Hemorrhoids, 04/01/1881.

PEAK, Wm. H. – C, 47 Wisconsin, 06/14/1881, Ohio, 61, Disease-eyes, 07/10/1891.

PIERRE, Bonnet – F, 5 Missouri, 10/10/1880, France, 68, Rheumatism, 06/09/1891.

QUEENAN, Jas. – H, 6 Missouri, 03/03/1891, Ireland, 54, Knee, 10/23/1891.

RAMOS, William – G, 5 Iowa Cav., 01/06/1877, Mexico, 43, Wound-right leg, 01/15/1891.

RANDOLPH, Joseph M. – E, 7 Iowa, 01/17/1880, Virginia, 52, Ulcer-leg, 03/30/1891.

RICHARDSON, James C. - __, 25 U. S. Colored Troop, 9/30/1887, Kentucky, 66, Loss-left leg, 06/11/1891.

RISENBERG, Henry – B, 20 Massachusetts, 08/11/1887, Germany, 54, Hemorrhoids, 02/09/1891.

ROBINSON, Joseph C. – D, 49 New York, 07/19/1883, England, 69, Rheumatism, 07/06/1891.

ROLFE, Benj. F. – B, Capt., 114 U. S. Colored Troop, 02/03/1887, New York, 55, Rheumatism, 01/22/1891.

SASS, Henry - __, S. M., 82 Illinois, 07/15/1886, Germany, 49, Rheumatism, 12/03/1891.

SCHILLING, Henry - A, 9 Wisconsin, 07/28/1881, Germany, 55, Rheumatism, 09/15/1891.

SCHIPPER, John – G, Sgt., 2 Missouri, 03/11/1879, Germany, 69, Rheumatism, 05/30/1891.

SCHMIDT, August – A, S., 15 Wisconsin, 04/05/1890, Germany, 53, Wound-left leg, 08/25/1891.

SCHRT, Charles H. – D, 3 Wisconsin, 04/05/1890, Germany, 59, Rheumatism, 02/09/1891.

SHOCK, Fred. – D, 16 Illinois, 12/11/1890, Germany, 65, Rheumatism, 04/20/1891.

SHORT, James – D, 104 New York, 07/16/1889, Ireland, 62, Asthma, 06/02/1891.

SLOYD, Charles – D, 1 Pennsylvania Light Art., 07/28/1884, Ireland, 64, Gunshot wound-leg, 06/01/1891. (Surname recorded out of alphabetical order, may be *F* instead of *S*.)

SMITH, Andrew – F, 24 Wisconsin, 12/21/1890, New York, 60, Cancer, 02/18/1891.

SMITH, Frank – C, 20 New York Cav., 01/01/1888, New York, 60, Deafness, 05/05/1891.

STABLES, Chas. – C, 7 Pennsylvania, 08/31/1871, Germany, 60, Wound-arm, 09/26/1891.

STAHL, Charles – B, Cpl., 1 Nebraska, 12/27/1884, Germany, 64, Rheumatism, 03/13/1891.

STETEL, John – B, 8 Iowa, 11/03/1889, Germany, 72, Old age, 05/21/1891.

STOER, Jacob – A, 1 Missouri, U. S. Reserve Corps, 07/26/1891, Germany, 57, Rheumatism, 08/14/1891.

TELYEA, Lewis – B, 39 Wisconsin, 12/19/1888, California, 76, Chronic diarrhoea, 08/03/1891.

THOMAS, Thos. G. – H, West Virginia, 07/22/1882, England, 60, Rheumatism, 05/21/1891.

VOCKE, George – C, 82 Illinois, 06/28/1889, Germany, 51, Heart disease, 06/11/1891.

WATSON, James H. – E, 7 Illinois, 12/22/1883, Ohio, 44, Disease-eyes, 02/23/1891.

WEBER, Mathias – K, 27 Wisconsin, 03/21/1880, Germany, 43, Rheumatism, 12/30/1891.

WEST, Clarence – C, 52 New York, 08/011891, New York, 42, Lung disease, 11/19/1891.

WHIPPLE, S. A. – A, 16 Wisconsin, 05/165/1891, New York, 50, Cancer, 11/03/1891.

WILLIAMS, Charles – A, 13 Pennsylvania Cav., 11/14/1886, Vermont, 42, Fracture-legs, 07/08/1891.

WOODS, James – A, 90 Illinois, 02/01/1889, Ireland, 73, Rheumatism, 02/25/1891.

YOUNG, Armer – G, 82 Pennsylvania, 01/26/1884, Pennsylvania, 44, Epilepsy, 03/24/1891.

Sources:

Report of the Board of Managers of the National Home for Disabled Volunteer Soldiers for the Year Ending June 30, 1891. Record of Disabled Volunteer Soldiers, Who Now Are and Have Been, Members of the National Home for Disabled Volunteer Soldiers, from July 1, 1890 to June 30, 1891. Washington: Government Printing Office, 1892.

Report of the Board of Managers of the National Home for Disabled Volunteer Soldiers for the Year Ending June 30, 1892. Record of Disabled Volunteer soldiers, Who Now Are and Have Been Members of the National Home for Disabled Volunteer Soldiers, from July 1, 1891 to June 30, 1892. Washington: Government Printing Office, 1893.

DEATHS IN 1892

FORMAT: NAME, COMPANY & REGIMENT, DATE OF ADMISSION, PLACE OF BIRTH, AGE, DEBILITY, DATE OF DEATH.

ALEXANDER, William – Fireman, U. S. Navy, 06/24/1887, Ireland, 56, General debility, 11/11/1892.

ANDERSON, Hans – H, 30 Wisconsin, 08/04/1884, Norway, 64, Rheumatism, 12/26/1892. (Data found in record for July 1, 1891 to June 30, 1892.)

ARKER, Joseph – M, 5 Pennsylvania Cav., 08/31/1871, Germany, 26, Injury-leg, 12/18/1892. (? Age or admission date.)

BAER, August – L, 4 Wisconsin Cav., 04/28/1886, Germany, 57, Wound-leg, 01/21/1892.

BARNES, Philander – I, 48 Indiana, 12/21/1890, Indiana, 43, Rheumatism, 05/13/1892.

BARRAY, John – I, 3 New York Cav., 09/07/1890, Ireland, 67, General debility, 05/30/1892.

BARRETT, Daniel – A, 3 Missouri Cav., 08/13/1890, Vermont, 55, Gunshot wound-back, 07/01/1892,

BOBANAN, Geo. W. – H, 2 U. S. Veteran Volunteers, 11/16/1891, New York, 49, Heart disease, 01/23/1892.

BRAND, Thomas H. – C, 7 Missouri Cav., 08/13/1889, England, 64, Blind, 10/16/1892.

BRANON, Michael – B, 4 Pennsylvania Cav., 08/08/1888, Pennsylvania, 71, Disease-eyes, 09/08/1892.

BROT_, Philip – F, 10 Illinois, 06/14/1882, Germany, 67, Rheumatism, 05/16/1892.

BROWN, George C, - __, Illinois Board of Trade Battery, 03/24/1891, New York, 48, Heart disease, 10/27/1892.

BRUCKNER, Henry – A, 8 U. S. Veteran Reserve Corps, 11/16/1877, Germany, 50 Hernia, 10/06/1892.

CAMPBELL, Corn'ls. – A 13 Missouri Cav., 12/08/1890, Scotland, 53, Rheumatism, 04/01/1892. (Status as to date of *death* or *discharge* omitted in record.)

CLAFFY, Thos. – A, C., 13 Wisconsin, 08/01/1887, Ireland, 51, Loss-left leg, 04/02/1892.

COE, Henry - __, 9 Wisconsin Battery, 03/08/1892, New York, 57, Rheumatism, 09/01/1892.

CRAWFORD, Steph. C. – I, Capt., 1 Indiana, Mexican War, 10/28/1887, Pennsylvania, 75, General debility, 09/23/1892.

CUMMINGS, William – G, 103 Ohio, 10/02/1892, Ohio, 57, Chronic rheumatism, 10/21/1892.

DAVIDSON, Grinton – H, 2 Illinois Light Art., 08/17/1892, Canada, 57, Chronic diarrhoea, 11/17/1892.

DAVIS, Mich'l – M, 5 New York Cav., 10/25/1888, New York, 45, Heart disease, 01/08/1892.

DENNISTON, Philip – K, 59 Indiana, 03/17/1887, Indiana, 64, Rheumatism, 04/30/1892.

DEVERNEY, Frank – F, 16 U. S. Army, 11/16/1891, Michigan, 59, Disease-eyes, 03/06/1892.

DOUGLASS, Wm. J. – F, 5 Minnesota, 02/07/1892, England, 50, Wound-left thigh, 05/15/1892.

EDWARDS, James – B, Minnesota Brackett's Battalion, 08/13/19892, England, 52, General debility, 12/03/1892.

EIER, Dan'l – L, 9 New Jersey, 01/16/1880, Bavaria, 66, Wound-head, 06/16/1892.

FENCIL, Joseph – H, 45 Wisconsin, 01/18/1892, Austria, 50, Rheumatism, 01/14/1892.

FISHER, Wm. – H, Sgt., 187 Ohio, 07/23/1889, Germany, 49, Rheumatism, 01/14/1892.

FITZGERALD, Daniel – H, 16 Kansas Cav., 02/12/1876, Ireland, 45, Wound-head, 12/12/1892.

FLOOD, Mich'l – C. passer, U. S. Navy, 12/08/1890, England, 46, Syphilis, 01/23/1892.

FLYNN, Edw. – H, 3 U. S. Veteran Reserve Corps, 10/21/1879, Ireland, 67, Piles, 03/13/1892.

FOGARTY, Patrick – H, 10 Illinois Cav., 05/21/1873, Ireland, 70, Injury-side, 11/10/1892

GASPER, John – E, 4 Wisconsin Cav., 10/26/1889, Germany, 61, Rheumatism, 04/27/1892.

GATZEL, P. Paul – E, 26 Wisconsin, 10/04/1867, Germany, 32(?), Loss-left leg, 01/24/1892.

GLANCEY, Owen L. – C, 53 Illinois, 08/18/1877, Ireland, 63, Hernia, 01/04/1892.

GRIPPIN, Alex. W. - __, 1 Battery, U. S. Veteran Reserve Corps, 01/06/1888, New York, 63, Varicose veins, 06/11/1892.

HARTNETT, Mich. – A, 12 Connecticut, 11/14/1889, Ireland, 50, Rheumatism, 04/14/1892. (Status as to date of *death* or *discharge* omitted in record.)

HEIZ, Xavier – C, 49 Illinois, 01/05/1882, Switzerland, 55, Rheumatism, 01/22/1892.

HENNESY, Patrick – B, 66 Ohio, 07/18/1878, Ireland, 58, Wound-leg, 10/11/1892.

HIBBERTS, Charles A. – __, Cpl., 20 Ohio Battery, 01/25/1891, Germany, 60, Deaf, 08/14/1892.

HOBBS, Prosper P. - __, 3 Indiana Battery, 08/11/1891, Indiana, 49, Paralysis, 08/13/1892.

HOLLAND, Rob't. – G, 41 Wisconsin, 06/15/1889, Ireland, 69, Rheumatism, 05/23/1892. (Status as to date of *death* or *discharge* omitted in record.)

HOLLAND, Timothy – Seaman, U. S. Navy, 06/24/1889, Ireland, 59, Rheumatism, 12/09/1892.

HOSP, Leo – C, 45 Wisconsin, 03/12/1882, Germany, 59, Rheumatism, 11/26/1892.

HOYT, Peaslee – C, 2 U. S. Dragoons, Mexican War, 09/24/1881. New Hampshire, 68, Hernia, 12/25/1892.

IDELL, Isaiah R. – E, 14 Wisconsin, 02/27/1892, Pennsylvania, 70, Cancer, 07/25/1892.

JACKSON, Jas. – B, 54 Illinois, 06/23/1888, Indiana, 68, General debility, 06/20/1892.

KECK, Conrad – G, Cpl., 9 Ohio, 12/13/1884, Germany, 55 Rheumatism, 01/26/1892. (Recorded in data covering last six months of 1892.)

KING, James – G, 13 U. S. Army, 03/15/1888, Ireland, 66, Rheumatism, 09/03/1892.

KINNEY, James – F, C., 2 Wisconsin Cav., 07/07/1889, Ireland, 67, Disease-stomach, 04/07/1892.

KLEINER, Sam'l. – A, 2 U. S. Veteran Volunteers, 03/14/1878, Switzerland, 43, Wound-side, 02/26/1892.

KOEPKE, August – C, 26 Wisconsin, 06/23/1888, Germany, 74, General debility, 09/23/1892.

LARING, Milton I. – E, 40 Massachusetts, 08/03/1887, Massachusetts, 66, Wound-hands, 11/08/1892.

LITHGOW, Geo. W. – G, 2 U. S. Veteran Reserve Corps, 01/02/1885, Pennsylvania, 54, Rheumatism, 02/25/1892.

MALONE, Henry – Landsman, U. S. Navy, 07/23/1887, New Jersey, 48, Rheumatism, 06/14/1892.

MCCABE, Edward – K, 82, Illinois, 07/07/1891, Ireland, 55, Rheumatism, 11/03/1892.

MCCLAUGHY, T. B. – G, 12 Wisconsin, 03/05/1892, New York, 67, Gunshot wound-leg, 10/11/1892.

MCFAUL, George B. – D, Lt., 76 U. S. Colored Troops, 05/17/1886, Ireland, 53, Rheumatism, 12/25/1892.

MILLER, Braxton – I, 45 Illinois, 05/05/1886, Indiana, 52, Disease-spine, 11/25/1892.

MILQUET, Gregoire – F, 14 Wisconsin, 09/17/1885, Belgium, 62, Wound-shoulder, 06/30/1892. (Recorded in data covering last six months of 1892.)

MOESSNER, Henry – H, 7 New York, 12/11/1890, Germany, 45, Rheumatism, 04/02/1892.

MORGAN, Josiah – D, 74 Illinois, 12/09/1891, New Hampshire, 81, Old age, 03/23/1892.

MORSE, Andrew J – C, Lt., 14 Ohio, 07/21/1890, New York, 58, Rheumatism, 11/04/1892.

MUELLER, Erhard – M, Qm., 17 Pennsylvania Cav., 03/09/1890, Germany, 53, Asthma, 01/30/1892.

MULLER, Joham - B, 2 Missouri, 05/01/1886, Germany, 72, Loss-right thigh, 02/13/1892.

MUNSLINGER, John - __, 10 Wisconsin Battery, 03/02/1870, Germany, 40, Wound-breast, 06/03/1892

MURPHY, John – H, Sgt., 17 U. S. Army, 08/26/1891, Ireland, 65, Rheumatism, 12/09/1892.

NELSON, Thomas A. – H, Musician, 10 Wisconsin, 04/26/1885, Wisconsin, 36, Rheumatism, 09/21/1892.

NOBLE, David P. – E, 19 Wisconsin, 08/26/1887, New York, 70, Paralysis, 04/02/1892.

O'DONNELL, Michael – C, 1 West Virginia Light Art., 10/25/1888, Ireland, 78, Bronchitis, 10/20/1892.

PUTZLER, Elias – D, 17 Wisconsin, 10/10/1878, Austria, 57, Injury-foot, 09/02/1892.

RAHLMAN, William – C, 24 Wisconsin, 03/23/1871, Germany, 46, Wound-thigh, 08/04/1892.

REIFF, Abra'm. – G, Sgt., 9 Pennsylvania Cav., 01/10/1881, Pennsylvania, 60, Disease-eyes, 01/10/1892.

RENGGA Adolph - __, Marine Brigade, Mississippi, 09/22/1889, Switzerland, 50, Varicose veins, 03/24/1892.

ROBINSON, RODY – E, 3 New Hampshire, 02/18/1879, Ireland, 35, Wound-arm, 11/25/1892.

SCHERMERHORN, J. D. – G, 2 New York Cav., 03/04/1891, New York, 59, Hernia, 01/28/1892.

SCHILLING, Henry – C, 22 Wisconsin, 08/16/1887, Germany, 59, Rheumatism, 08/30/1892.

SIMPSON, Thomas - __, 13 Wisconsin Battery, 05/24/1867, Ireland, 40, Diarrhoea, 10/26/1892.

SLATER, William – K, 12 Wisconsin, 07/07/1890, England, 67, Varicose veins, 10/18/1892.

SLOSSON, Thomas J. – M, 10 Illinois Cav., 12/08/1891, New York, 50, Rheumatism, 12/31/1892.

SMITH, George – H, 14 Illinois Cav., 01/29/1884, Scotland, 52, Heart disease, 10/25/1892.

SMITH, George – K, 9 Massachusetts, 12/22/1887, Germany, 53 Rheumatism, 11/20/1982.

SNYDER, Chauncey – D, 115 New York, 04/28/1886, New York, 74, Deaf, 10/06/1892

SONNENBERG, Ernst - __, 8 District of Columbia, 10/27/1884, Germany, 62, Heart disease, 09/05/1892.

STAHL, William – H. 9 Wisconsin, 10/06/1889, Germany, 59, Asthma, 12/07/1892.

STARKS, Peter – I, 43 Wisconsin, 11/02/1891, Holland, 54, Chronic diarrhoea, 08/07/1892.

STEINE, Henry – B, 49 Illinois, 12/29/1872, Germany, 53, Rheumatism, 03/24/1892.

STUART, Charles F. – C, 47 Pennsylvania, 01/09/1883, Pennsylvania, 63, Rheumatism, 11/24/1892.

TEARNEY, Edward – I, 46 Illinois, 08/11/1882, Ireland, 54, Paralysis, 10/22/1892.

TROAN, Ole E. – I, 15 Wisconsin, 04/08/1869, Norway, 25, Shell wound-leg, 03/24/1892. (Recorded in data covering last six months of 1892.)

ULLRICH, Joachim – I, 18 Wisconsin, 07/02/1888, Germany, 58, Asthma, 05/11/1892.

VALENTINE, W. H. H. – B, S. 32 Wisconsin, 06/06/1892, New York, 50, Paralysis, 06/28/1892.

WOODS, Robert – I, 4 U. S. Army, 03/01/1890, Ireland, 65, Injury-ankle, 07/10/1892.

WRIGHT, Joel – B, 35 Iowa, 06/18/1884, Maryland, 54, Rheuma-tism, 01/24/1892.

WYSS, Ulrich – H, Musician, 1 Iowa, 05/20/1879, Switzerland, 40, Wound-leg, 09/15/1892.

Sources:

Report of the Board of Managers of the National Home for Disabled Volunteer Soldiers for the Year Ending June 30, 1892. Record of Disabled Volunteer Soldiers, Who Now Are and Have Been, Members of the National Home for Disabled Volunteer Soldiers, from July 1, 1891 to June 30, 1892. Washington: Government Printing Office, 1893.

The Miscellaneous Documents of the House of Representatives for the First Session of the 53rd Congress, 1893-94. #3151. Record of Disabled Volunteer Soldiers, Who Now Are And Have Been, Members of the National Home for Disabled Volunteer Soldiers, from July 1, 1892 to June 30, 1893. Washington: Government Printing Office, 1894. (Extracted from Annual Reports – National Homes for Disabled Volunteer Soldiers.)

FORMAT: NAME, COMPANY & REGIMENT, DATE OF ADMISSION, PLACE OF BIRTH, AGE, DISABILITY, DATE OF DEATH.

ANDERSON, G. C. – F, 12 Wisconsin, 05/26/1886, Norway, 52, Rheumatism, 07/18/1893.

BECKER, Robert – K, Cpl., 26 Wisconsin, 09/12/1893, Prussia, 73, Rheumatism, 10/13/1893.

BELCHAM, William – Gunner, U. S. Navy, 10/26/1888, Gibraltar, 62, Hernia, 03/02/1893.

BELLAMY, C. M. – A, 106 Illinois, 12/26/1893, New York, 60, Rheumatism, 12/26/1893.

BERGMAN, Martin – G, 12 Missouri, 09/30/1878, Germany, 39, Wound-arm, 03/20/1893.

BIXBY, Sylvester S. – C, 50 New York Engineers, 10/09/1888, Pennsylvania, 50, Ulcer, 07/16/1893.

BOWKER, Eben – F, 16 Wisconsin, 12/16/1887, New York, 63, Blind, 02/02/1893.

BOYD, Mathew - F, Capt., 73 Indiana, 11/03/1892, Indiana, 55, Injury-leg, 08/08/1893.

BOYLE, James – F, 106 New York, 11/19/1891, Ireland, 65, Abscess, 02/14/1893.

BRENNAN, John – A, 155 New York, 06/17/1867, Ireland, 40, Rheumatism, 02/02/1893.

BRIGLER, Morgan – H, 45 Wisconsin, 01/10/1874, Switzerland, 55, Rheumatism, 04/03/1893.

BROWN, Ephr. – I, 18 Wisconsin, 05/07/1885, England, 56, Disease-eyes, 11/08/1893.

BROWN, James – F, 57 Illinois, 11/01/1891, Ireland, 50 Bronchitis, 02/04/1893.

BROWN, Theo. C. – L, 1 Illinois Light Art., 03/17/1885, New Hampshire, 65, Lung disease, 11/02/1893.

BUNCH, Thomas H. – A, Capt., 9 Tennessee Cav., 04/18/1885, Tennessee, 46, Wound-leg, 04/03/1893.

CALLAHAN, Michael - F, 100 Illinois, 01/01/1888, Ireland, 60, Rheumatism, 10/14/1893.

CHAMBERS, Thomas - __, S. M., 11 Minnesota, 03/09/1889, Ireland, 57, Old age, 08/01/1893.

CLARK, Alva M – D, 15 Illinois, 07/25/1891, Vermont, 49, Gunshot wound-shoulder, 03/20/1893.

CLARK, Charles, C. – K, 59 Illinois, 04/11/1890, Massachusetts, 78, Injury-hip, 05/09/1893.

CLARK, George – D, 2 Pennsylvania, Cav., 07/25/1892, Pennsylvania, 73, Old age, 10/04/1893.

CLEMENT, William H. H. – H, 5 New York, 08/20/1892, New York, 53, Asthma, 07/18/1893.

COLLINS, John – B, 23 Illinois, 04/19/1880, Ireland, 54, Rheumatism, 09/29/1893.

CONNELLY, George – K, 20 Illinois, 03/12/1878, Ireland, 58, Wound-hip, 06/14/1893.

CONNER, John F. – F, 16 Massachusetts, 05/08/1888, Scotland, 57, Paralysis, 01/06/1893.

CONNER, John – Fireman, U. S. Navy, 03/23/1886, Ireland, 62, Injury-knee, 06/20/1893.

DALTON, John H. – G, 37 Wisconsin, 07/05/1892, Ireland, 60, Deaf, 11/02/1893.

DAVIS, John A. – K, 49 Wisconsin, 10/22/1892, New York, 43, Syphilis, 03/29/1893.

DENCH, Jul. – K, 29 Wisconsin, 11/11/1889, Germany, 78, Old age, 10/04/94 (Recorded as '94 in '93 data.)

DESELL, William – 12, 2 Battery U. S. Veteran Reserve Corps, 11/13/1874, Germany, 57, Varicose veins, 12/21/1893.

DETWEILER, Jacob – H, Cpl., 18 Missouri, 12/09/1879, Switzerland, 47, Rheumatism, 01/18/1893.

DICK, Alex – E, 67 Ohio, 11/15/1882, Scotland, 54, Diarrhoea, 09/18/1893.

DICKASON, Joseph H. - __, 23 U. S. Veteran Reserve Corps, 10/12/1883, New York, 53, Rheumatism, 04/06/1893.

DIPPLE, Alb. W. – E, 31 Wisconsin, 09/21/1893, Pennsylvania, 53, Rheumatism, 12/17/1893.

DORRANCE, Hugh – E, 1 New York Mounted Rifles, 03/21/1893, Scotland, 63, Heart disease, 03/26/1893.

DOYLE, John – F, 98 Pennsylvania, 01/18/1892, New York, 44, Rheumatism, 04/12/1893.

DOYLE, John – K, 4 Maine, 10/13/1886, Maine, 48, Wound-leg, 01/03/1893.

DUENKE, Casper – A, 15 Missouri, 06/09/1877, Switzerland, 64, Hernia, 12/28/1893.

DUVERNAY, William- B, 1 Michigan Sharpshooters, 12/12/1882, Michigan, 33, Diarrhoea, 08/25/1893.

FARR, Andrew J. – B, 66 Illinois, 05/13/1885, New York, 47, Rheumatism, 06/01/1893.

FENTON, Patrick – B, 45 Illinois, 08/31/1893, Ireland, 63, Chronic rheumatism, 10/12/1893.

FILLIO, Nelson – F, 1 Michigan Light Art., 08/02/1883, New York, 65, Chronic Diarrhoea, 10/27/1893.

FJOSER, Swenning – D, 30 Wisconsin, 01/19/1887, Norway, 66, Hernia, 05/21/1893.

FRANK, Henry A. – G, 38 Ohio, 05/01/1892, Germany, 47, Hernia, 04/18/1893.

GALVIN, William – G, 80 Illinois, 10/25/1888, Ireland, 52, Varicose veins, 04/14/1893.

GASTINGER, Robert – B, 106 Ohio, 08/21/1884, Germany, 63, Wound-leg, 08/08/1893.

GENTCHELL, Adel. – A, 29 New York, 03/21/1870, Germany, 37, Disease-brain, 12/09/1893.

GEROUX, George – B, 3 New York Prov. Cav., 12/08/1887, Canada, 46, Lumbago, 10/28/1893.

GILDEY, James – F, 47 New York, 11/02/1892, New York, 46, Injury-hands, 03/25/1893.

GOETZ, John – E, 9 Wisconsin, 06/19/1880, Germany, 54, Chronic Rheumatism, 12/05/1893.

GREER, James – F, 90 Pennsylvania, 11/04/1885, Ireland, 66, Rheumatism 10/24/1893.

GROBMAN, J. C. F. – H, Sgt., 11 Pennsylvania Cav., 06/30/1881, Germany, 57, Wound-leg, 07/03/1893.

GROVER, Isaac – K, 3 Wisconsin Cav., 09/22/1891, New York, 69, Chronic diarrhoea, 08/28/1893.

HANAFIN, James – G, 35 Indiana, 08/19/1870, Ireland, 30(?), Shell wound-hip, 01/30/1893.

HANNAH, John – H, 13 Wisconsin, 12/19/1892, New York, 51, Injury-side, 07/21/1893.

HAUCK, John – K, 54 Illinois, 12/09/1868, Germany, 55, Hernia, 12/22/1893.

HAYS, John – D, Sgt., 14 Maine, 10/13/1882, England, 42, Gunshot wound-shoulder, 06/29/1893.

HILL, Jackson – D, 18 U. S. Colored Troop, 10/05/1886, Indiana, 39, Paralysis, 07/03/1893.

JENSEN, Chris – I, 82, Illinois, 04/01/1891, Denmark, 66, Old age, 03/10/1893.

JOHNSON, Alex. – D, 30 Wisconsin, 03/04/1890, Norway, 56, Fracture-leg, 06/02/1893.

JOHNSON, Peter J. – I, 37 Wisconsin, 12/08/1888, Sweden, 63, Asthma, 07/21/1893.

JONES, Oliver – E, 11 U. S. Colored Troop, 08/26/1890, Michigan, 44, Rheumatism, 06/08/1893.

KIELEY, Patrick – H, 31 Wisconsin, 03/19/1873, Ireland, 65, Disease-eyes, 11/17/1893.

KIRSCHNER, Ferd. – H, 26 Wisconsin, 07/21/1871, Germany, 59, Rheumatism 06/04/1893.

KNEISEL, Charles – G, 14 Illinois, 05/25/1884, Germany, 54, Wound-knee, 01/14/1893.

KOEHLER, Anton – G, 94 New York, 09/22/1891, Germany, 52, Gunshot wounds, 10/27/1893.

KREHL, Frederick – B, 2 Pennsylvania Heavy Art., 08/22/1889, Germany, 65, Hernia, 03/31/1893.

KRIEGER, Peter – F, 7 Michigan, 04/01/1885, Germany, 62, Wound-thigh, 05/09/1893.

LANGAN, Thomas – Gunner, U. S. Navy, 04/13/1888, Ireland, 68, Diarrhoea, 07/07/1893.

LEWIS, Henry R. – F, 152 New York, 03/06/1891, Ireland, 56, Heart disease, 01/02/1893.

LILLEBERG, Charles – Landsman, U. S. Navy, 11/03/1888, Sweden, 62, Rheumatism, 08/19/1893.

LUMBE, William S. – H, 21 Wisconsin, 12/19/1884, England, 65, Wound-back, 01/09/1893.

LUTZELSCHWAB, Charles – K, 82 Illinois, 04/01/1885, Switzerland, 54, Injury-head, 03/29/1893.

MANS, Ulrich – C, Sgt., 45 Wisconsin, 04/26/1893, Prussia, 65, Asthma, 04/30/1893.

MCCANN, John – G, 1 Michigan Sharpshooters, 10/01/1889, Canada, 69, Old age, 09/25/1893.

MCGLEN, Charles – F, 2 U. S., Mexican War, 02/25/1893, Ireland, 70, Piles, 03/24/1893.

MCKAY, John C. – G, Lt., 7 Pennsylvania Cav., 09/22/1891, Pennsylvania 57, Asthma, 03/07/1893.

MCMILLAN, Donald – A, 1 U. S. Army, 03/11/1870, Scotland, 47, Varicose veins, 12/04/1893.

MILDE, Charles - G, Sgt., 14 Illinois, 10/2/4/1882, Germany, 56, Wound-face, 11/25/1893.

MILLER, Chris. W. – C, 8 Wisconsin, 02/25/1885, Germany, 54, Atrophy, 07/01/1893.

MILLER, Jacob – D, 9 U. S. Veteran Volunteers, 1/11/1880, Switzerland, 49, Chronic rheumatism, 12/30/1893.

MILLS, William C. – B, Capt., 128 Indiana, 05/14/1887, Ohio, 60, General debility, 01/14/1893.

MURPHY, James – K, Cpl., 143 Illinois, 07/21/1892, Ireland, 66, Wounds, 02/21/1893.

NABHOL, Frederick – B, 27 Pennsylvania, 06/12/1885, Germany, 42, Gunshot wound- head, 05/17/1893.

NELSON, James R. – K, 13 Wisconsin, 01/02/1887, New York, 67, Rheumatism, 06/14/1893.

NELSON, Lars M. - C, Cpl., 6 Wisconsin, 08/24/1893, Norway, 58, Phthisis, 09/07/1893.

OBER, Peter A. – K, 5 Massachusetts, 07/29/1885, Sweden, 43, Rheumatism, 03/10/1893.

O'CALLAGHAN, James – E, 10 Michigan Cav., 12/08/1892, Ireland, 70, Hernia, 10/02/1893.

ORAN, John – C, 156 Illinois, 05/21/1890, Maryland, 47, Rheumatism, 04/15/1893.

OWENS, Charles A. – G, 36 U. S. Army, 10/28/1892, New York, 49, Rheumatism, 12/27/1893.

PALMETER, David – F, 100 New York, 04/27/1887, New York, 70, Asthma, 03/15/1893.

PATTERSON, William E. – E, 3 Maryland Cav., 08/14/1890, Virginia, 51, Deaf, 02/18/1893.

REDBURG, Charles – L, 31 Ohio, 10/16/1868, Prussia, 34(?), Rheumatism, 11/05/1893.

RENNER, John – Landsman, U. S. Navy, 10/27/1888, Austria, 57, Deaf, 02/04/1893.

RICE, Daniel – E, 4 U. S. Army Cav., 03/28/1893, Vermont, 60, Rheumatism, 08/30/1893.

ROTTSCHEIT, J. P. – B, 52 Wisconsin, 12/11/1890, Germany, 64, Rheumatism, 04/22/1893.

RYAN, Jerry - __, Illinois Cogswell's Battery, 08/29/1886, Illinois, 46, Deaf, 05/11/1893.

SANFORD, John D. – H, 83 Pennsylvania, 09/21/1890, Ohio, 46, Imbecile, 01/03/1893.

SAUTERS, Frank – F, 5 Iowa Cav., 04/27/1887, Germany, 64, Hernia, 09/01/1893.

SCHLOSSMACHER, P. – H, 1 Illinois Light Art., 12/21/1881, Germany, 63, Disease-eyes, 06/29/1893.

SCHMIDT, Jul. – Landsman, U. S. Navy, 07/21/1874, Germany, 68, Rheumatism, 07/24/1893.

SCHOTT, Chris – D, 23 Wisconsin, 12/11/1892, Germany, 49, Rheumatism, 03/17/1893.

SCHUBARTH, Hennan – 77, 2 Battery, U. S. Veteran Reserve Corps, 11/06/1880, Germany, 63, Hernia, 03/22/1893.

SHAPELY, Hiram H. – G, Sgt., 13 New York Heavy Art. 10/19/1893, Ohio, 55, Cancer, 10/31/1893.

SHEEREN, John – U. S. Marine Corps, 11/26/1884, Ireland, 54, Paralysis-leg, 04/12/1893.

SHERIDAN, Patrick B – D, 177 New York, 10/18/1893, Ireland, 50, Kidney disease, 11/12/1893.

SLOAN, Bernard - __, 7 New York Battery, 01/08/1892, New York, 48, Heart disease, 01/10/1893.

SMITH, Isr. E. – A, 200 Pennsylvania, 06/07/1893, Pennsylvania, 49, Rheumatism, 07/12/1893.

SMITH, John P. – Landsman, U. S. Navy, 03/17/1890, Germany, 62, Asthma, 05/02/1893.

SPENCER, Robert H. – D, 34 New York, 11/19/1873, New York, 67, Chronic Rheumatism, 04/25/1893.

SPENCER, Robert H. – A, Lt., 14 New York Heavy Art., 11/19/1873, New York, 67, Rheumatism, 04/25/1893.

SPORER, Fritz – D, 8 Illinois Cav., 05/26/1892, Germany, 55, Varicose veins, 02/20/1893.

STRAUB, Theo – D, 15 New York Heavy Art., 11/16/1877, Germany, 36, Wound-left hand, 05/09/1893.

SULLIVAN, Flor. - __, Recruiting Service U. S. Army, 06/08/1885, Ireland, 49, Rheumatism, date of death not recorded.

TEMPLIN, Fred – B, 41 New York, 09/02/1890, Germany, 56, Defective vision, 10/07/1893.

TOMPKINS, George W. – C, Cpl., 3 Wisconsin Cav., 09/26/1883, New York, 60 Hernia, 07/24/1893.

TUCKER, Charles F. – L, Sgt., 29 Indiana, 10/29/1889, Michigan, 46, Rheumatism, 11/13/1893.

TWIGGS, David - __, 2 Minnesota Battery, 08/31/1887, Wisconsin, 58, Rheumatism, 07/24/1893.

UNI, John F. – H, 95 New York, 04/18/1893, Switzerland, 57, Cystitis, 05/27/1893.

VISGAR, William – A, 184 New York, 04/19/1889, New York, 44, Gunshot wound-hip, 11/05/1893.

VOHL, Frederick – C, 9 Wisconsin, 01/15/1893, Germany, 48, Varicose veins, 06/20/1893.

WALSER, Benedict – G, 57 Illinois, 08/08/1882, Germany, 57, Rheumatism, 10/07/1893.

WEIKEL, Peter – H, 6 U. S. Veteran Volunteers, 09/20/1884, Germany, 74, Rheumatism, 10/31/1893.

WEILAND, Charles – H, 47 Ohio, 05/06/1882, Germany, 54, Wound-left hand, 08/23/1893.

WENKEL, Chris – B, 6 Wisconsin, 02/02/1887, Germany, 65, Cystitis, 12/15/1893.

WHITFIELD, George S. – L, Sgt., 14 Rhode Island Heavy Art., 09/24/1891, New York, 48, Epilepsy, 05/27/1893.

WILDT, Fred. – H, 23 U. S. Veteran Reserve Corps, 08/21/1883, Germany, 70, Varicose veins, 12/16/1893.

WILEY, George – G, 4 U. S. Veteran Volunteers, 01/22/1878, Ireland, 56, Disease-eyes, 02/17/1893.

Sources:

The Miscellaneous Documents of the House of Representatives for the First Session of the 53rd Congress, 1893-94. #3151. Record of

Disabled Volunteer Soldiers, Who Now Are And Have Been, Members of the National Home for Disabled Volunteer Soldiers, from July 1, 1892 to June 30, 1893. Washington: Government Printing Office, 1894. (Extracted from Annual Reports – National Homes for Disabled Volunteer Soldiers.)

The Miscellaneous Documents of the House of Representatives for the Third Session of The 53rd Congress, 1894-95. #3329. Record of Disabled Volunteer Soldiers, Who Are And Have Been, Members of the National Home for Disabled Volunteer Soldiers, from July 1, 1893 to June 30, 1894. Washington: Government Printing Office, 1895. (Extracted from Annual Reports – National Homes for Disabled Volunteer Soldiers.)

DEATHS IN 1894

FORMAT: NAME, COMPANY & REGIMENT, DATE OF ADMISSION, PLACE OF BIRTH, AGE, DISABILITY, DATE OF DEATH.

AMBACHER, John - G, 45 Wisconsin, 03/02/1873, Bavaria, 62, Rheumatism, 08/08/1894.

ATWOOD, William D, - A, 4 Massachusetts Cav., 11/19/1872, Vermont, 52, Diarrhoea, 01/04/1894.

BACHUS, Henry – D, 2 Wisconsin, 11/11/1885, Germany, 67, Ulcers-legs, 09/03/1894.

BAIER, Andreas – E, 98 Pennsylvania, 08/19/1879, Germany, 64, Wound-ankle, 11/03/1894.

BAISON, Nich. – D, 7 U. S. Army, 04/02/1888, Switzerland, 48, Hernia, 05/29/1894.

BARNES, John – C, 72, Ohio, 11/18/1880, New York, 36, Wound-foot, 11/21/1894.

BARTELS, Fred – C, 5 Wisconsin, 10/30/1886, Germany, 44, Paralysis, 11/02/1894.

BAYLOR, Elij. M. – A, 14 Illinois, 10/15/1884, Ohio, 47, Gunshot wound-side, 06/05/1894.

BETZEL, Charles – Assistant Surgeon, U. S. Army, 05/18/1892, Germany, 83, Old age, 06/12/1894.

BODE, Henry – K, 30 Massachusetts, 05/20/1890, Germany 60, Double hernia, 06/14/1894.

BORCHERS, Lud. – D, 52 New York, 02/28/1871, Germany, 49, Hernia, 11/24/1894.

BRANDT, Charles – C, 6 Connecticut, 07/28/1889, Germany, 75, Rheumatism, 08/05/1894.

BREMER, John – B, 9 Illinois Cav., 09/03/1894, Germany, 65, Asthma, 11/08/1894.

BULGER, Edward – G, 1 Minnesota Cav., 07/23/1883, Ireland, 57, Disease-eyes, 04/27/1894.

BUSH, Melancth – E, 17 Vermont, 02/22/1893, New York, 53, Paralysis, 07/13/1894.

BYRNE, Thomas – E, 90 Illinois, 07/21/1890, New York, 44, Loss-right eye, 02/14/1894

BYWATER, Charles – G, 11 Wisconsin, 08/13/1893, England, 49, Apoplexy, 10/14/1894.

CHANDLER, William P. – A, 16 Michigan, 04/22/1869, Ireland, 34(?), Chronic dysentery, 01/31/1894.

CHIPMAN, J. Q. A. – __, 28 New York Battery, 04/27/1892, Pennsylvania, 47, Fistula, 01/15/1894.

CLARK, Robert B. – C, Lt., 87 New York, 06/16/1886, New York, 57, Hernia, 03/05/1894.

CLARK, William H. – B, Cpl., 157 New York, 06/19/1893, New York, 52, General debility, 07/24/1894.

CLAY, George S. – D, Lt., 15 Michigan, 10/12/1894, Michigan, 54, Lumbago, 12/29/1894.

CLEVELAND, M. – A, New York Militia, War of 1812, 04/11/1889, Vermont, 89, Old age, 03/05/1894.

COLLINS, Thomas – B, 5 U. S. Army Cav., 05/20/1887, Canada, 39, Injury-foot, 05/27/1894.

CONWAY, Shad – G, 54 Massachusetts, 09/05/1893, North Carolina, 50, Asthma, 02/17/1894.

COON, Charles – A, 154 New York, 07/28/1886, Vermont, 46, Heart disease, 02/10/1894.

COHOS, Michael – C, 207 Pennsylvania, 11/04/1880, Canada, 45, Paralysis, 4/26/1891. (Recorded '91 in '94 data.)

CORS, Adolph – L, 1 Missouri Light Art., 04/13/1889, Germany, 69, Wound-shoulder, 05/03/1894.

DAY, William – C, Sgt., 6 Wisconsin, 10/26/1893, New York, 57, Gunshot-wound leg, 03/29/1894.

DUGELMAN, August – H, 32 Wisconsin, 10/02/1891, Germany, 65, Old age, 03/31/1894.

DURGIN, Anson D. – B, 22 Massachusetts, 11/14/1889, New Hampshire, 55, Rheumatism, 10/12/1894.

DURNEY, Thomas – E, 4 New York Heavy Art., 06/15/1889, Ireland, 64, Hemorrhoids, 07/20/1894.

ELLIS, John – __, 15 Mexican War, 08/09/1886, England, 61, Sunstroke, 09/17/1894.

ENGEL, Joseph – B, 37 Wisconsin, 06/15/1893, Germany, 56, Paralysis, 06/07/1894.

ERBART, John – A, 35 Wisconsin, 08/10/1876, Germany, 61, Deaf, 10/24/1894.

FILLER, Henry – K, 98 Pennsylvania, 09/29/1876, Switzerland, 52, Wound-elbow, 07/06/1894.

FINCK, Daniel – F, 45 Wisconsin, 05/01/1887, Germany, 62, Rheumatism, 03/29/1894.

FRANKS, Baxter – E, 145 Illinois, 06/07/1894, Ohio, 52, Bronchitis, 07/18/1894.

FRIEDERICH, John – 115, 2 U. S. Veteran Reserve Corps Battery, 11/01/1889, Germany, 50, Rheumatism, 07/25/1894.

GAFFNEY, Math. A. – I, Cpl., 9 U. S. Veteran Volunteers, 09/22/1889, Connecticut, 66, Rheumatism, 06/29/1894.

GILBOY, James – F, 12 Illinois Cav., 03/31/1886, Ireland, 50, Loss-arm, 12/14/1894.

GILLESPIE, John – F, 80 New York, 01/27/1891, Ireland, 45, Rheumatism, 06/10/1894.

GLEASON, George – D, 2 Michigan Cav., 03/04/1890, Michigan, 57, Chronic diarrhoea, 08/23/1894.

GLEASON, John – H, 9 Connecticut, 10/24/1893, Ireland, 61 Malaria, 07/17/1894.

GUNNERWINE, G. D. – A, Cpl., 2 Pennsylvania Heavy Art., 10/02/1891, Germany, 69, Injury-shoulder, 04/22/1894.

HADDEN, Hamilton – C, 4 U. S. Inf., Mexican War, 08/26/1890, Ireland, 80, Old age, 02/17/1894.

HAUPTMAN, Wesley – D, Maryland & D.C. Battalion, Mexican War, 11/11/1893, Missouri, 65, Old age, 03/23/1894.

HAWLEY, George H. – F, 8 Illinois, 01/12/1884, New York, 43, Chronic diarrhoea, 10/08/1894.

HENDERSON, John S. – G, 173 New York, 06/26/1893, Germany, 80, Old Age, 11/03/1894.

HENDERSON, Samuel – C, 57 Massachusetts, 08/13/1892, Indiana, 65, Rheumatism, 07/04/1894.

HEINTZE, Fred – G, 63 Illinois, 05/23/1892, Missouri, 46, Rheumatism, 10/06/1894.

HERTS, Andrew – D, 57 Illinois, 10/05/1886, Sweden, 59, Rheumatism, 09/03/1894.

HOGAN, Charles A. – D, 1 Wisconsin Heavy Art., 10/22/1892, Wisconsin, 47, Rheumatism, 06/26/1894.

HUGGINS, Plon. H. – E, 2 Michigan, 05/20/1890, Ohio, 54, Hemorrhoids, 08/30/1894.

HUNT, Nelson – H, 4 Wisconsin, 03/06/1882, New York, 56, Disease-eyes, 07/08/1894.

JOHNSON, Barent – C, 142 Illinois, 04/27/1887, Norway, 71, Rheumatism, 04/07/1894.

JUDGE, Charles – G, 69 Ohio, 06/23/1883, Ireland, 52, Hernia, 09/18/1894.

KELLER, Michael – B, 65 New York, 11/06/1883, Germany, 55, Rheumatism, 09/11/1894.

KELLER, Samuel – E, 1 U. S. Veteran Reserve Corps, 05/01/1892, Switzerland, 61, General debility, 11/29/1894.

KING, Charles S. – Mate, U. S. Navy, 05/19/1891, New York, 53, Defective vision, 11/07/1894.

LANFER, Rudolph – G, 93 Pennsylvania, 10/08/1885, Switzerland, 66, Disease-lungs, 04/05/1894.

LAWRENCE, Alph. B. – H, 4 Wisconsin Cav., 02/07/1894, New York, 66, Heart disease, 11/28/1894.

LINGELBACH, William – A, 9 U. S. Veteran Volunteers, 08/15/1890, Germany, 49, Fracture-hip, 12/23/1894.

MARTIN, Michael – C, 24 New York Cav., 11/05/1894, Ireland, 77, Old age, 11/17/1894.

MCCUSKER, James – M, 1 Connecticut Heavy Art., 06/10/1884, Ireland, 53, Rheumatism 04/07/1894.

MCGUIRE, James – Seaman, U. S. Navy, 03/21/1887, Ireland, 49, Rheumatism 07/26/1894.

MCINTYRE, Charles E. – H, 8 Ohio, 12/26/1893, New York, 58, Gunshot wound-leg, 01/28/1894.

MCINTYRE, John – G, 37 Wisconsin, 01/30/1871, Ireland, 46, Wound-right leg, 05/11/1894.

MCKELVEY, William J. – M, 11 Pennsylvania Cav., 09/03/1884, Pennsylvania, 52, Injury-chest, 02/24/1894.

MCMANUS, James – B, 12 Illinois, 08/05/1878, Ireland, 60, Hernia, 03/10/1894.

METZKER, Fred – D, 2 Ohio Heavy Art., 07/06/1890, Pennsylvania, 56, Disease-ankle, 07/10/1894.

MILLERT, Anton – B, Capt., 107 Ohio, 10/01/1887, Germany, 75, Hernia, 03/11/1894.

MOORE, James – G, Cpl., 3 New York, 07/18/1894, England, 59, Varicose veins, 12/25/1894.

MOTT, George H. – D, 4 Michigan Cav., 11/01/1879, New York, 52, Rheumatism, 04/03/1894.

MORAN, Michael – L, 2 Minnesota Cav., 02/03/1887, Ireland, 69, Rheumatism, 07/16/1894.

MOUNT, Joseph F. – C, Lt., 40 New Jersey, 04/07/1892, New Jersey, 56, Paralysis, 04/20/1894.

NEELEY, William – C, 69 Illinois, 10/30/1893, Canada, 53, Tuberculosis, 08/18/1894.

NELSON, Charles – A, 187 New York, 12/29/1885, Denmark, 62, Rheumatism, 03/13/1894.

NIEBAUER, George H. – C, Missouri Consolidated Battalion 31 & 32 Inf., 10/04/1893, Germany, 67, Varicose veins, 09/17/1894.

O'HARA, John – F, 9 Ohio Cav., 03/25/1887, Ireland, 47, Hernia, 0/26/1894.

OLESON, John – F, 4 New York, 11/21/1888, Sweden, 53, Rheumatism, 11/10/1894.

PARKER, Charles F. – L, 1 Wisconsin Cav., 01/02/1878, Massachusetts, 55, General debility, 10/17/1894.

PATTEN, James – D, 7 New York Heavy Art., 10/14/1892, Ireland, 60, Rheumatism, 11/10/1894.

RAUNA, Joseph – E, 83 New York, 05/08/1888, France, 56, Asthma, 12/10/1894.

REGAN, Christy – H, 44 Illinois, 03/06/1881, Ireland, 60, Rheumatism, 01/28/1894.

RICHARDS, Fred. – M, 9 New York Heavy Art., 04/01/1885, Germany, 63, Injury-ankle, 09/01/1894.

RILEY, William H. – F, 10 U. S. Army, 10/19/1886, Illinois, 38, Rheumatism, 10/09/1894.

ROBERT, William – H, 19 Wisconsin, 05/06/1876, Connecticut, 42, Rheumatism, 06/11/1894.

ROBINSON, Henry – Seaman, U. S. Navy, 06/12/1894, Ireland, 57, Injury-leg, 10/25/1894.

RODGERS, James – D, 11 Missouri Cav., 06/05/1894, Ireland, 47, Malaria, 09/18/1894.

RODRIQUEZ, Joseph C. – K, Capt., 5 U. S. Veteran Reserve Corps, 11/05/1890, Cuba, 57, Hernia, 04/14/1894.

ROWAN, James A. – A, 4 Indiana Cav., 10/123/1890, Pennsylvania, 58, Rheumatism, 01/21/1894.

RUGGLES, James P. – H, Sgt., 2 U. S. Army Cav., 03/06/1883, Massachusetts, 40, Wounds-body, 11/21/1894.

SAIRS, ELIAS – A, 9 Mexican War, 11/14/1894, New York, 71, Old age, 12/13/1894.

SCHAEFFER, Charles – A, 35 Wisconsin, 05/23/1867, Germany, 26(?), Epilepsy, 09/08/1894.

SCHALLER, Jacob - __, Cpl., 2 Wisconsin Battery, 12/05/1883, Germany, 57, Rheumatism, 04/22/1894.

SCOTT, Rich – F, 23 Illinois, 10/14/1873, Ireland, 50, Wound-shoulder, 11/12/1894.

SCOTT, Thomas – H, 29 U. S. Colored Troop, 10/20/1893, Maryland, 53, Asthma, 06/25/1894.

STEIMES, Nicholas – B, 9 Wisconsin, 08/31/1887, Germany, 67, Rheumatism, 06/29/1894.

STEVENS, George F. – C, 64, Illinois, 01/01/1880, Virginia, 67, Lumbago, 12/10/1894.

SULLIVAN, Jermiah – E, 12 Connecticut, 02/26/1893, Ireland, 53, Injury-ankle, 06/04/1894.

TECHEL, Chris. – C, 68 New York, 07/21/1875, Germany, 61 Hernia, 09/07/1894.

VAN GAMERT, John – F, 50 Wisconsin, 11/21/1888, Holland, 61, Rheumatism, 05/09/1894.

WALSH, Michael J. – M, 10 Missouri Cav., 06/28/1877, Ireland, 43, Wound-arm, 01/27/1894.

WEIKBACHER, Val. – K, 35 Wisconsin, 07/29/1885, Germany, 51, Disease-eyes, 07/21/1894.

WEST, John – G, 16 Illinois Cav., 08/18/1893, Maine, 85, Old age, 08/24/1894.

WHITING, Charles A. – Unassigned, 29 Massachusetts, 09/04/1893, Massachusetts, 48, Hernia, 10/10/1894.

WICHART, Emil – K, 162 New York, 05/08/1887, Germany, 51, Rheumatism, 10/30/1894.

WILLIS, Thomas J. – P, Capt., Illinois Dodson's Independent Cav., 12/16/1884, England, 72, Gunshot wound-leg, 06/24/1894.

WISSE, William – C, 5 Missouri, 1/27/1868, Holland, 58, Varicose veins, 04/23/1894.

WRIGHT, Henry - __, Unassigned, U. S. Veteran Reserve Corps, 10/02/1893, Canada, 52, Rheumatism, 02/05/1894.

WUERTZBERGER, A. - A, 82, Illinois, 09/15/1883, Germany, 65, Injury-leg, 08/27/1894.

ZAPFE, August – E, Cpl., 26 Wisconsin, 10/09/1891, Germany, 61, Gunshot wound-side, 11/02/1894.

ZELLMER, Julius – H, 2 Wisconsin Cav., 02/10/1893, Germany, 54, Rheumatism, 03/23/1894.

ZICK, William – F, 2 Missouri, 06/25/1885, Germany, 60, Rheumatism 07/27/1894.

Sources:

The Miscellaneous Documents of the House of Representatives for the Third Session of the 53rd Congress, 1894-95 #3329. Record of Disabled Volunteer Soldiers Who Are And Have Been, Members of the National Home for Disabled Volunteer Soldiers, from July 1, 1893 to June 30, 1894. Washington: Government Printing Office, 1895. (Extracted from Annual Reports – National Homes for Disabled Volunteer Soldiers.)

The Miscellaneous Documents of the House of Representatives for the First Session of the 54th Congress, 1895-96. #3412. Record of Disabled Volunteer Soldiers, Who Are And Have Been, Members of the National Home for Disabled Volunteer Soldiers, from July 1, 1894 to June 30, 1895. Washington: Government Printing Office, (Extracted from Annual Reports – National Homes for Disabled Volunteer Soldiers.)

DEATHS IN 1895

FORMAT: NAME, COMPANY & REGIMENT, DATE OF ADMISSION, PLACE OF BIRTH, AGE, DISABILITY, DATE OF DEATH.

ALSOP, Charles – A, Illinois, Thielman's Independent. Cav., 11/15/1890, England, 51, Injury-back, 03/08/1895.

ARCHER, John – B, 1 New York Light Art., 06/12/1894, Ireland, 67, Old age, 10/19/1895.

AVERILL, George E. – C, 12 Vermont, 04/22/1885, Vermont, 48, Hemorrhoids, 03/24/1895.

BABCOCK, Charles – G, Cpl., 37 Wisconsin, 05/26/1886, Wisconsin, 42, Catarrh, 02/14/1895.

BACON, James F. – I, 17 Illinois Cav., 07/28/1886, New York, 56, Paralysis, 12/22/1895.

BAHR, August – F, 20 Ohio, 02/03/1887, Germany, 52, Disease-eyes, 05/11/1895.

BAKER, Frederick – C, 7 Connecticut, 10/06/1889, Germany, 52, Rheumatism, 09/20/1895.

BAKER, Michael – M, Cpl., 10 Michigan Cav., 01/21/1884, Germany, 38, Hemorrhoids, 08/03/1895.

BEHLING, Charles – A, 5 U. S. Veteran Reserve Corps, 05/04/1895, Germany, 53, Rheumatism, 08/28/1895.

BENEDICT, Anthony – C, 25 New York, 07/28/1888, France, 53, Wound-left leg, 07/30/1895.

BENNETT, George – M, 1 California Cav., 08/17/1891, Germany, 68, Rheumatism, 01/28/1895.

BERGMANN, Fred. – I, 45 Wisconsin, 09/22/1891, Germany, 64, Rheumatism, 12/15/1895.

BREITENSTEIN, F. – D, 41 Missouri, 04/08/1885, Germany, 68, Rheumatism, 01/19/1895.

BRENNAN, John – C, 113 Ohio, 06/21/1894, Ireland, 64, Heart disease, 02/15/1895.

BROWN, Edward A. – A, 3 Pennsylvania Heavy Art., 08/02/1889, New Jersey, 47, Rheumatism, 07/04/1895.

BUEL. James M. – M, Lt., 12 Indiana Cav., 10/17/1889, New York, 59, Rheumatism 02/26/1895.

BURGETT, Harry – K, Sgt., 68 U. S. Colored Troop, 10/07/1887, Missouri, 46, Gunshot wound-hand, 12/27/1895.

BURNS, Charles – A, 4 Delaware, 11/17/1869, Ireland, 28(?),
Rheumatism 04/15/1895.

BURROUGHS, John – K, 57, 03/11/1885, Massachusetts, 65,
Rheumatism, 08/13/1895.

BUSEKIST, Carl – K, 7 New York, 04/10/1878, Germany, 66,
Wound-left leg, 12/16/1895.

CAMPBELL, John – C, 2 U. S. Army Art., 07/02/1890, New
Jersey, 71, General debility, 04/21/1895.

CASWELL, John A. – G, 1 Minnesota Cav., 03/29/1889, New
York, 59, Paralysis, 11/09/1895.

COTTER, William – Seaman, U. S. Navy, 10/02/1887, Ireland, 61,
Varicose veins, 09/29/1895.

COUILLARD, George – C, 2 Wisconsin, 08/23/1894, Maine, 62,
Catarrh, 08/12/895.

COY, John H. – G, 39 Missouri, 06/19/1893, Germany, 73, Old age,
06/12/1895.

DAY, Nelson V. – C, 20 New York Cav., 11/20/1889, New York,
59, Hernia, 06/07/1895.

DEWEY, Charles P. – M, Lt., 4 New York Heavy Art., 05/13/1892,
New York, 55, Disease-spine, 01/10/1895.

DOLAN, Patrick – D, Cpl., 2 New York Cav., 12/08/1881, Ireland,
50, Rheumatism, 12/18/1895.

DUFFY, Anthony – Coal. Passer, U. S. Navy, 11/30/1889, Ireland,
60, Rheumatism, 11/21/1895.

FAERNEN, Michael – E, 13 U.S. Army, 04/10/1895, Ireland, 60,
Heart disease, 11/18/1895.

FIFER, Joseph – Landsman, U. S. Navy, 10/28/1892, Germany, 57,
General debility, 05/21/1895.

FORGEY, Alf. V. – M. Mate, U. S. Navy, 04/28/1891, Ohio, 44,
General debility, 04/20/1895.

FOSTER, William E. - A, Sgt., 23 Pennsylvania, 08/18/1884,
Pennsylvania, 52, Inflammation-lungs, 05/07/1895.

GALE, John – G, 51 Illinois, 08/07/1886, France, 64, Hernia,
06/18/1895.

GERITY, James – A, 44 Wisconsin, 07/03/1893, Ireland, 73,
Rheumatism, 03/21/1895.

GERNDT, Fred. W. – C, 82 Illinois, 09/29/1881, Germany, 54,
Wound-breast, 12/02/1895.

GIBBONS, John – H, 65 Illinois, 07/27/1894, England, 65, Gunshot wound-arm, 01/21/1895.

GLINES, Eleaz. H. – B, 4 Wisconsin Cav., 10/27/1889, Vermont, 66, Hemorrhoids, 03/01/1895.

HAAGE, Frederick – D, 28 Wisconsin, 04/05/1876, Germany, 58, Hernia, 05/06/1895.

HAFNER, Lewis – K, 27 Missouri, 05/28/1889, Germany, 51, Rheumatism, 03/24/1895.

HARRIS, James F. – K, Cpl., 127 U. S. Colored Troop, 06/12/1895, Pennsylvania, 53, Heart disease, 06/17/1895.

HASKELL, Hiram - __, 2 U. S. Veteran Reserve Corps, 05/09/1882, Maine, 69, General debility, 08/22/1895.

HANLEY, John F. – H, 6 Ohio, 12/23/1890, N. F., 54, Asthma, 02/23/1895.

HEES, Frederick – H, 82 Illinois, 11/19/1881, Germany, 61, Wound-head, 01/28/1895.

HOLLAND, Robert – C, 41 Wisconsin, 06/15/1889, Ireland, 69, Rheumatism, 08/01/1895.

HOSE, August - H, 2 Wisconsin Cav., 09/07/1882, Germany, 66, Hernia, 02/07/1895.

HUEG, William – I, 46 New York, 09/27/1888, Germany, 64, Rheumatism, 01/23/1895.

KAELTY, Patrick - __, 2 U. S. Veteran Reserve Corps Battery, 08/14/1877, Ireland, 50, Disease-spleen, 01/08/1895.

KELLY, James – I, 5 Maine, 08/26/1876, Ireland, 60, Varicose veins, 08/04/1895.

KIMBERK, L. G. – D, 127 Illinois, 04/29/1895, New York, 82, Rheumatism, 12/01/1895.

KITT, John B. - __, Illinois, Chicago Mercantile Battery, 07/28/1889, England, 60, Vertigo, 03/02/1895.

LEAREY, John – Landsman, U. S. Navy, 09/01/1894, New York, 56, General debility, 01/15/1895.

LEBER, George – C, 2 Illinois Light Art., 10/09/1891, Germany, 74, Rheumatism, 05/22/1895.

LEE, Michael – I, 151 Illinois, 02/12/1894, Ireland, 47, Piles, 01/20/1895.

LINDEMAN, J. H. – Unassigned, U. S. Art,. Mexican War, 07/28/1887, Germany, 68, Rheumatism, 05/24/1895.

LODERHOSE, Jacob – E, 23 U. S. Veterans Reserve Corps, 04/27/1891, Germany, 52, Heart disease, 09/26/1895.

LOEFFLER, Math. – E, 26 New York, 05/12/1886, Germany, 53, Rheumatism, 05/24/1895.

LONG, James – G, 82 Ohio, 02/03/1893, Ireland, 46, Varicose veins, 02/17/1895.

LOSEY, Belemus H. – K, 9 Michigan, 07/12/1895, New York, 55, Cancer, 08/09/1895.

MALONE, James – E, 19 Wisconsin, 08/14/1877, Ireland, 62, Old age, 04/21/1895.

MARBES, Jacob - __, 2 Wisconsin Battery, 08/05/1895, Germany, 67, General debility, 08/18/1895.

MARTIN, Thomas – F, 12 Illinois Cav., 08/09/1894, Delaware, 60, Disease-eyes, 08/01/1895.

MATHEWS, Milton – F, 61 Pennsylvania, 06/02/1886, Pennsylvania, 61, Rheumatism, 11/04/1895.

MAY, William B. – K. 2 Michigan, 12/27/1884, England, 62, Hernia, 02/05/189

MCCLURE, Carl S. – Seaman, U. S. Navy, 08/16/1894, New York, 62, General debility, 05/27/1895.

MCCORMICK, Patrick – C, 110 Ohio, 09/11/1881, Ireland, 66 Wound-hand, 07/13/1895.

MCCREARY, Obediah – D, 22 Pennsylvania, 03/04/1890, Pennsylvania, 43, Wound head, 11/24/1895.

MCDONALD, James – C, 27 Wisconsin, 12/26/1893, New York, 60, Defective vision, 08/26/1895.

MCDONALD, John – H, Cpl., 4 Massachusetts Heavy Art., 05/20/1890, Ireland, 65, Fracture-leg, 01/18/1895.

MCFEE, John – B, 1 New York Cav., 12/27/1881, Ireland, 63, Rheumatism, 08/13/1895.

MCGILL, Henry – F, 5 West Virginia, 09/04/1886, Scotland, 61, Disease-lungs, 10/05/1895.

MCLEAN, George – I, 4 Missouri Reserve Corps, 07/07/1893, England, 58, Rheumatism, 08/29/1895.

MEILENTZ, Gustav – K, 41 Missouri, 07/22/1895, Germany, 61, Hernia, 12/14/1895.

MILLER, Chris. – E, 1 Minnesota, 05/28/1889, Germany, 57, Rheumatism, 03/05/1895.

MURPHY, Jeremiah – K, 2 New Hampshire, 10/05/1877, Ireland, 60, Gunshot wound- hand, 04/03/1895.

NAVEL, Charles – E, Musician, 12 New York Cav., 11/26/1894, Germany, 75, Defective vision, 06/21/1895.

NEWBY, William L. – C, Sgt., 65 U.S. Colored Troops, 09/04/1895, Indiana, 56, Chronic diarrhoea, 12/29/1895.

NICHOLS, John – I, 44 Indiana, 08/08/1893, Connecticut, 63, Chronic rheumatism, 03/03/1895.

O'DELL, Andrew J. – C, 1 Wisconsin Cav., 03/23/1895, Wisconsin, 52, Rheumatism, 04/12/1895.

OLSON, Arne – C, 28, Wisconsin, 03/04/1895, Norway, 54, Cancer-stomach, 03/24/1895.

PEIRONNET, J. H. – H, Lt., 46 Illinois, 05/29/1895, New York, 50, Rheumatism, 08/28/1895.

PFEIFER, Jacob – D, 2 Missouri Light Art., 07/21/1892, Germany, 63, General debility, 05/20/1895.

PITT, Nich. – B, Cpl., 133 New York, 09/05/1887, New York, 63, Defective vision, 05/11/1895.

RAPP, Anthony – D, 4 Indiana Cav., 07/12/1895, New York, 56, Heart disease, 10/03/1895.

REAGAN, Thomas – F, 58 Illinois, 12/16/1875, Ireland, 34, Gunshot wound-shoulder, 03/01/1895.

RICE, Franklin W. – A, Cpl., 24 Wisconsin, 10/22/1880, Wisconsin, 35, Hernia, 07/31/1895.

RICKS, Ludwig – Landsman, U. S. Navy, 12/27/1890, Prussia, 56, Lumbago, 06/08/1895.

RIORDAN, John – H, 17 U. S. Army, 12/14/1869, Ireland, 37, Gunshot wound-arm, 03/30/1895.

ROCHFORT, Philip – E, Cpl., 13 Wisconsin, 01/11/1872, Ireland, 53, Pneumonia, 07/25/1895.

ROGERS, Richard S. – 151, 2 U. S. Veteran Reserve Corps Battery, 05/29/1894, England, 53, Paralysis, 01/28/1895.

SCHAEFER, John – H, 188 Ohio, 05/08/1888, Germany, 53, Rheumatism, 08/09/1895.

SCHUTZ, John – L, 17 Illinois Cav., 09/07/1890, Germany, 59, General debility, 10/09/1895.

SCOLES, Rus. B. – H, Sgt., 14 Iowa, 11/01/1894, Ohio, 58, Chronic catarrh, 02/19/1895.

SHAY, Daniel – A, 102 New York, 04/04/1891, Ireland, 78, Hernia, 03/26/1895.

SHORT, Patrick – D, 37 Wisconsin, 10/21/1887, Ireland, 58, Rheumatism, 06/06/1895.

SMITH, Daniel W. – K, 160 New York, 08/13/1890, Ohio, 55, Heart disease, 01/29/1895.

SMITH, Joseph – K, 1 California Cav., 05/23/1885, Pennsylvania, 69, Asthma, 06/05/1895.

SPRECH, Xavier – F, 4 U. S. Veteran Volunteers, 10/04/1869, Germany, 49, Chronic rheumatism, 05/22/1895.

STEEN, Nath'l – F, Sgt., 5 Wisconsin, 02/10/1892, New York, 55, Bronchitis, 12/21/1895.

STRAUB, George – L, 13 New York Heavy Art., 01/18/1892, Germany, 66, Hernia, 07/12/1895.

THOMAS, John – F, 39 Wisconsin, 05/04/1893, England, 75, Heart disease, 07/05/1895.

TRACEY, Thomas – A, 16 U. S. Army, 11/21/1891, Ireland, 52, Piles, 01/14/1895.

TRIEBSES, Gottf. – L, 1 Missouri Light Art., 11/12/1880, Prussia, 68, Hernia, 08/15/1895.

UNMIZIK, Frank – G, 17 Wisconsin, 09/16/1884, Germany, 64, Rheumatism, 01/19/1895.

VERDEAUX, Charles – E, 41 Missouri, 08/20/1880, France, 42, Chronic rheumatism, 03/19/1895.

WAGNER, Casper – G, 57 Illinois, 04/28/1886, Germany, 54, Frozen feet, 10/04/1895.

WAGNER, Daniel – D, 123 New York, 09/29/1888, France, 71, Chronic rheumatism, 05/13/1895.

WILLIAM, Charles - __, U. S. Marine Corps, Mexican War, 08/12/1886, Germany, 62, Rheumatism, 03/10/1895.

WILMS, Martin - F, Musician, 1 Wisconsin, 07/06/1889, Germany, 63, Malaria, 07/13/1895.

WORCESTER, Thomas – A, 1 Wisconsin Heavy Art., 02/27/1887, Maine, 59, Rheumatism, 11/15/1895.

Sources:

The Miscellaneous Documents of the House of Representatives for the First Session of The 54th Congress, 1895-1896. #3412. Record of Disabled Volunteer Soldiers, Who Are And Have Been, Members of the National Home for Disabled Volunteer Soldiers, from July 1, 1894 to June 30, 1895. Washington: Government Printing Office, 1896. (Extracted from Annual Records – National Homes for Disabled Volunteer Soldiers.)

The Miscellaneous Documents of the House of Representatives for the Second Session of The 54th Congress, 1896-97. #3516. Record of Disabled Volunteer Soldiers, Who Are And Have Been, Members of the National Home for Disabled Volunteer Soldiers, from July 1, 1895 to June 30, 1896. Washington: Government Printing Office, 1897. (Extracted from Annual Records – National Homes for Disabled Volunteer Soldiers.)

DEATHS IN 1896

FORMAT: NAME, COMPANY & REGIMENT, DATE OF ADMISSION, PLACE OF
BIRTH, AGE, DISABILITY, DATE OF DEATH.

ADAMS, Charles – 227, 1 U. S. Veteran Reserve Corps Battery,
  07/25/1894, Pennsylvania, 65, Gunshot wound-side,
  01/18/1896.

AMY, Michael – C, 11 Michigan, 04/07/1887, New Hampshire, 61,
  Disease-lungs, 05/06/1896.

ARMSTRONG, Edward – I, 51 Pennsylvania, 08/27/1874, Ireland,
  64, Disease-bladder, 02/12/1896.

ARNOLD, John – A, 38 Wisconsin, 03/17/1885, Germany, 68,
  Rheumatism, 07/08/1896.

BABSON, Washington – E, 25 Maine, 12/16/1887, Maine, 63,
  Chronic diarrhoea, 07/28/1896.

BARNUM, William W. – B, 7 Wisconsin, 07/02/1890, Vermont,
  69, Deafness, 08/22/1896.

BARTHOLIN, W. P. – E, Sgt., 1 Nebraska Cav., 07/27/1896, Denmark, 70, Senile debility, 12/26/1896.

BARTHUN, William – G, 14 Illinois, 06/16/1886, Germany, 60,
  Wound-thigh, 06/12/1896.

BARTLETT, William – A, 134 Illinois, 10/24/1893, Vermont, 70,
  Heart disease, 11/12/1896.

BATE, Andrew J. – I, Sgt., 20 Massachusetts, 09/20/1895,
  Massachusetts, 54, Hernia, 02/26/2896.

BATFIELD, Richard – Seaman, U. S. Navy, Mexican War,
  06/21/1895, New York, 77, Rheumatism, 08/19/1896.

BECKER, John – B, 7 New York, 07/21/1876, Germany, 46,
  Wound-left arm, 11/12/1896.

BENDER, John – B, Cpl., 9 New Jersey, 10/08/1896, New Jersey,
  52, Consumption, 11/15/1896.

BENJAMIN, Edward W. – E, 37 Illinois, 02/06/1878, New York,
  50, Hernia, 04/29/1896.

BENNETT, Alfred – B, 144 Indiana, 11/30/1892, Ohio, 71, Rheumatism, 08/25/1896.

BEST, George A. – I, 7 U. S. Army, 06/18/1889, New York, 39,
  Rheumatism, 06/10/1896.

BIRMINGHAM, Patrick T. – E, Cpl., 2 Connecticut Art.,
  10/27/1889, Ireland, 65, Rheumatism, 04/28/1896.

BLY, Edward P. – F, 16 Wisconsin, 04/25/1890, New York, 70, Old age, 02/24/1896.

BRENNAN, John – C. Passer, U. S. Navy, 10/02/1893, Ireland, 65, Hemorrhoids, 01/24/1896.

BRENNAN, John – G, 1 Indiana Heavy Art., 06/02/1893, Ireland, 76, Chronic rheumatism, 08/13/1896.

BRICKEY, Ernest – F, 15 Missouri, 08/27/1874, Germany, 41, Varicose veins, 03/30/1896.

BRIZZIE, William A. – B, 27 Massachusetts, 09/03/1895, Massachusetts, 73, Hernia, 02/19/1896.

BUCHANAN, James – G, 10 New York Cav., 04/04/1877, Ireland, 34, Blind, 11/05/1896.

CARROLL, Patrick – E, 140 New York, 08/22/1877, Ireland, 62, Rheumatism 04/10/1896.

CHENDORFF, Charles – Seaman, U. S. Navy, Mexican War, 06/28/1891, Sweden, 75, Loss-left eye, 11/16/1896.

CHRISTNOCK, M. – L, 5 Iowa Cav., 01/25/1893, Germany, 67, Wound-shoulder, 08/07/1896.

CIEMENTS, James – H, 59 Illinois, 08/17/1891, New York, 74, Rheumatism, 05/31/1896.

CONNELLY, Michael – B, 6 New Jersey, 03/24/1895, Ireland, 58, Hernia, 06/01/1896.

CONNOLLY, Patrick – U. S. Marine Corps, 09/01/1896, Ireland, 68, Heart disease, 10/25/1896.

COWAN, Michael – G, 154 Illinois, 11/01/1889, Ireland, 64, Rheumatism, 04/08/1896.

CUTLER, Riley H. – D, 22 Wisconsin, 08/03/1888, Ohio, 52, Rheumatism, 12/09/1896.

DALEY, Dennis – E, 11 Massachusetts, 10/17/1893, Ireland, 64, Gunshot wound-arm, 03/31/1896.

DALZIN, Martin – A, Minnesota Backett's Battalion Cav., 02/26/1887, Germany, 53, Rheumatism, 08/08/1896.

DAVIS, Benjamin – C, 2 Illinois Light Art., 07/04/1884, England, 58, Injury-shoulder, 05/29/1896.

DIELMAN, Charles, I, Cpl., 100 New York, 12/29/1884, New York, 42 Rheumatism, 02/24/1896.

DIETRICH, Henry – F, 26 Wisconsin, 04/25/1889, Germany, 65, Rheumatism, 10/10/1896.

DOWNIE, James – Seaman, U. S. Navy, 10/06/1890, Scotland, 62, Neuralgia, 10/31/1896.

DOYLE, John – C, U. S. Veteran Reserve Corps, 10/27/1889, Ireland, 58, Ulcers, 10/21/1896.

ELSNER, Charles – L, 2 Iowa Cav., 05/01/1894, Germany, 69, Hernia, 12/17/1896.

ERICKSON, Eric – D, 57 Illinois, 05/20/1879, Sweden, 57, General debility, 06/25/1896.

FISCHENICK, Peter – I, 1 Louisiana Cav., 07/21/1890, Prussia, 64, Fracture-left leg, 11/11/1896.

FORBES, Alexander – B, 97 Pennsylvania, 08/18/1893, Scotland, 60, Lumbago, 11/28/1896.

FOSTER, John – I, 155 Illinois, 01/11/1896, Germany, 56, Heart disease, 03/28/1896.

FUCHS, Anton – I, 1 Wisconsin Heavy Art., 05/26/1886. Germany, 70, Rheumatism, 02/07/1896.

GANDY, Otho W. – C, Cpl., 13 Missouri Cav., 09/01/1892, Iowa, 46, Epilepsy, 05/04/1896.

GENTES, Charles – E, 2 Maryland, 11/19/1869, Canada 43, Gunshot wound-shoulder, 07/19/1896.

GIBBONS, James A. – H, 3 Wisconsin Cav., 10/01/1880, N. B., 57, Paralysis, 09/26/1896.

GIES, George – H, 178 New York, 06/19/1892, Germany, 54, Gunshot wound-legs, 04/27/1896.

GILL, Eugene C. – B, 42 Wisconsin, 11/06/1895, New York, 49, Wound-face, 09/03/1896.

GORDON, William I. – D, 5 Ohio, 11/17/1890, Scotland, 62, Piles, 08/19/1896.

GRADY, Robert – K, 19 Illinois, 11/29/1888, New York, 53, Disease-bladder, 02/18/1896.

GRAVE, Malo – G, 3 New York Cav., 10/02/1887, Bavaria, 64, Injury-side, 02/29/1896.

GREGORY, Charles R. – G, 11 U. S. Veteran Reserve Corps, 12/16/1884, Germany, 58, Rheumatism, 10/21/1896.

GREVE, Albert – C, 37 Ohio, 06/21/1894, Germany, 54, Gunshot wound-side, 11/11/1896.

GRIMES, Frank – C, 9 U. S. Colored Troops Heavy Art., 06/05/1894, Ohio, 48, General debility, 05/01/1896.

GUNDRY, Richard – I, Cpl., 2 Wisconsin, 11/14/1892, New York, 50, Injury-side, 12/28/1896.

HANSON, Peter – K, 42 Illinois, 07/30/1884, Norway, 59, Rheumatism, 07/02/1896.

HERBERGER, Urban – F, 8 U. S. Veterans Volunteers, 06/14/1880, Germany, 53, Rheumatism, 05/28/1896.

HIGGINS, George W. – M, 4 Michigan Cav., 07/23/1887, Indiana, 50, Chronic rheumatism, 07/20/1896.

HILT, Peter – G, 15 New York Heavy Art., 01/07/1879, Germany, 63, Rheumatism, 05/23/1896.

HOFFMAN, Paul – H, 75 Illinois, 10/13/1881, Germany, 49, Wound-head, 01/08/1896.

HUGHES, Edward – Seaman, U. S. Navy, 10/27/1889, England, 63, Defective vision, 09/29/1896.

HURTLE, Charles – D, 15 Illinois Cav., 12/10/1878, Germany, 55, Rheumatism, 08/27/1896.

IMANS, Anth. M. H. – H, 17 Wisconsin, 11/15/1890, Holland, 63, Chronic diarrhoea, 05/23/1896.

JAGGER, Henry – F, Cpl., 17 New York, 05/28/1890, Germany, 55, Rheumatism, 12/27/1896.

JOHNSON, Henry – M, 5 U. S. Colored Troops Heavy Art., 9/29/1888, Virginia, 48, Rheumatism, 11/17/1896.

JONES, Daniel H. – G, 9 Illinois Cav., 06/11/1889, New York, 56, Hernia, 08/11/1896.

JONES, William B. – K, Cpl., 17 Michigan, 05/31/1877, New York, 36, Gunshot wound-thigh, 07/13/1896.

JUCH, Charles – D, Musician, 9 Wisconsin, 07/26/1882, Germany, 52, Rheumatism, 07/19/1986.

KAISER, Charles – D, 8 Maryland, 05/01/1879, Germany, 42, Wound-leg, 03/10/1896.

KEEFE, Edward – F. 2 Minnesota, 06/08/1883, Ireland, 70, Disease-liver, 10/18/1896.

KEIPP, Franz – G, 9 Wisconsin, 04/14/1885, Germany, 70, Sunstroke, 03/12/1896.

KELLY, Emmon – L, 2 Minnesota Cav., 05/14/1892, New York, 66, Old age, 06/09/1896.

KELLY, Thomas – L, 6 Iowa Cav., 01/12/1883, Ireland, 50, Chronic diarrhoea, 04/22/1896.

KLEIN, John – E, 35 Wisconsin, 12/22/1877, Germany, 46, Rheumatism, 12/23/1896.

KOLLER, Conrad – I, 29 Wisconsin, 05/08/1888, Germany, 66, Rheumatism, 12/14/1896.

KRENTZER, Jacob – I, 25 New York Cav., 06/13/1895, Germany, 70, General debility, 07/26/1896.

LANE, Albert G. – A, 6 West Virginia, 05/06/1893, Ohio, 71, General debility, 11/08/1896.

LANGNER, John G. – D, 21 Pennsylvania, 07/06/1874, Prussia, 48, Disease-eyes, 10/18/1896.

LIDLE, Charles – D, C. S., 14 Illinois Cav., 04/07/1881, Germany, 55, Rheumatism, 09/10/1896.

LOCKWOOD, Joseph – Seaman, U. S. Navy, 11/14/1892, Ireland, 53, Asthma, 11/20/1896.

LUSK, David – C, Sgt., 24 Indiana, 06/03/1886, Pennsylvania, 63, Rheumatism, 04/26/1896.

MAASS, John C. – D, Capt., 17 Wisconsin, 02/04/1888, Germany, 55, General debility, 10/04/1896.

MAYER, Daniel E. –D, Capt., 27 Iowa, 07/26/1891, Germany, 70, Rheumatism, 03/09/1896.

MAXWELL, William – L, 17 Illinois, 06/03/1886, Pennsylvania, 73, Hernia, 01/13/1896.

MAXWELL, William – K, 129 Illinois, 06/03/1886, Pennsylvania, 73, Hernia, 01/18/1896.

MCBRAIR, JOHN – A, 102 New York, 11/18/1895, Scotland, 86, Defective hearing, 12/28/1896.

MCCAFFERY, James – D, 27 U. S. Army, 03/25/1874, Ireland, 74, Injury-hand, 03/27/1896.

MCCARTY, John – A, 24 Wisconsin, 05/01/1887, N. F., 49, Rheumatism, 11/10/1896.

MCCLASKEY, WILLIAM – K, Lt., 139 New York, 07/06/1890, Ireland, 52, Piles, 12/07/1896.

MCCORMICK, John – G, 29 Indiana, 06/18/1888, Illinois, 55, Erysipelas, 09/13/1896.

MCGARY, Thomas – E, 44 Wisconsin, 12/28/1895, Ireland, 68, Chronic consti.(constipation). 08/01/1896.

MELODY, Thomas – B, 26 Illinois, 07/26/1890, Scotland, 60, Rheumatism, 02/07/1896.

MELROSE, Charles H. – B, 179 Ohio, 01/12/1888, Scotland, 58, Rheumatism, 07/13/1896.

MERZ, John - __, Cpl., Missouri Independent Volunteers, 06/21/1873, Germany, 58, Injury-left shoulder, 03/16/1896.

NELSON, John – I, 13 Wisconsin, 02/24/1890, England, 63, Rheumatism, 08/27/1896.

NEWTON, Isaac - __, 3 Wisconsin Battery, 08/05/1895, New York, 71, Injury-testicle, 02/05/1896.

OBENBRENER, Joseph – E, 38 Wisconsin, 11/20/1895, Germany, 50, Chronic rheumatism, 03/05/1896.

PALMER, George – A, Sgt., 12 New York Cav., 09/06/1895, New York, 68, Wound- hand, 05/08/1896.

PARCEL, John – D, 19 New York, 05/29/1895, Ireland, 58, Injury-back, 01/01/1896.

PAYBERG, Charles A. – I, 1 Massachusetts, 10/27/1884, Denmark, 41, Chronic rheumatism, 08/15/1896.

PLANT, Francis J. – F, 14 Michigan, 11/13/1884, New York, 61, Paralysis, 02/18/1896.

PREIS, George – F, 58 Illinois, 06/18/1885, Bavaria, 65, Asthma, 09/16/1896.

PROUD, William – F, 97 New York, 03/26/1887, Ireland, 62, Rheumatism, 01/24/1896.

RADER, Jacob – G, 45 Wisconsin, 12/22/1890, Germany, 57, Rheumatism, 12/25/1896.

REED, James E. – M, Sgt., 1 New York Mounted Rifles, 12/08/1891, New York, 51, Hernia, 06/23/1896.

REGAN, Michael – E, 17 Wisconsin, 06/22/1891, Ireland, 68, Lumbago, 08/18/1896.

RICE, Horace – I, Lt., 7 Illinois Cav., 05/23/1893, New York, 53, General debility, 07/02/1896.

RIEL, Sebastian – C, 1 Wisconsin Cav., 06/07/1889, Germany, 56, Rheumatism, 10/06/1896.

ROSENBAUM, Charles – F, 11 Wisconsin, 08/03/1887, Germany, 61, Sunstroke, 05/21/1896.

RUSSELL, George W. – H, Cpl., 1 U. S. Veteran Reserve Corps, 08/05/1896, New York, 58, Cancer, 11/14/1896.

RUSSELL, William W. – A, Lt., 64 New York, 07/28/1886, New York, 54, Wound-left arm, 03/18/1896.

SARVIS, Hiram – B, 46 Wisconsin, 09/22/1891, Canada, 69, Rheumatism, 06/08/1896.

SCHAUMBERGER, A. – I, 3 New York Prov. Cav., 06/23/1888, Germany, 51, Injury-legs, 10/14/1896.

SHAWEN, James W. – E, 114 Illinois, 04/27/1887, Virginia, 67, Rheumatism, 07/21/1896.

SHEPARD, Martin V. – I, 63 Ohio, 08/08/1895, New York, 63, Lung disease, 12/05/1896.

SHIPNER, Charles – F, 1 Pennsylvania Light Art., 06/29/1882, Germany, 55, Rheumatism, 10/15/1896.

SIEGRIST, Henry – C, 26 Wisconsin, 09/04/1894, Switzerland, 51, Rheumatism, 03/01/1896.

SMITH, John – B, 6 Connecticut, 06/07/1889, Canada, 49, Lung disease, 03/12/1896.

SMITH, Patrick – Seaman, U. S. Navy, 11/05/1887, Ireland, 56, Rheumatism, 09/21/1896.

SNELL, Stephen – F, 30 Wisconsin, 05/16/1896, New York, 58, Heart disease, 07/17/1896.

STAUDINGER, Joseph – D, Musician, 147 New York, 12/28/1888, Austria, 60, Imbecility, 08/15/1896.

STUART, John H. – B, 46 Wisconsin, 12/28/1895, Scotland, 80, Senility, 10/06/1896.

SULLIVAN, Jeremiah – B, 2 U. S. Army, 04/24/1886, Ireland, 51, Loss-left arm, 08/07/1896.

TEABO, Franklin – H, 29 Maine, 08/05/1895, Canada, 65, Hernia, 06/10/1896.

TERRITT, John – A, 73 Pennsylvania, 08/29/1884, Ireland, 60, Rheumatism, 07/13/1896.

THOMPSON, William – I, 86 New York, 12/18/1890, England, 68, Hernia, 06/05/1896.

TROY, Edward – D, 28 Wisconsin, 05/14/1887, Ireland, 57, Heart disease, 03/15/1896.

TUFTS, William N. – B, 20 Massachusetts, 11/27/1893, Massachusetts, 57, Cancer, 03/30/1896.

VOLKNER, Albert – H, 9 Wisconsin, 08/26/1884, Prussia, 62, Hernia, 12/03/1896.

WATERMAN, John – E, 10 Wisconsin, 06/23/1888, New York, 56, Wound-hip, 05/29/1896.

WEST, Andrew W. – G, 3 Missouri Cav., 06/24/1895, Pennsylvania, 58, Catarrh, 02/28/1896.

WHITE, Isaac N. – L. 8 Illinois Cav., 0912/1893, Pennsylvania, 67, Heart disease, 07/04/1896.

WIEDNER, Benedict – B, 2 Michigan, 04/29/1895, Switzerland, 61, Gunshot wound-shoulder, 06/12/1896.

WILCOX, Nathan F. – G, 57 Pennsylvania, 11/17/1891, Pennsylvania, 74, Senile debility, 07/20/1896.

WITZ, Frederick – A, 2 Maryland, 06/28/1872, Germany, 50, Gunshot wound-arm, 10/10/1896.

YORK, John B. – __, U. S. Marine Corps, 06/12/1888, Scotland, 66, Hernia, 07/31/1896.

ZILLMER, Chris. - I, 1 Wisconsin Cav., 12/05/1888, Germany, 58, Chronic rheumatism, 06/26/1896.

Sources:

The Miscellaneous Documents of the House of Representatives for the Second Session of the 54th Congress, 1896-97. # 3516. Record of Disabled Volunteer Soldiers, Who Are And Have Been, Members of the National Home for Disabled Volunteer Soldiers, from July 1, 1895 to June 30, 1896. Washington: Government Printing Press, 1897. (Extracted from Annual Records – National Homes for Disabled Volunteer Soldiers.)

The Miscellaneous Documents of the House of Representatives for the Second Session of the 55th Congress, 1897-98. #3664. Record of Disabled Volunteer Soldiers, Who Are And Have Been, Members of the National Home for Disabled Volunteer Soldiers, from July 1, 1896 to June 30, 1897. Washington: Government Printing Office, 1898. (Extracted from Annual Records – National Homes for Disabled Volunteer Soldiers.)

DEATH IN 1897

FORMAT: NAME, COMPANY & REGIMENT, DATE OF ADMISSION, PLACE OF BIRTH, AGE, DISABILITY, DATE OF DEATHL.

ACKER, Peter – G, 57 Illinois, 07/19/1893, Germany, 69, Paralysis, 10/03/1897.

BAHEL, William – H, 13 Pennsylvania, 10/09/1896, Pennsylvania, 57, Paralysis, 03/27/1897.

BALL, Charles C. H. – I, 20 Indiana, 11/19/1880, Sax., 57, Fracture-shoulder, 01/23/1897.

BANSON, Gilbert – H, 42 Wisconsin, 05/23/1893, Norway, 57, Asthma, 05/10/1897.

BARKER, Thomas N. – H, Cpl., 102 U. S. Colored Troops, 03/17/1890, New Hampshire, 46, Shell wound-head, 09/13/1897.

BAUMGARTNER, A. – A, Cpl., 37 Ohio, 03/15/1889, Germany, 61, Rheumatism, 06/04/1897.

BEUERMAN, Frank – K, 5 Michigan, 11/21/1888, Germany, 60, Injury-left side, 12/27/1897.

BLAKE, Thomas – K, 84 Illinois, 03/26/1880, Ireland, 57, Wound-left hand, 04/26/1897.

BOGK, William – A, 26 Wisconsin, 10/08/1894, Prussia, 73, Rheumatism, 12/02/1897.

BRAUNLEIN, Michael – I, 17 Wisconsin, 12/05/1876, Germany, 38, Gunshot wound-hip, 07/10/1897.

BREWER, J. M. – F, 27 Illinois, 07/27/1892, Germany, 61, Disease-eyes, 11/05/1897.

BROWN, Charles – K, Musician, 7 New York, 10/07/1881, Germany, 56, Rheumatism, 12.09/1897.

BROWN, Peter – B, 24 Illinois, 04/29/1896, Bavaria, 63, Rheumatism, 05/10/1897.

BURDICK, Ira W. – K, 2 New York Heavy Art., 05/11/1897, New York, 60, Cystitis, 08/12/1897.

BURDICK, William – Unassigned, 3 Wisconsin, 07/22/1895, New York, 69, Injury-hand, 06/08/1897.

BURLINGAME, George – F, 23 Illinois, 05/19/1897, New York, 56, Hernia, 09/04/1897.

BURTCH, Simon P. – F, 1 Illinois, Mexican War, 10/27/1888, Canada, 79, Old age, 02/06/1897.

CABORN, Richard – G, Cpl., 43 Wisconsin, 06/21/1895, England, 63, Catarrh, 09/22/1897.

CHANLEY, William – D, 1 U. S. Army Art., 09/03/1881, Ireland, 67, Rheumatism, 02/16/1897.

CLEVELAND, John H. – F, 33 Illinois, 10/08/1894, New York, 62, Rheumatism, 05/07/1897.

COLLINS, John – C, 2 District of Columbia, 05/23/1893, Ireland, 66, Disease-eyes, 01/17/1897.

COMFORT, Thomas – H, 27 Michigan, 10/24/1893, New York, 51, Gunshot wound-side, 05/06/1897.

COOK, Adam – A, 88 New York, 11/07/1891, England, 66, Old age, 02/10/1897.

COOPER, Henry – F, 21 Pennsylvania, 06/27/1877, Pennsylvania, 38, Wound-lung, 04/28/1897.

COPELAND, Ben. F. – A, Lt., 11 Indiana, 12/09/1896, Indiana, 60, Kidney disease, 01/19/1897.

CUMMINS. John – K, 2 Kansas Cav., 12/01/1882, New York, 69, Hernia, 01/09/1897.

DALY, Thomas – D, 47 Illinois, 05/01/1885, Ireland, 59, General debility, 04/06/1897.

DAMES, Charles – E, 27 Iowa, 07/21/1886, New York, 51 Rheumatism, 03/04/1897.

DANIEL, Louis A. – C, 12 Vermont, 07/21/1890, Canada, 56, Defective vision, 04/12/1897.

DELESS, Harry – C, 24 Michigan, 07/27/1896, New York, 47, Rheumatism, 06/26/1897.

DETREUX, Frederick – I, Cpl., 98 Pennsylvania, 10/02/1887, Germany, 43, Gunshot wound-side, 02/21/1897.

DILL, William S. - __, 7 Wisconsin Light Art., 09/16/1884, New York, 61, Rheumatism, 04/15/1897.

DOBERT, Carl – C, 17 Wisconsin, 11/11/1883, Germany, 57, Injury-shoulder, 08/31/1897.

DUNN, George – Seaman, U. S. Navy, 10/14/1890, Ireland, 53, Heart disease, 11/03/1897.

EASTMAN, Abiel – Seaman, U. S. Navy, 05/07/1891, New York, 63, Paralysis, 12/23/1897.

EELS, Jackson – C, 7 Illinois Cav., 12/26/1893, Illinois, 66, Rheumatism, 07/06/1897.

EVANS, John H. – F, 195 Pennsylvania, 09/23/1883, Pennsylvania, 46, Kidney disease, 08/26/1897.

FARRER, Charles – G, Cpl., 46 New York, 07/31/1897, Germany, 56, Phthisis, 10/11/1897.

FENSKE, A. – G, 65 Illinois, 04/11/1890, Prussia, 56, Varicose veins, 11/19/1897.

FRANKLIN, John B. – M, Cpl., 2 Ohio Cav., 09/13/1895, Kentucky, 75, Paralysis, 11/10/1897.

GARDNER, Charles P. – K, Musician, 1 Wisconsin Cav., 07/14/1896, Massachusetts, 78, Rheumatism, 03/28/1897.

GEMARIS, John – D, 14 Ohio, 08/12/1881, Austria, 60, Heart disease, 11/20/1897.

GILMAN, William R. – I, 3 Minnesota, 12/13/1890, New York, 57, Bronchitis, 11/12/1897.

GRIFFITH, John – A, 22 Wisconsin, 07/07/1886, England, 60, Injury-head, 04/26/1897.

HANSLEMAN, George – A, Michigan Provost Guard, 10/18/1893, Germany, 71, Hernia, 05/30/1897.

HAUETER, Jacob – D, Cpl., 44 Indiana, 10/02/1887, Switzerland, 64, Paralysis, 09/17/1897

HARTLEY, William B. – D, 141 Pennsylvania, 07/02/1896, Pennsylvania, 60, Cancer-face, 01/02/1897.

HAYFORD, Charles W. – C, 105 New York, 06/21/1894, New York, 55, Hernia, 01/08/1897.

HEFFERMAN, James C. - A, 127 New York, 10/14/1892, New York, 53, Rheumatism, 12/25/1897.

HEIMERS, Henry – G, 9 Pennsylvania Reserves, 09/21/1887, Germany, 51, Wound-left side, 02/101/1897.

HEINKEL, John – B, 59 Illinois, 01/05/1884, Germany, 56, Deaf, 12/19/1897.

HELMER, Charles – B, 8 Ohio Cav., 02/25.1891, Germany, 51, Spine disease, 01/24/1897.

HEUBLEIN, John – E, 45 Wisconsin, 06/14/1880, Germany, 54, Chronic rheumatism, 04/06/1897.

HOGARTY, Michael – H, 12 Wisconsin, 01/20/1891, New York, 69, Gunshot wound-left leg, 10/05/1897.

HOLT, Henry H. – K, 15 Illinois, 07/15/1884, Ohio, 40, Rheumatism, 01/28/1897.

HOLWAY, Watson – E, Sgt., 8 Maine, 04/25/1890, Maine, 56, Paralysis, 09/01/1897.

HOMMER, M. – E, 9 Wisconsin, 07/27/1895, Germany, 72, Hernia, 07/28/1897.

HOULIHAN, Martin – C, 16 U. S. Army, 11/12/1887, Ireland, 54, Injury-right arm, 01/29/1897.

HUNT, John A. – C, 4 Wisconsin Cav., 05/02/1896, New York, 51, General debility, 02/28/1897.

JACOBS, John – H, 156 Illinois, 08/26/1895, Prussia, 62, Rheumatism, 01/14/1897.

JOERNT, Henry – C, 9 Wisconsin, 06/08/1887, Germany, 47, Asthma, 11/22/1897.

JOHNSON, Edward – K, 9 Massachusetts, 06/07/1889, Ireland, 54, Hernia, 01/04/1897.

JOHNSON, George – Seaman, U. S. Navy, 02/02/1892, New York, 55, Rheumatism, 10/27/1897.

JOHNSON, Gustav – E, 46 Illinois, 02/28/1878, Sweden, 59, Wound-right hand, 09/02/1897.

JOHNSON, Thomas – K, 25 Illinois, 12/07/1875, Ireland, 45, Gunhot wound-groin, 10/22/1897.

JOHNSON, William – A, 17 Wisconsin, 07/15/1885, Ireland, 53, Rheumatism, 12/09/1897.

JUNGE, Ferdinand – B, 9 Wisconsin, 02/03/1887, Germany, 57, Rheumatism, 10/02/1897.

KEITH, Michael – D, 2 Michigan, 10/05/1890, Ireland, 50, Rheumatism, 10/25/1897.

KELLY, John – A, 57 Pennsylvania, 11/05/1896, Canada, 53, Rheumatism, 08/24/1897.

KELLY, John – K, 35 New York, 10/25/1897, New York, 57, Diabetes, 10/30/1897.

KENT, Robert - __, Cpl., 5 Ohio Independent Battery, 09/24/1885, England, 55, Injury-hands, 05/16/1897.

KNIPP, Gerhard – A, 9 Missouri, 07/16/1889, Germany, 64, Gunshot wound-breast, 05/17/1897.

KOCH, George – G, 9 New Jersey, 08/01/1885, Germany, 60, Wound-right shoulder, 12/26/1897.

KRASKY, Moritz – E, 58 New York, 08/28/1892, Germany, 54, Rheumatism, 06/27/1897.

KRAUSS, Charles – G, 23 U. S. Veteran Reserve Corps, 09/01/1889, Germany, 62, Rheumatism, 03/21/1897.

KREGER, Anthony – Unassigned, 198 Ohio, 05/28/1892, Bavaria, 72, Rheumatism, 03/20/1897.

LEHMKUHL, William – H, 45 New York, 08/18/1884, Germany, 58, Chronic rheumatism, 1012/1897.

LENTZ, Herman – C, Lt., 3 New York Art., 02/18/1884, Germany, 54, Typhoid fever, 02/19/1897.

LIES, Alva – F, 8 Illinois Cav., 01/17/1884, Germany, 55, Rheumatism, 08/14/1897.

LINDSEY, Samuel F. – C, 2 Ohio Heavy Art., 11/26/1897, Ohio, 49, Heart disease, 12/11/1897.

MADER, Frank – B, 2 Missouri, 10/17/1885, Germany, 49, Rheumatism, 03/01/1897.

MALLING, Franklin - __, C. S., 1 Iowa Cav., 12/24/1882, Ohio, 46, Rheumatism, 08/04/1897.

MARTIN, James - __, 5 New York Art., 09/22/1883, Ireland, 62, Rheumatism, 07/17/1897.

MAURER, John - C, 6 Minnesota, 11/07/1882, Germany, 62, Sunstroke, 11/28/1897.

MCCONNELL, Charles – G, 12 Wisconsin, 03/17/1897, Ireland, 68, Wound-head, 03/29/1897.

MCCREADY, William – K, 17 Iowa, 01/23/1882, Ohio, 52, Hernia, 01/03/1897.

MCGINNIS, John - __, 17 Indiana Art., 04/22/1879, Ireland, 30, Rheumatism, 11/09/1897.

MCGINTY, Patrick – G, 14 Wisconsin, 02/03/1887, Ireland, 45, Catarrh, 08/16/1897.

MCMAHON, Peter – H, 6 West Virginia Cav., 09/27/1882, Ireland, 40, Rheumatism, 03/03/1897.

MCMILLER, William – D, 153 New York, 11/21/1884, New York, 58, General debility, 02/26/1897.

MICHALBACH, Joe. – G, 1 Oregon Cav., 05/19/1876, Germany, 54, Hernia, 05/07/1897.

MILLER, William C. P. – K, 44 Wisconsin, 05/15/1891, Germany, 59, Varicose veins, 08/26/1897.

MILLER, William J. – C, 11 Minnesota, 06/20/1891, Pennsylvania, 55, Lung disease, 12/06/1897.

MORTON, James – B, 24 Michigan, 06/23/1884, Ireland, 61, Rheumatism, 07/28/1897.

O'CONNELL, Daniel – B, 3 U. S. Army, 11/22/1889, Ireland, 52, Rheumatism, 11/05/1897.

ORVIS, John A. – E, 62 Illinois, 01/21/1896, Connecticut, 63, Diarrhoea, 08/03/1897.

PEEL, John – F, 19 U. S. Army, 09/02/1881, Ireland, 64, Old age, 11/08/1897.

PETERSON, Ole – K, 33 U. S. Veteran Reserve Corps, 09/03/1884, Norway, 62, Gunshot wound-right arm, 06/26/1897.

POTTS, William – G, 24 Wisconsin, 02/17/1886, England, 57, Rheumatism, 06/06/1897.

PRICE, Richard – I, 27 Wisconsin, 08/24/1880, Wisconsin, 52, Rheumatism, 01/30/1897.

RAABE, August – A, 3 Ohio Cav., 12/11/1883, Germany, 51, Hernia, 09/28/1897.

RAUM, Ashard – E, 16 New York Cav., 11/26/1890, Germany, 46, Injury-foot, 05/13/1897.

REAGAN, Joseph – Unassigned, 19 Massachusetts, 10/23/1890, Ireland, 52, Gunshot wound, 07/24/1897.

REILLY, James E. – K, 5 Wisconsin, 01/26/1897, Pennsylvania, 50, Constipation, 07/07/1897.

RICHARDSON, Henry – B, 29 U. S. Colored Troops, 08/24/1894, Kentucky, 55, Rheumatism, 11/03/1897.

RIELL, George – D, 1 New Jersey Mexican War, 01/23/1886, Germany, 62, Chronic rheumatism, 09/05/1897.

RIGG, Anthony – A, 22 Iowa, 03/16/1886, Pennsylvania, 45, Injury-left hand, 08/30/1897.

ROTH, Lorenzo – A, 22 New York Cav., 10/18/1883, Germany, 66, Injury-right arm, 03/26/1897.

RYAN, James – C, 2 Illinois Light Art., 11/16/1877, Ireland, 59, Injury-hip, 01/23/1897.

SAWDEY, Francis – E, Cpl., 43 Wisconsin, 06/17/1883, New York, 55, Rheumatism, 03/21/1897.

SAWYER, Charles S. – D, 4 Wisconsin Cav., 08/28/1895, Michigan, 56, Heart disease, 11/25/1897.

SCHAFFER, JOHN – H, 97 Pennsylvania, 07/01/1888, Germany, 66, Rheumatism 08/09/1897.

SCHMIDT, Jacob – C, 178 New York, 05/21/1867, Germany, 43, Hernia, 05/18/1897.

SCHMITT, Peter – C, Sgt., 5 Maryland, 07/21/1887, Germany, 62, Heart disease, 10/11/1897.

SCHNELL, John – C, 9 Wisconsin, 12/17/1874, Germany, 46, Scorbutus, 03/07/1897.

SCHOONMAKER, M. – F, Sgt., 2 U. S. Veteran Volunteers, 7/26/1895, New York, 50, Heart disease, 05/05/1897.

SELLERS, Alexander – D, 27 Michigan, 04/12/1871, Scotland, 66, General debility, 09/25/1897.

SHERMAN, Hiram – F, 3 New York Light Art., 11/19/1890, New York, 47, Gunshot wound-thigh, 01/03/1897.

SHOEMAKER, Charles – C, 12 Maine, 10/18/1893, Germany, 49, Fracture-left ankle, 12/10/1897.

SHURE, Hans – K, Cpl., 88 Illinois, 07/31/1896, Illinois, 54, Lumbago, 08/12/1897.

SIMMONS, C. – D, 5 Wisconsin, 04/21/1886, New York, 68, Rheumatism, 09/20/1897.

SMITH, Dexter – A, 8 U. S. Veteran Reserve Corps, 01/11/1883, New Hampshire, 61, Rheumatism, 07/22/1897.

SPEARMAN, Francis – B, 1 New York Engineers, 05/13/1885, Germany, 79, Rheumatism, 01/08/1897.

STOCK, Frederick W. – E, Sgt., 21 Wisconsin, 05/06/1886, New York, 58, Chronic rheumatism, 08/01/1897.

STOCKLIN, Ambrose – F, 10 Kansas, 07/24/1885, Germany, 64, Rheumatism, 09/21/1897.

STOYLES, William – A, 4 Ohio, 08/29/1890, England, 58, Gunshot wound-right arm, 01/20/1897.

STROBEL, Jacob – K, 1 U. S. Veteran Volunteers, 1/09/1889, Germany, 60, General debility, 08/06/1897.

STUBBS, James C. – B, 26 Illinois, 10/14/1892, Indiana, 45, Blind, 01/06/1897.

SUDBROCK, Henry – I, 106 Ohio, 11/17/1886, Prussia, _5, Rheumatism, 08/18/1897.

SWANSON, Peter – D, 57 Illinois, 05/08/1887, Sweden, 45, Heart disease, 02/07/1897.

SWEET, John – K, Cpl., 50 Wisconsin, 05/27/1887, N. S., 64, Sciatica, 05/31/1897.

TAPPEN, Sylvester – G, 28 Michigan, 06/29/1897, Michigan, 49, Phthisis, 09/29/1897.

THORNTON, Michael - __, 5 New York Art., 09/17/1897, Ireland, 67, Chronic rheumatism, 10/26/1897.

TOOMEY, Ambrose – E, 17 Massachusetts, 06/18/1889, Massachusetts, 54, Lumbago, 04/26/1897

TOWNSEND, George – A, 95 Illinois, 06/15/1896, England, 70, Partial paralysis, 07/09/1897.

TROSTER, John – B, 13 Illinois Cav., 08/29/1895, Germany, 51, Rheumatism, 08/11/1897.

UMSTATTER, John J. – E, 46 New York, 09/01/1887,Germany, 61, Rheumatism, 05/13/1897.

VALENTINE, Edward – D, 52 New York, 03/24/1894, Denmark, 51, Paralysis, 11/08/1897.

VAN SLYKE, Peter – __, 7 Wisconsin Light Art., 06/08/1887, New York, 53, Rheumatism, 05/13/1897.

WABER, Henry – K, 1 Oregon, 04/06/1881, Germany, 62, Chronic rheumatism, 01/02/1897.

WAILEN, Peter – I, 105 Illinois, 12/09/1882, Ireland, 48, Hernia, 01/26/1897.

WALL, Charles – I, Cpl., 15 Missouri, 11/01/1894, Germany, 66, Chronic rheumatism, 02/04/1897.

WANN, William S. - __, Musician, 184 Ohio, 06/19/1896, Ohio, 48, Nervous prost. (prostration) 05/16/1897.

WARNESS, Franz – Gunner, U. S. Navy, 01/25/1893, Norway, 60 Loss-left eye, 10/30/1897.

WENTWORTH, Henry – E, 8 Illinois Cav., 07/02/1889, New York, 71, Kidney disease, 12/29/1897.

WOLFF, M. B. - __, 9 Wisconsin Art., 01/27/1891, New York, 49, Rheumatism, 12/30/1897.

WOODARD, H. J. - __, 18 New York Light Art., 03/28/1896, New York, 70, Chronic bronchitis, 06/25/1897.

WOODWARD, Isaac – E, 27 Massachusetts, 03/28/1895, Massachusetts, 58, Chronic diarrhoea, 02/01/1897.

WUNDERLICH, R. – 62, 2 U. S. Veteran Reserve Corps Battery, 10/26/1891, Germany, 59, Varicose veins, 03/07/1897.

Sources:

The Miscellaneous Documents of the House of Representatives Second Session of the 55th Congress, 1897-98. #3664. Record of Disabled Volunteer Soldiers, Who Are And Have Been, Members of the National Home for Disabled Soldiers, from July 1, 1896 to June 30, 1897. Washington: Government Printing Office, 1898. (Extracted from Annual Records – National Homes for Disabled Volunteer Soldiers.)

The Miscellaneous Documents of the House of Representatives Third Session of the 55th Congress, 1898-99. #3785. Record of Disabled Volunteer Soldiers, Who Are And Have Been, Members of the National Home for Disabled Soldiers, from July 1, 1897 to June 30, 1898. Washington: Government Printing Office, 1899. (Extracted from Annual Records - National Homes for Disabled Volunteers Soldiers.)

DEATHS IN 1898

FORMAT: NAME, COMPANY & REGIMENT, DATE OF ADMISSION, PLACE OF BIRTH, AGE, DISABILITY, DATE OF DEATH.

ALDEN, Edwin – F, 42 Massachusetts, 07/02/1896, Connecticut, 50, Heart disease, 04/29/1898.

ALDEN, Samuel E. – G, 51 Massachusetts, 08/15/1896, Massachusetts, 72, Heart disease, 02/09/1898.

ALLEN, William – K, 188 New York, 07/12/1896, New York, 65, Rheumatism, 04/05/1898.

BAKER, Theodore – Seaman, U. S. Navy, 04/13/1897, Germany, 59, Disease-tongue, 07/07/1898.

BARRETT, R. P. – D, 2 Wisconsin, 11/11/1889, New York, 56, General debility, 04/21/1898.

BATLEY, Richard A. – E, Sgt., 1 Virginia, Mexican War, 09/13/1885, Virginia, 65, Hernia, 12/07/1898.

BELL, Alex. – I, 95 Illinois, 09/20/1895, Scotland, 67, Heart disease, 06/09/1898. (Data in July 1, 1898 to June 30, 1899 record.)

BENNETT, Stephen – Seaman, U. S. Navy, 10/17/1885, New York, 64, Lumbago, 08/26/1898.

BERTH, James – K, 2 Kentucky, 08/27/1877, Ireland, 56, Hernia, 10/02/1898.

BLOOM, Frederick – D, 90 Illinois, 09/30/1893, Germany, 63, Gunshot wound-leg, 06/14/1898.

BRAINARD, George - __, Illinois Cooley's Art., 08/10/1897, New York, 79, Heart disease, 03./13/1898.

BRESLAND, Joseph – G, 9 New Hampshire, 03/24/1887, Ireland, 49, Gunshot wound- right leg, 02/28/1898.

BROGLE, Robert – F, 3 Pennsylvania Heavy Art., 05/19/1883, Germany, 62, Rheumatism, 09/03/1898.

BROWN, Isaac C, - F, Lt., 1 Pennsylvania, Mexican War, 06/24/1884, Pennsylvania, 67, Rheumatism, 05/10/1898.

BROWN, Joseph – B, 10 New York Cav., 10/11/1893, New York, 51, Chronic rheumatism, 11/23/1898.

BUTTERFIELD, William E. - A, Lt., 61 New York, 10/26/1887, New York, 51, Piles, 04/05/1898.

CAMPBELL, Charles – I, 52 Illinois, 03/26/1887, Ireland, 72, Loss-left eye, 12/11/1898.

CANTWELL, Thomas – L, 3 Wisconsin Cav., 02/19/1896, Ireland, 56, Hernia, 03/03/1898.

COERSMEYER, Henry – A, 142 New York, 07/27/1887, Germany, 60, Hernia, 04/07/1898.

COLLINS, William – Landsman, U. S. Navy, 03/30/1885, New York, 54, Rheumatism, 01/07/1898.

CONWAY, Anthony – E, Cpl., 35 Wisconsin, 08/09/1890, Ireland, 57, Disease-feet, 07/01/1898.

CORBETT, James – B, 1 Illinois Art., 04/21/1891, England, 60, Hernia, 04/15/1898.

CORKINS, John – E, 7 Kansas Cav., 08/12/1878, New York, 41, Injury-leg, 01/25/1898.

CREAGAN, Michael – B, 146 Illinois, 1/29/1883, Ireland, 53, Wound-left leg, 12/12/1898.

DAILEY, John H. – L, Cpl., 16 Wisconsin, 10/31/1888, Canada, 74, Rheumatism, 08/16/1898.

DASHIELL, Henry – K, 4 Illinois Cav., 12/26/1894, Indiana, 59, Chronic diarrhoea, 06/24/1898.

DAVENPORT, G. F. – K, 153 Illinois, 02/26/1893, New York, 62, Chronic diarrhoea, 02/24/1898.

DELENORY, Daniel – L, 15 Kansas Cav., 01/30/1891, Ireland, 60, Loss-left eye, 03/08/1898.

DENNIS, Stephen – K, 17 Indiana, 04/11/1889, France, 66, Rheumatism, 05/23/1898.

DONAHOO, John J. – K, 3 Ohio, 12/05/1893, Pennsylvania, 52, Gunshot wound-right leg, 04/15/1898.

DONOVAN, Dennis – Landsman, U. S. Navy, 08/27/1886, Ireland, 49, Rheumatism, 12/03/1898.

DOODY, Jeremiah – E, 12 New York Cav., 11/11/1888, Ireland, 52, Bronchitis, 08/28/1898.

DUVAL, James M. – E, 11 Illinois Cav., 06/03/1876, Norway, 55, Piles, 04/18/1898.

EDWARD, James – G, 11 U. S. Veteran Reserve Corps, 08/23/1894, Ireland, 59, Rheumatism, 07/25/1898.

ELTING, Lewis B. - B, 91, Illinois, 02/24/1890, New York, 56, Wound-foot, 03/13/1898.

EVELESHEIMER, P. - L, Qm., 13 Wisconsin, 11/21/1888, New York, 69, Old age, 07/25/1898.

FALES, Henry W. - __, Cpl., 1 Vermont Heavy Art., 08/25/1897, Vermont, 68, Spine-disease, 01/22/1898.

FALKENSTEIN, Henry - H, 193 Pennsylvania, 03/03/1890, Germany, 42, Rheumatism, 06/29/1898. (Data in July 1, 1898 to June 30, 1899 record.)

FARBER, Phillip - K, 4 Missouri Cav., 05/26/1896, Germany, 67, Senility, 12/114/1898.

FARNER, William H. - C, 48 Wisconsin, 05/01/1894, Wisconsin, 46, Sciatica, 06/27/1898.

FELTON, John - C, 146 Illinois, 10/27/1889, Pennsylvania, 70, Hernia, 08/25/1898.

FLEMING, James - B, 22 Wisconsin, 08/17/1886, Ireland, 41, General debility, 10/23/1898.

FRANK, Henry - D, Cpl., 45 Wisconsin, 04/02/1891, Germany, 61, Rheumatism, 08/05/1898.

FRENCH, Ezra B. - C, 1 Michigan Engineers, 11/30/1892, New York, 72, Old age, 02/14/1898.

GORDON, Thomas - __, 10 Wisconsin Art., 08/06/1885, England, 69, General debility, 09/02/1898.

GREEN Francis M. - L, Sgt., 21 U. S. Veterans Volunteer Engineers, 05/23/1893, Ohio, 62, Varicose veins, 07/28/1898.

HAGERUP, Anthony E, - Ensign, U. S. Navy, 06/09/1897, Norway, 59, Injury-shoulder, 05/23/1898.

HAMPSON, George - H, 42 Illinois, 06/06/1895, Pennsylvania, 77, Cataract, 05/27/1898.

HANSON, George - __, Illinois, Chicago Board of Trade Art., 07/24/1893, Sweden, 66, Rheumatism, 08/31/1898.

HARNER, Ferdinand - K, Sgt., 2 U. S. Veteran Reserve Corps, 08/06/1885, Germany, 64, Sunstroke, 12/02/1898.

HARRINGTON, M. - I, 51 Pennsylvania, 01/03/1885, Ireland, 60, Fracture-ankle, 12/17/1898.

HARRISON, Robert – K, 147 New York, 06/30/1869, Scotland, 45, Gunshot wound-right arm, 11/21/1898.

HARVEY, James – H, 8 U. S. Veteran Volunteers, 1/30/1876, Ireland, 53, Rheumatism, 09/26/1898.

HAYES, James – G, 6 Wisconsin, 10/19/1890, Connecticut, 49, Gunshot wound-thigh, 05/12/1898.

HELLER, Thomas S. – G, 1 Iowa Cav., 10/16/1897, Pennsylvania, 57, General debility, 07/08/1898.

HESS, David – B, 3 Wisconsin, 08/14/1878, New York, 53, General debility, 10/11/1898.

HETHER, William - B, 3 New York Art., 01/15/1893, Ireland, 56, Heart disease, 04/13/1898.

HIGGINS, Isaac – C, 20 Wisconsin, 12/06/1881, Ireland, 68, Injury-left hand, 05/08/1898.

HILL, Richard – F, 17 Wisconsin, 10/23/1886, Ireland, 66, Rheumatism, 07/17/1898.

HOFF, Adolph – G, 1 Missouri Engineers, 02/15/1887, Prussia, 60, Rheumatism, 01/23/1898.

HOFFER, Fred – H, Pennsylvania Independent Art., 09/11/1884, Pennsylvania, 67, Heart disease, 10/13/1898.

HOUSE, George – Landsman, U. S. Navy, 01/04/1893, Germany, 50, Varicose veins, 04/05/1898.

JENKINS, William – H, 142 Indiana, 07/31/1897, Indiana, 68, Defective sight, 05/16/1898.

JOHNSON, Charles L. – C, 4 Missouri Cav., 09/07/1878, Canada, 42, Rheumatism, 03/07/1898.

JOHNSON, John P. – C, Cpl., 15 Indiana, 09/23/1898, Ohio, 59, Heart disease, 09/30/1898.

JUSTICE, Charles – Seaman, U. S. Navy, 10/06/1888, Ireland, 55, Kidney disease, 05/28/1898.

KARTES, Peter – F, 17 Wisconsin, 01/17/1898, Germany, 62, General debility, 01/23/1898.

KEARNEY, Thomas – E, 5 U. S. Army Cav., 03/12/1887, Ireland, 63, Heart disease, 11/18/1898.

KEATING, Patrick – F, 17 Wisconsin, 10/24/1896, Ireland, 69, Chronic Rheumatism, 10/02/1898.

KELLY, John – L, 2 Wisconsin Cav., 02/04/1898, Ireland, 56, Varicose veins, 06/28/1898.

KERNIN, Edward J. – K, 1 Maine Heavy Art., 08/15/1894, Maine, 52, Gunshot wound- shoulder, 02/23/1898.

KEWN, James – F, 6 Pennsylvania Heavy Art., 07/05/1885, Ireland, 64, Hernia, 07/17/1898.

KEYES, Ezra A. – A, 16 Wisconsin, 10/19/1886, New York, 56, Disease-lungs, 08/12/1898.

KIRCHNER, Martin – E, 25 Iowa, 10/30/1886, Germany, 50, Gunshot wound-left arm, 06/04/1898.

KLUMB, Valentine - H, 2 Wisconsin Cav., 04/10/1883, Germany, 44, Wound-right foot, 01/18/1898.

KOENIG, N. – E, 45 Illinois, 03/11/1898.Germany, 70, Paralysis, 03/28/1898.

KRUM, Charles – H, 4 Illinois Cav., 08/24/1893, Germany, 67, Rheumatism, 07/28/1898.

LAASS, GEORGE – C, 9 U. S. Veteran Volunteers, 10/08/1878, Germany, 70, Gunshot wound-leg, 11/18/1898.

LESLIE, Alexander – F, 9 Illinois Cav., 09/07/1874, Ireland, 40, Varicose veins, 07/18/1898.

LEUTHART, Thomas – K, 82 Illinois, 12/17/1881, Switzerland, 59, Wound-left leg, 09/02/1898.

LINK, Eli – Unassigned, 1 U. S. Army Veteran Engineers, 07/29/1871, England, 53, Injury-back, 03/31/1898.

LINK, Henry – F, 15 Missouri, 08/14/1873, Germany, 43, Gunshot wound-left leg, 06/30/1898. (Data in July 1, 1898 to June 30, 1899 record.)

LITCHFELD, Henry – H, 144 Illinois, 07/30/1894, Germany, 53, Rheumatism, 02/21/1898.

LOVEY, John – B, 1 Wisconsin Heavy Art., 10/12/1891, England, 72, Old age, 06/12/1898.

LYNCH, James J. – E, Cpl., 2 New Hampshire, 07/17/1895, Canada, 65, Asthma, 12/06/1898.

MASCHKA, Anthony – A, 40 Missouri, 07/29/1884, Austria, 55, Rheumatism, 09/14/1898.

MCCORMICK, William – D, 48 Indiana, 10/09/1888, Illinois, 43, Gunshot wound-left leg, 03/07/1898.

MCGLING, John – F, 48 Wisconsin, 07/15/1886, Ireland, 69, Rheumatism, 04/29/1898.

MCSHERRY, Daniel – Seaman, U. S. Navy, 06/03/1891, Ireland, 62, Injury-right hip, 11/21/1898.

MCVETY, Robert – F, 108 New York, 08/26/1895, Canada, 52, Gunshot wound-hip, 07/07/1898

MELBER, Frederick – F, 4 U. S. Veteran Volunteers, 09/13/1892, Germany, 58, Injury-shoulder, 02/10/1898.

MELGA, Christian – I, 29 Illinois, 07/29/1885, Norway, 61, Rheumatism, 12/11/1898.

MEYER, Nicholaus – B, 165 Ohio, 08/26/1895, Bavaria, 71, Apoplexy, 04/30/1898.

MILLANE, John – B, 1 Kansas, 06/20/1870, Ireland, 49, Hernia, 06/08/1898.

MOOERS, Charles C. – K, Lt., 46 Ohio, 05/05/1896, Ohio, 56, Diabetes, 06/29/1898.

MOORE, William J. – C, 1 Minnesota Heavy Art., 8/24/1892, Illinois, 52, Rheumatism, 02/18/1898.

MORSE, William – D, Cpl., 1 Minnesota Heavy Art., 12/08/1892, Maine, 64, Disease-liver, 07/22/1898.

MOTHERWAY, John – E, 1 Wisconsin Heavy Art., 08/26/1895, New York, 51, Rheumatism, 10/05/1898.

MOWER, Lyman - __, U. S. Army General Service, 06/05/1877, Vermont, 60, Epilepsy, 01/08/1898.

MULLENHOUER, Charles – G, 8 Indiana, 03/04/1891, Germany, 65, Rheumatism, 03/05/1898.

NEUHAUSS, G. – D, 15 New York Heavy Art., 09/22/1889, Germany, 66, General debility, 03/09/1898.

O'BRIEN, William – D, 17 Wisconsin, 07/06/1875, Ireland, 45, Deafness, 05/21/1898.

O'CONNER, William – F, 72 Illinois, 05/13/1885, New York, 45, Hernia, 10/14/1898.

PEARSON, GEORGE – M, 3 Wisconsin Cav., 05/01/1894, England, 51, General debility, 11/18/1898.

PEASE, Oscar C. – E, Lt., 89 Illinois, 06/05/1891, Illinois, 52, Gunshot wound-thigh, 04/01/1898.

POIRON, John C. – A, 6 Wisconsin, 10/27/1876, Germany, 56, Gunshot wound-right leg, 02/02/1898.

PRENTICE, William – F, 15 Illinois Cav., 11/29/1879, Canada, 58, Rheumatism, 12/14/1898.

PROCTOR, William – A, 4 Illinois Cav., 0511/1897, Ireland, 69, General debility, 01/08/1898.

RAAB, William – K, 5 Michigan, 10/18/1897, Germany, 70, Gunshot wound-back, 09/11/1898.

RAFTLE, Jacob – B, 53 Illinois, 06/21/1887, Germany, 59, General debility, 04/27/1898.

RANDALL, M. N. – I, 32 Wisconsin, 06/19/1896, Vermont, 66, General debility, 11/16/1898.

REED, George W. – I, 103 Ohio, 09/12/1893, Pennsylvania, 49, Paralysis, 01/14/1898.

REGLAN, Fred. – L, 1 Illinois Art., 12/04/1870, Germany, 60, Hernia, 06/14/1898.

REMLINGER, Frank – F, 10 U. S. Veteran Reserve Corps, 07/10/1884, Germany, 57, Varicose veins, 08/03/1898.

REYNOLDS, B. W. - __, 6 Wisconsin, Art., 08/16/1898, Ohio, 54, Paralysis, 10/02/1898.

RICE, Peter H. – A, Sgt., 1 Wisconsin Art., 06/27/1882, New York, 52, Rheumatism, 12/18/1898.

ROBB, James M. – B, 2 West Virginia, 04/03/1896, Pennsylvania, 52, Asthma, 01/12/1898.

ROBSON, George – D, 6 Wisconsin, 03/20/1877, Canada, 52, Deaf, 11/06/1898.

ROLAND, William – G, 16 Illinois, 12/10/1897, Illinois, 55, Hernia, 03/18/1898.

RONK, Julius L – Landsman, U. S. Navy, 08/16/1884, New York, 44, Diphtheria, 01/31/1898.

SABINE, G. C. – M, 1 Maine Cav., 06/17/1891, Maine, 54, Heart disease, 09/12/1898.

SADLER, Thomas – E, 7 New York, 04/04/1887, England, 54, Kidney disease, 08/25/1898.

SCHMIDT, Heinrich – E, Sgt., 29 Massachusetts, 09/04/1894, Germany, 58, Rheumatism, 08/29/1898.

SCHROETER, Theo. – H, 106 Ohio, 01/16/1887, Germany, 63, Ulcer-left leg, 01/29/1898. (Data in July 1, 1898 to June 30, 1899 record.)

SEISER, John D – M, 9 Illinois Cav., 12/14/1888, Germany, 66, Rheumatism, 11/15/1898.

SEX, Michael – D, 69 Pennsylvania, 08/02/1875, Ireland, 50, Blindness, 10/12/1898.

SIMON, John – B, 1 Louisiana, 1/26/1894, Germany, 71, Chronic rheumatism, 02/23/1898.

SKELLY, Matthew – Seaman, U. S. Navy, 11/03/1888, Ireland, 50, Rheumatism, 07/24/1898.

SMITH, Richard – E, 100 Illinois, 04/28/1886, England, 68, Wound-head, 03/19/1898.

SNYDER, Peter – D, 26 Illinois, 03/09/1880, Germany, 60, Scurvy, 04/04/1898. (Data in July 1, 1898 to June 30, 1899 record.)

STEPHENSON, G. W. – B, 99 New York, 12/18/1889, New York, 68, Rheumatism, 07/18/1898.

STETTESSI, Peter – K, Musician, 9 Wisconsin, 03/02/1889, Switzerland, 51, Epilepsy, 12/01/1898.

STOUT, Ebenezer - __, Lt., 19 New York Art., 06/14/1892, New York, 70, Rheumatism, 12/10/1898.

STROM, H. P. – G, 1 Maryland, 08/22/1893, Sweden, 63, Hernia, 11/28/1898.

SUMBARDO, D. R. – K, 9 Indiana, 05/22/1897, Connecticut, 53, Rheumatism, 03/06/1898.

TAYLOR, Albert – D, 1 Pennsylvania Heavy Art., 10/31/1885, Pennsylvania, 38, Heart disease, 05/08/1898.

THOMAS, William - __, Qm. Sgt., 1 Wisconsin Cav., 08/25/1897, Ohio, 78, Senile debility, 08/21/1898.

TORGUSON, William O. – H, 27 Wisconsin, 08/13/1893, Norway, 69, Rheumatism 07/09/1898.

TRENKLE, Ferdinand - __, 34 Iowa, 05/11/1896, Germany, 63, Heart disease, 11/10/1898.

TUTTLE, William H. – Seaman, U. S. Navy, 05/07/1898, New York, 71, Rheumatism, 07/04/1898.

VARS, Joseph L. – K, 5 Illinois Cav., 03/26/1887, New York, 66, Loss-hand, 05/15/1898.

WALKER, D. A. – C, 33 Massachusetts, 10/02/1893, Massachusetts, 53, Diarrhoea, 08/12/1898.

WALLERMAN, George – B, 51 Wisconsin, 09/11/1889, Prussia, 67, Loss-right eye, 08/19/1898.

WATERS, HIRAM – I, 44 Wisconsin, 08/28/1888, New York, 63, Hemorrhoids, 09/17/1898.

WEBBER, JOHN J. - __, Qm. Sgt., 16 New York Cav.,
03/07/1887, Switzerland, 49, Bronchitis, 05/24/1898.
WELLS, John W. – H, 37 Wisconsin, 07/07/1886, New York,
60, Heart disease, 08/28/1898.
WHIPPLE, John P. – A, 27 Wisconsin, 10/18/1897, Maine,
77, General debility, 03/03/1898.
WHITE, Earl A. – F, 1 Illinois Art., 10/21/1893, Connecticut,
71, Blind, 09/02/1898.
WHITMORE, Fred – A, 11 New York Heavy Art.,
09/09/1898, New York, 57, Phthisis, 09/26/1898.
WILLIAMS, Asa – A, Lt., 12 Illinois, 06/15/1892, Massachusetts, 61, Injury-right leg, 04/25/1898.
WILLIAMS, William - __, Illinois Chicago Board of Trade
Art., 06/28/1891, New York, 59, Rheumatism,
04/17/1898.
WILLIE, B. F. – I, Cpl., 2 U. S. Veteran Reserve Corps,
12/02/1883, Massachusetts, 55, General debility,
09/29/1898.
WILSON, William – F, 1 Massachusetts Heavy Art.,
08/13/1897, England, 63, Disease-tongue, 01/09/1898.
WORDEN, Henry – D, 1 Louisiana, Mexican War,
09/28/1876, New York, 54, Hemorrhoids, 02/04/1898.

Sources:

The Miscellaneous Documents of the House of Representatives Third Session of the 55th Congress, 1898-99. #3785. Record of Disabled Volunteer Soldiers, Who Are and Have Been, Members of the National Home for Disabled Volunteer Soldiers, from July 1, 1897 to June 30, 1898. Washington: Government Printing Office, 1899. (Extracted from Annual Reports – National Homes for Disabled Volunteer Soldiers.)

The Miscellaneous Documents of the House of Representatives First Session of the 56th Congress, 1899-00. #3958. Record of Disabled Volunteer Soldiers, Who Are And Have Been, Members of the National Home for Disabled Volunteer Soldiers, from July 1, 1898 to June 30, 1899. Washington: Government Printing Office, 1900. (Extracted from Annual Reports – National Homes for Disabled Volunteer Soldiers.)

DEATHS IN 1899

FORMAT: NAME, COMPANY & REGIMENT, DATE OF ADMISSION, PLACE OF BIRTH, AGE, DISABILITY, DATE OF DEATH.

ALLEN, John C. - A, Cpl., 9 Minnesota, 04/05/1890. Maine, 55, Varicose veins, 02/06/1899.

AMUNDSON, H. – K, 37 Wisconsin, 07/28/1886, Norway, 57, Asthma, 08/31/1899.

APPRADARIS, F. – E, 4 Ohio Cav., 04/22/1887, Prussia, 70, Rheumatism, 10/25/1899.

ASZFALZ, Sebastian - D, 5 Minnesota, 08/07/1883, Germany, 56, Heart disease, 01/03/1899.

ATKINS, George – C, 1 Michigan Cav., 07/27/1891, Michigan, 67, Blindness, 11/30/1899.

BACKUS, Frank – G, 13 Wisconsin, 04/29/1893, New York, 62, Varicose veins, 09/30/1899.

BAHN, John – F, 5 Wisconsin, 08/27/1895, Germany, 70, Injury-head, 08/06/1899.

BAKER, Joseph – A, 15 U. S. Veteran Reserve Corps, 06/18/1885, Germany, 53, Wound-head, 07/23/1899.

BARRETT, Michael – G, 61 Massachusetts, 03/05/1896, New York, 48, Heart disease, 03/29/1899.

BELLOMY, J. D. – D, 5 West Virginia, 10/26/1899, Ohio, 72, Heart disease, 01/22/1899.

BELLWAY, George – G, 3 Wisconsin, 04/12/1883, Canada, 43 Rheumatism, 08/09/1899.

BLAHAN, Patrick – I, 153 Illinois, 03/29/1888, Ireland, 57, Injury-right shoulder, 04/07/1899.

BOHR, John J. – F, 65 Illinois, 04/11/1890, Germany, 68, Loss-left eye, 09/04/1899.

BONNEY, Oliver - A, 13 Wisconsin, 07/12/1891, Canada, 79 Rheumatism, 12/25/1899.

BOOTH, A. H. – E, Cpl., 35 Wisconsin, 08/12/1878, Canada, 51, Rheumatism, 10/27/1899.

BRADFORD, O. K. – G, 6 Massachusetts, 01/27/1888, New Hampshire, 56, Rheumatism, 01/08/1899.

BRETHAN, John – A, 1 Michigan Art., 06/07/1877, Canada, 47, Rheumatism, 04/29/1899.

BREWSTER, John H. – E, 141 Illinois, 11/03/1897, New York, 76, Deaf, 06/15/1899.

BRINGER, Henry – E, 2 Missouri Art., 05/25/1889, Germany, 55, Hernia, 04/06/1899.

BROCKEL, Nicholas – B, 48 Wisconsin, 12/01/1888, Germany, 51, Hemorrhoids, 02/05/1899.

BROTHER, E. F. - __, Lt., 198 Pennsylvania, 08/01/1899, Pennsylvania, 70, Rheumatism, 10/19/1899.

BUETTNER, Henry – B, Cpl., 82 Illinois, 09/10/1878, Germany, 50, Gunshot wound-head, 06/23/1899.

BUTLER, Michael – Seaman, U. S. Navy, 12/16/1887, Ireland, 50, Rheumatism, 05/28/1899.

CAMPBELL, John – Seaman, U. S. Navy, 01/20/1897, New York, 71, Blind, 04/11/1899.

CARROLL, Mathew – B, Cpl., 90 Illinois, 08/15/1886, Ireland, 54, Rheumatism, 05/22/1899.

CHINN, Jacob – E, 30 Wisconsin, 05/03/1897, England, 62, Wound-right hand, 11/02/1899.

CLANCY, John – I, Cpl., 5 Minnesota, 02/17/1870, Ireland, 38, Lung disease, 10/02/1899.

COOK, Walter – C, 39 Wisconsin, 08/09/1899, Germany, 85, Rheumatism, 11/10/1899.

COYLE, Charles – B, Sgt., 34 New Jersey, 06/04/1884, Ireland, 47, Rheumatism, 03/03/1899.

CROAK, Thomas – E, 3 Wisconsin Cav., 10/23/1898, Ireland, 64, Old age, 06/30/1899.

CULLEN, Patrick – E, Cpl., 1 Wisconsin Cav., 11/11/1897, Ireland, 62, Heart disease, 05/29/1899.

DEBREY, John A. – G, Cpl., 10 New York, 08/10/1897, France, 53, Asthma, 02/06/1899.

DOLAN, John – F, 69 Pennsylvania, 09/15/1876, Ireland, 64, Ulcers, 07/27/1899.

DUANE, Daniel J. – A, Lt., 3 Iowa, 05/19/1897, Ireland, 59, Gunshot wound-right thigh, 06/03/1899.

DYE, Havey N. – G, 1 New York Marine Art., 06/03/1897, New York, 73, Rheumatism, 01/28/1899.

EBERT, Julius – Seaman, U. S. Navy, 05/09/1899, Germany, 58, Heart disease, 12/14/1899.

EHRHARDT, Charles – K, 82 Illinois, 08/17/1877, France, 69, Rheumatism, 11/11/1899.

EICH, E. – F, 5 New Hampshire, 11/23/1894, Germany, 58, Varicose veins, 11/15/1900. (Data in July 1, 1899 to June 30, 1900 record.)

FISHER, M. – D, 44 Indiana, 11/02/1888, Switzerland, 68, Hernia, 11/15/1899.

FLANDERS, A. C. – B, 10 Minnesota, 08/26/1885, New Hampshire, 66, General debility, 06/16/1899.

FOX, John B. – D, 134 Illinois, 06/15/1899, New York, 57, Rheumatism, 10/12/1899.

FRANTZ, Fred – H, 42 Wisconsin, 06/23/1888, Germany, 66, Rheumatism, 10/25/1899.

FRITZ, John B. – E, 88 Illinois, 07/28/1888, Ohio, 46, Epilepsy, 04/23/1899.

FRY, Thomas J. – F, 10 Wisconsin, 06/01/1897, Pennsylvania, 60, Paralysis, 02/19/1899.

GRADY, Patrick – E, 47 Illinois, 07/21/1886, Ireland, 58, Asthma, 05/28/1899.

GRAY, John – B, 1 Washington, 09/20/1897, Ireland, 65, Injury-right arm, 11/09/1899.

GRIFFIN, Roscoe T. – A, 9 U. S. Veteran Reserve Corps, 03/31/1896, Maine, 54, Injury-throat, 06/27/1899.

GROSHONG, William – C, Musician, 15 Wisconsin, 02/01/1881, New York, 54, Disease-eyes, 06/07/1899.

GUILFOIL, Martin – F, 60 New York, 06/07/1894, Pennsylvania, 46, Fracture-clavicle, 05/04/1899.

HALE, Charles A. – F, Capt., 5 New Hampshire, 06/12/1899, Maine, 58, Paralysis, 08/19/1899.

HAMILTON, A. J. – K, 6 Michigan Heavy Art., 09/04/1882, Ohio, 53, General debility, 11/18/1899.

HAMMOND, R. C. – E, 5 Wisconsin, 08/25/1898, New York, 50, General debility, 11/20/1899.

HARTING, George – I, 25 Wisconsin, 06/25/1890, Germany, 53, Rheumatism, 01/26/1899.

HARTLEY, F. J. – G, 82 Illinois, 06/23/1888, Germany, 51, Hemorrhoids, 05/03/1899.

HEPPE, John W. – I, 1 Michigan, 03/31/1890, Germany, 69, Epilepsy, 03/04/1899.

HEGELMAIER, Gott. – H, 48 Indiana, 08/27/1886, Germany, 56, Rheumatism, 03/27/1899.

HILL, Edgar P. - __, Col., 23 Wisconsin, 12/19/1890, Vermont, 64, Paralysis, 06/09/1899.

HINES, Andrew J. – A, 42 Wisconsin, 09/08/1898, Scotland, 74, Heart disease, 02/23/1899.

HOBBS, Benjamin – C, 12 Maryland, 02/17/1882, Maryland, 48, Injury-head, 11/09/1899.

HODGKINS, Rufus - __, 1 U.S. Art., Indian War, 02/24/1899, Maine, 80, Injury-hip, 05/16/1899.

HOELECKE, William - __, Capt., Detached U. S. Veteran Volunteers, 04/23/1880, Prussia, 53, Paralysis, 07/21/1899.

HOHN, David F. – A, Cpl., 19 Illinois, 08/03/1895, Germany, 55, Chronic rheumatism, 05/30/1899.

HOPKINS, Sewell W. – Seaman, U. S. Navy, 05/07/1898, Maine, 56, Sciatica, 01/05/1899.

HORTON, William H. – I, 2 New York Cav., 03/07/1896, New York, 61, Rheumatism, 01/05/1899.

JEWITT, Edward E. – F, 124 Ohio, 09/20/1887, Massachusetts, 59, Hernia, 03/17/1899.

JOHNSON, John – Seaman, U. S. Navy, 12/13/1892, Norway, 63, Chronic Rheumatism, 01/07/1899.

JONES, David I. – A, 17 U. S. Army, 11/10/1893, Wisconsin, 55, Asthma, 04/07/1899.

JURAEZ, William – D, Sgt., 97 New York, 06/26/1894, Mexico, 60, Rheumatism, 02/16/1899.

KAST, Nicholas – K, 2 Kansas, 07/21/1888, Germany, 54, Gunshot wound-left arm, 11/21/1899.

KEARN, William – I, 1 Wisconsin Cav., 09/22/1889, New York, 74, Gunshot wound-left leg, 04/01/1899.

KEEFE, John – C, 4 Illinois Cav., 10/18/1893, Canada, 50, Rheumatism, 07/09/1899.

KELLY, John S. – E, Cpl., 15 Illinois, 05/14/1899, Illinois, 56, Hernia, 09/10/1899.

KEMPF, Charles W. - __, Maj., 5 Wisconsin, 11/22/1898, Germany, 61, Injury-spine, 01/11/1899.

KENNEDY, Michael – K, 24 Missouri, 08/22/1885, Ireland, 50, Injury-side, 05/26/1899.

KING, John S. – K, 18 Wisconsin, 12/26/1893, New York, 72, Fracture-ankle, 06/11/1899.

KISNER, B. – D, 6 Wisconsin, 09/25/1889, Germany, 69, Gunshot wound-right hand, 10/31/1899.

KLAUS, William – F, 43 Illinois, 11/06/1883, Germany, 48, Blind-left eye, 02/07/1899.

KLEINE, O. L. E. - __, 9 Wisconsin Art., 10/25/1893, Sax., 71, Lumbago, 04/16/1899.

KUNTZ, Adam – A, Cpl., 26 Wisconsin, 12/22/1890, Germany, 64, General debility, 11/04/1899.

LARNEY, John - Seaman, U. S. Navy, 06/28/1891, Ireland, 73, Rheumatism, 04/25/1899.

LAWSON, Lewis – B, Cpl., 17 Illinois Cav., 04/18/1895, Illinois, 49, Paralysis, 04/12/1899.

LOPER, Peter H. – F, 4 U. S., Mexican War, 07/16/1889, Ohio, 59, Rheumatism, 02/15/1899.

LOYD, Enols – G, 1 Michigan Art., 12/23/1890, Maryland, 64, Loss-right eye, 03/10/1899.

MAHER, Thomas – F, 24 Wisconsin, 10/19/1886, Ireland, 63, Rheumatism, 03/23/1899.

MALONEY, J. E. – D, 56 Ohio, 06/19/1896, Ohio, 50, Injury-right hand, 07/23/1899.

MANSON, Aaron – I, 8 Illinois, 06/03/1886, Sweden, 49, Chronic diarrhoea, 03/27/1899.

MARX, Philip – E, 18 Wisconsin, 03/24/1887, Germany, 63, Rheumatism, 11/06/1899.

MCCABE, John – Landsman, U. S. Navy, 07/07/1896, Pennsylvania, 51, Loss-right eye, 11/28/1899.

MCCARTHY, James – H, 9 Connecticut, 02/11/1882. Ireland, 53, Injury-back, 12/13/1899.

MCCARTY, Dennis – B, 23 Illinois, 07/16/1883, Ireland, 65, Gunshot wound-left leg, 06/18/1899.

MCCLAIN, A. W. – D, Sgt., 138 Indiana, 03/31/1894, Indiana, 50, Loss-right foot, 11/15/1899.

MCCLAINTHAN, John – G, 3 Ohio, 03/17/1887, Ohio, 45, Hemorrhoids, 01/07/1899.

MCGEEN, Thomas – F, 5 Wisconsin, 08/03/1887, New York, 47, Rheumatism, 09/01/1899.

MCINENLY, James – D, 5 Wisconsin, 03/19/1887, Canada, 54, Gunshot wound-right thigh, 05/18/1899.

MCINTYRE, Neil – G, 13 Maryland, 01/15/1893, Scotland, 59, Rheumatism, 08/22/1899.

MCKENNA, John C. – Seaman, U. S. Navy, 12/22/1891, Ireland, 57, Rheumatism, 04/12/1899.

MECKIEN, Adolph – C, Cpl., 68 New York, 03/21/1888, Germany, 63, Rheumatism, 02/25/1899.

METCALF, Abraham – C, 53, Kentucky, 11/07/1887, Pennsylvania, 43, Rheumatism, 11/14/1899.

MEYER, John W. – H, 35 Wisconsin, 02/06/1887, Germany, 62, Rheumatism, 03/09/1899.

MEYERS, J. D. – D, 1 Maryland, 11/08/1892, Switzerland, 65, Varicose veins, 11/04/1899.

MILLER, James – I, 2 Illinois Art., 01/06/1885, Scotland, 53, Rheumatism, 10/24/1899.

MONROE, Richard – E, 49 New York, 11/05/1894, N. S., 56, Injury-shoulder, 03/27/1899.

MOORE, J. Adderly – G, 95 Illinois, 09/17/1897, Pennsylvania, 57, Rheumatism, 09/25/1899.

MOORE, Patrick – K, 14 Ohio, 10/15/1893, Ireland, 62, Inflammaory rheumatism, 05/19/1899.

MORGAN, Charles – K, Cpl., 19 Illinois, 08/14/1896, Illinois, 51, Deaf, 02/23/1899.

MORLEY, John G. – B, 95 Illinois, 06/15/1889, England, 57, General debility, 12/24/1899.

MORRIS, Levi – Seaman, U. S. Navy, 05/27/1898, New York, 73, Injury-left hip, 07/20/1899.

MUNGER, R. D. – G, 11 Illinois, 02/25/1893, Massachusetts, 62, Rheumatism, 04/26/1899.

OBERMEYER, Jacob – C, 45 Wisconsin, 06/08/1892, Bavaria, 66, Liver disease, 01/10/1899.

O'NEIL, John – H, 100 Pennsylvania, 10/08/1879, Ireland, 58, Asthma, 09/10/1899.

PARKS, B. F. - __, Lt. Col., 13 Illinois, 04/08/1889, Michigan, 59, Injury-left leg, 11/11/1899.

PENDERS, William - __, 1 New York Sharpshooters, 12/26/1893, New, York, 53, Heart disease, 05/28/1899.

PEPPER, H. L. – A, 48 Wisconsin, 06/19/1896, Pennsylvania, 73, Heart disease, 07/01/1899.

PETERS, Henry - __, 21 Indiana, Art., 01/02/1885, Prussia, 55, Anchylosis-ankle, 01/09/1899.

PIERCE, John H. – H, Lt., 44 Illinois, 10/23/1890, Massachusetts, 57, Gunshot wound·right leg, 11/20/1899.

PIERCOTT, Joseph – C, 9 Wisconsin, 08/26/1895, Prussia, 68, Chronic Rheumatism, 07/06/1899.

POLLOCK, Thomas – A, 66 Ohio, 08/21/1890, Ohio, 46, Injury-left foot, 08/06/1899.

POWELL, J. N. – C, 18 Wisconsin, 06/12/1894, Ohio, 51, Gunshot wound-shoulder, 01/28/1899.

PRICE, S. F. – D, 17 Illinois, 06/08/1887, Pennsylvania, 66, Rheumatism, 10/20/1899.

QUINN, James – I, 59 Ohio, 04/04/1893, Ireland, 52, Rheumatism, 01/11/1899.

RAKUTZ, Hermann – I, 35 Wisconsin, 05/05/1896, Prussia 74, Senility, 03/07/1899.

RAVENELL, P. – G, 2 Louisiana, Mexican War, 03/15/1899, Louisiana, 82, Hernia, 11/15/1899.

REED, John – I, 76 Pennsylvania, 10/06/1889, Pennsylvania, 43, Heart disease, 07/20/1899.

RICHARDSON, L. S. – D, Capt., 3 Massachusetts Heavy Art., 08/10/1893, Massachusetts, 56, Gunshot wound-ankle, 03/21/1899.

ROGGEN, Frederick – D, 12 Maine, 09/21/1876, Germany, 62, General debility, 11/26/1899.

ROSCHE, Philip – L, 25 New York, 10/24/1895, Germany, 68, Heart disease, 02/04/1899.

ROZAS, John C. – F, Cpl., 1 Louisiana, 08/10/1891, Cuba, 49, Epilepsy, 02/11/1899.

RUTHMAN, C. – K, 2 U. S. Army Cav., 05/08/1892, Germany, 56, Injury-right arm, 12/31/1899.

RYAN, Timothy – G, 90 Illinois, 09/09/1867, Ireland, 34, Loss-right leg, 02/07/1899.

SAEGER, John – B, Sgt., 51 Wisconsin, 08/10/1897, Germany, 68, Senility, 11/11/1899.

SAMPLES, John W. – F, 3 Illinois Cav., 04/08/1891, Illinois, 51, Rheumatism, 02/21/1899.

SCHIBLER, Alois – F, 74 Pennsylvania, 09/24/1884, Germany, 60, Rheumatism, 06/07/1899.

SCHLEICHER, A. - K, Cpl., 45 Wisconsin, 09/28/1894, Germany, 73, Blindness, 07/27/1899.

SCHLUTER, Hermann - __, Maj., 9 Wisconsin, 02/12/1884 or '81, Germany, 66, Hemorrhoids, 08/05/1899.

SCHREFTLER, C. C. – B, 56 Illinois, 07/26/1898, Ohio, 59, Paralysis, 01/22/1899.

SHAW, John J. – G, 16 Wisconsin, 06/18/1894, New York, 71, Old age, 04/25/1899.

SHIELDS, N. S. - __, French's Infantry, Michigan, Black Hawk War, 08/01/1899, Kentucky, 89, Old age, 08/24/1899.

SHOOTY, Charles – A, 26 Michigan, 12/12/1881, Belgium, 61, Hernia, 01/02/1899.

SHRIBER, August – H, 32 Illinois, 01/29/1895, Germany, 74, Old age, 07/06/1899.

SINCLAIR, George W. – B, 5 Wisconsin, 08/04/1882, Massachusetts, 59, Rheumatism, 11/16/1899.

SPERLING, Johann – M. 1 Wisconsin Heavy Art., 04/01/1887, Pennsylvania, 58, Rheumatism, 10/21/1899.

STEWART, James – K, 3 New Jersey, 06/26/1888, Ireland, 46, Injury-right shoulder, 11/06/1899.

SULLIVAN, John – I, 24 Wisconsin, 09/30/1873, Ireland, 40, Hernia, 03/30/1899.

SZULCZENSKI, John – C, Cpl., 31 New York, 02/19/1886, Prussia, 50, General debility, 12/28/1899.

TALCOTT, J. W. – F, 14 Wisconsin, 05/22/1897, Massachusetts, 61, Gunshot wound-left leg, 06/20/1899.

TOMA, Joseph – F, 1 Wisconsin, 04/25/1892, Germany, 70, Rheumatism, 02/22/1899.

TRUMAN, George W. – G, 50 Wisconsin, 06/17/1898, Connecticut, 71, Senile, 04/18/1899.

TRUMPER, Henry – K, 30 Massachusetts, 10/19/1896, Germany, 50, Asthma, 02/25/1899.

TSCHEEPE, Moritz – C, 24 Wisconsin, 08/27/1898, Germany, 56, Paralysis, 10/26/1899.

VAN TREES, John – K, 12 Kansas, 02/05/1880, Indiana, 51, Dyspepsia, 07/28/1899.

WALLACE, James – Seaman, U. S. Navy, 11/14/1889, Scotland, 50, Rheumatism, 09/17/1899.

WARDLE, George – C, 2 Pennsylvania Cav., 04/08/1885, England, 63, Gunshot wound-right shoulder, 08/10/1899.

WARREN, Theodore – H, 43 Massachusetts, 06/17/1893, Massachusetts, 50, Rheumatism, 02/27/1899

WELLS, Emory F. – E, 17 Wisconsin, 11/03/1888, Connecticut, 67, Lung disease, 06/11/1899.

WESLOWSKI, A. – F, 22 Michigan, 03/29/1876, Michigan, 33, Chronic diarrhoea, 09/16/1899.

WILLIAMS, James H. – D, 122 Illinois, 03/24/1892, Mississippi, 73, Hernia, 01/06/1899.

WILLIARD, Robert – D, 11 Connecticut, 01/11/1882, Ireland, 62, Gunshot wound-right thigh, 02/05/1899.

WING, R. S. H. – G, 4 U. S. Army Art., 03/02/1891, Ohio, 46, Hernia, 11/02/1899.

WISE, John – I, 6 U. S. Army Cav., 08/25/1898, Ireland, 60, Hernia, 07/11/1899.

WOODRUFF, James T. – E, 7 Iowa, 10/28/1899, Virginia, 72, Heart disease, 11/05/1899.

Sources:

The Miscellaneous Documents of the House of Representatives First Session of the 56th Congress, 1899-00. #3985. Record of Disabled Volunteer Soldiers, Who Are And Have Been, Members of the National Home for Disabled Volunteer Soldiers, from July 1, 1898 to June 30, 1899. Washington: Government Printing Office, 1900. (Extracted from Annual Reports – National Homes for Disabled Volunteer Soldiers.)

The Miscellaneous Documents of the House of Representatives Second Session of the 56th Congress, 1900-01 #4136. Record of Disabled Volunteer Soldiers, Who Are And Have Been, Members of the National Home for Disabled Volunteer Soldiers, from July 1, 1899 to June 30, 1900. Government Printing Office, 1901. (Extracted from Annual Reports – National Homes for Disabled Volunteer Soldiers.)

AFTERWORD

AFTERWORD

A Memorial Note to: *The Lady and Her Respected Sisters in their Great Mission*

Lydia Ely (Hewitt), born December 3, 1833 in Homer, Michigan, daughter of Ambrose Ely and Eliza Minerva Ely, born Hawley. She came to Milwaukee in 1840 with her mother and father. In 1852 she married G. P. Hewitt, Jr. She was an artist and an advocate of art appreciation. Most importantly she was the skilled leader of the *Ladies of Milwaukee* who unswervingly saw to the needs of the Civil War veterans of Wisconsin.

She was one of the few of that group that lived on into the early part of the 20th century until her death 12/21/1914. Her grave is found on the ELY family plot in Forest Home Cemetery, Milwaukee, Wisconsin.

All Branches:

After WWI, the Veterans Bureau was created to meet the hospitalization and rehabilitation needs of younger veterans. The National Home and the Veterans Bureau merged to become the U. S. Veterans Administration by order of President Hoover in July 1930. The Board of Managers no longer existed and identification of branches as *Home* began to change to that of *Hospital* then to that of *Medical Center*.

The Northwestern Branch:

The *Soldiers' Home* officially became *Veterans' Administration Hospital* in 1930. And later became the *Veterans Administration Medical Center*. The branch was renamed *Wood, Wisconsin* in 1937 in honor of the last president of the Board of Managers, General George H. Wood, a Spanish War veteran. In 1985, the name was changed to *Clement J. Zablocki Veterans Administration Medical*

Center and later changed to *Clement J. Zablocki Veterans Affairs Medical Center.* Congressman Zablocki's district included the Center. He was supportive of legislation that impacted positively on the welfare of the veteran. The cemetery retained the name of General Wood – *Wood National Cemetery.*

There is one lake left on the grounds, *Wheeler Lake,* and it was relocated when the new hospital was built in 1966. The other lakes had been removed by landfill. The original farmhouses no longer exist. The *Beer Hall (Canteen)* built in 1888 was shut down by Congress in 1908. The *Pavilion,* which provided a place for outside band concerts, was torn down in the 1960s. The *Old Men's Barracks* which was later used as segregated housing for colored veterans has been demolished.

The acreage of the grounds was reduced. A part of the Grounds was taken for an expressway and another part provided the land upon which the Milwaukee County Stadium was built.

208

MEDICAL TERMS

MEDICAL TERMS

The following medical terms were found in the preceding data as to cause of death or disability of soldier. These terms are defined as understood during the second half of the nineteenth century.

ABSCESS A collection of pus localized within an organ or in an area of the body, e. g., liver, brain, or muscles in the lower back (lumbar region).

ACUTE MANIA A type of insanity noted by sudden behavioral expressions of excitement that may escalate to violence.

ALBUMINURIA The presence of a body protein called albumin in the urine that often is a result of kidney disease.

ALCOHOLISM The habit of ingesting excessive amounts of alcoholic drinks resulting in nervous conditions.

ANAEMIA (Anemia) A condition noted by deficiency in amount of blood, or a reduction of red corpuscles in the blood, or a reduction of hemoglobin in the blood. Symptoms include pallor of the face, lips, tongue, and palpitations of the heart. Some causes are bloodletting, severe mental work, lack of exercise, poor diet, and lead poisoning.

ANCHYLOSIS (Ankylosis) A condition noted by a *stiff joint* caused by the abnormal union of the bones at a joint, e.g., knee or ankle.

APOPLEXY The effects of a sudden change in the flow of blood or the plugging of the flow of blood of an organ, e.g., brain, lung, or liver. The term is generally used to indicate the cause of a cerebral *stroke.*

ASPHYXIA A condition caused by the body's inability to process air into the lungs e.g., in drowning or inhalation of poisonous gases.

ASTHMA Also called *Phthisic.* A condition manifested by reoccurring difficult breathing. It is accompanied by wheezing respiration indicating stressful attempts to breathe.

ATROPHY A wasting away of tissue resulting in a reduction in size of a part of the body caused by a lack of nutrition to the part and/or disuse of the part

BLADDER DISEASE A general term used to describe a disorder of the hollow organ behind the pubic bone used in the body as a holding space for urine.

BLIND The state of not having the sense of sight – total lack of vision

BLINDNESS Also called *Amaurosis.* A general term noting a lack of sight without a noticeable change in the appearance of the eye. Some causes are alcohol, tobacco, and lead poisoning, kidney disease, diabetes, and brain disease.

BRAIN DISEASE A general phrase used to denote a medical problem relating to the structure and/or function of the brain.

BRIGHT'S DISEASE A general phrase used to denote acute and chronic diseases of the kidneys often associated with *dropsy* and *albuminuria.*

BRONCHITIS An inflammation of the mucous membranes of the bronchial tubes. Symptoms include fever, cough and chest pain. The *acute* type is most often found in children. The *chronic* type may follow multiple bouts of the *acute* type - serious problems with breathing arises. There is great difficulty moving secretions from the mucous membranes needed to clear the airways.

CANCER A general term for a malignant growth.

CARBUNCLE An inflammation of subcutaneous tissue. It is like a *boil* except that it is larger, somewhat flat, and has multiple pus pro ducing heads.

211

CARDIAC DISEASE A general phrase used to denote a medical problem relating to the structure and/or function of the heart.

CATARACT A disease of the eye causing blindness due to loss of the clearness of the lens and/or its covering.

CATARRH A general term for inflammation of a mucous membrane with subsequent discharge as in the common cold – may be *acute* or *chronic.*

CEREBRAL CONGESTION Abnormal amounts of blood in the brain – often the cause of a *stroke.*

CEREBRAL HEMORRHAGE The rupture of a blood vessel in the brain, a cause of *apoplexy.*

CHILLS A feeling of cold with shivering of the body usually followed by a fever.

CHOLERA MORBUS Also called *Sporadic Cholera* or *Simple Cholera.* A general phrase given to diseases that cause nausea and vomiting and diarrhea accompanied with severe cramps. It is often epidemic in the summer. Believed to be caused by eating ripe fruits and vegetables that are difficult to digest.

CHOREA Also called *St. Vitus' Dance.* A nervous condition noted by involuntary movements of the muscles of the body. Its causes are multiple and seen more often in women than in men. Teething in young children and developmental changes in puberty are considered common causes. And it often occurs in persons with *rheumatism.*

COLLAPSE OF LUNGS A condition in which the lungs or a part of a lung is unable to stay inflated due to pressure changes in the chest. It is noted by pain and difficult breathing and is frequently found in cases of *bronchopneumonia.*

CONCUSSION OF THE BRAIN A condition caused by a fall or a violent blow to the head. First symptoms are unconsciousness and shock, and later headache and vomiting. Considered a possible cause of feeble-mindedness.

CONGESTION OF THE BRAIN An abnormal collection of blood in the brain generally caused by *concussion of the brain.* It may also indicate an acute episode of mental instability.

CONGESTION OF THE LUNGS An abnormal collection of blood in the lungs generally found in persons with heart disease.

CONGESTIVE CHILLS A general phrase noting a *chill* due to some unknown disease process in the body.

CONSTIPATION Also called *Costiveness.* A condition is which the large intestine is not emptied of fecal matter daily. It can cause congestion of the bowels, liver, and/or stomach.

CONSTRICTION OF THE LARYNX A tightness or stricture causing a narrowing of the upper part of the windpipe due to in-flammatory disorders or muscle spasms.

CONSUMPTION Also called *Phthisis Pulmomalis.* A general term indicating a wasting away of the body. Commonly used to identify *pulmonary tuberculosis.*

CONSUMPTION OF BOWELS Also called *Tuberculosis of the Bowels.* The ulceration found in the mucous membranes of intes-tines due to break down of tissue during formation of tubercles. Believed to be caused by swallowing infected pulmonary debris from the upper airways.

CONVULSION A sudden involuntary general muscular contrac-tion .of voluntary muscles. Believed to be caused by toxic agents. affecting the nervous system.

COXARUM MORBUS Also called *Hip Joint Disease, Coxalgia, and Coxitis.* Most often a *scrofulous* affection found in bones of the hip joint. Suppuration and formation of fistulas occur in advanced stages. *Rheumatism* of *old age* may be the cause of this suppuration but fistulas are not manifest in advanced stages.

CYSTITIS An inflammation of the bladder. In chronic form called *catarrh* of the bladder.

DEAF A condition in which there is a loss of hearing which ranges from minimal loss to total loss.

DEBAUCH An episode of excessive indulgence of alcoholic drinks or food.

DEFECTIVE VISION A general phrase noting varying degrees of loss of the sense of sight.

DELIRIUM TREMENS An acute nervous state brought on by the chronic intake of excessive alcoholic drinks. It is noted by great agitation and confusion often accompanied with hallucinations. Although it is considered to be alcoholic poisoning, the symptoms become evident after alcohol intake is withdrawn.

DIABETES A term most often used to indicate *Diabetes Mellitus.* A disease noted by the discharge of large quantities of urine containing sugar. Thirst and appetite increase. Cause unknown. Complications are multiple: pulmonary tuberculosis, gangrene, cataract, and neuritis. If death does not follow complications, it occurs as a result of diabetic coma.

DIARRHOEA (Diarrhea) A looseness and increased frequency of the bowels, accompanied with abdominal cramps and weakness. It is not a disease in itself but is a symptom of many diseases, e.g., cholera, and intestinal worms. It is classified as *acute* or *chronic.*

DIPHTHERIA A contagious disease in which the air-passages, particularly the throat, become covered with a thick membrane. Symptoms include sore throat, stiff neck, fever, vomiting, lassitude and exhaustion. A grave disease

DISEASE OF THE FEET A general phrase indicating a contagious disease of the skin of the feet believed to be caused by ringworm.

DISEASE OF THE TONGUE A general phrase noting an abnormal change in the tissue and/or color of tissue of the tongue itself, e.g., cancer. Some changes in the tongue are indicative of other diseases of the body but they are not considered to be a disease of the tongue.

DROPSY An abnormal collection of fluid in body cavities or in the tissue under the skin. A sign of a possible disease state of the blood, kidneys, liver, and /or heart.

DROPSY-CELLULAR Also called *Anasarca* A generalized *dropsy* noted by bloating all over the body.

DROPSY OF THE CHEST Also called *Hydrothorax*. An abnormal collection of fluid in the pleural cavity – found in individuals with heart disease and/or kidney disease.

DYSENTERY A general term for an inflammation of the large intestine noted by small frequent passage of mucus and blood considered infectious in origin. It was often found in army camps.

DYSPEPSIA Also called *Dyspepsy*. A condition of disturbed digestion or indigestion, cause unknown.. The primary symptom is discomfort over the upper and/or mid abdomen after eating. *Dyspeptic* individuals had been known to become invalids over time.

ENLARGEMENT OF THE HEART The thickening of the muscular walls of the heart affecting one part or the whole organ. Generally believed to be due to disease of valves of the heart or to Bright's disease.

ENTERITIS An inflammation of the mucous lining of the small intestine which is noted by abdominal pain, nausea and vomiting, and diarrhea. It has many causes chiefly bacteria, poisons, and debauchery.

EPILEPSY Also called *Fits* or *Falling Sickness*. A nervous condition of the brain noted by convulsions and unconsciousness. Many possible causes are cited: hereditary tendency, syphilis, uterine disease, masturbation, indigestion, intestinal worms, and head injuries.

EPILEPTIC CONVULSIONS A sudden attack or *fit*. There are two general categories relating to symptoms. One in which the individual looses consciousness, falls down, and manifests involuntary muscular contractions is called a *grand mal* seizure. And *petit mal* seizures noted by a brief loss of consciousness and involuntary movement. of the facial muscles.

ERYSIPELAS A common disease not considered contagious. It begins with general symptoms of chills, nausea and vomiting, and fever. Followed by an inflammatory response generally on the face that is characterized by a burning pain and tenderness to the touch. If the inflammation moves to a vital organ the individual may become mortally ill.

EXHAUSTION A condition of extreme fatigue in which it is difficult to maintain life. It may be due to long standing disease and/or nervous condition.

EXPOSURE The state of being open to bodily harm, e.g., the lack of coverings for the hands and/or feet in the winter.

EYE DISEASE A general phrase for an inflammation of the eye most often caused by bacterial growth in the conjunctiva (the membrane that covers the outside surface of the eyeball).

FATTY DEGENERATION OF HEART The deposit of fatty particles in the heart that replace muscle tissue thereby reducing the ability of the heart to function normally. It is noted in the obese person by poor circulation, and in extreme cases, dropsy.

FEVER An increased heat of the body that is widely spread. The pulse is quicker; there is dullness, weakness, chilliness, and disinclination to take food. It is generally a response to infectious agents.

FISTULA An abnormal, deep, narrow canal in body tissue from which pus or other body liquids drain.. It follows incomplete healing of ulcers or wounds.

FRACTURE A breaking of a bone or a broken bone.

FROZEN The state of being in which the body or parts of the body have been exposed to extreme cold over a long period of time resulting in loss of circulation and death of tissue.

GANGERUS (Gangrenous) An eroded non-healing sore of the nature of gangrene, .i.e., resulting in death of tissue.

GASTRITIS An inflammation of the mucous membranes of the stomach that may be either *acute* or *chronic*. The *acute* type, noted by a burning sensation in the stomach, may be a complication of a condition caused by an infectious disease or food poisoning. Excessive eating and drinking of alcoholic beverages – not the result of frequent episodes of the acute type - usually causes the chronic type, noted by a dull pain in the stomach after eating.

GASTROSIS Also called *Gastroxia,* An excessive secretion of hydrochloric acid by the stomach, a condition which characterizes a form of *dyspepsia.* Or a general term noting any disease of the stomach.

GENERAL DEBILITY A phrase indicating the absence or reduction of the normal functional ability of the body.

GENERAL PARALYSIS OF THE INSANE A progressive loss of normal physical and mental capacity ending in death believed to be associated with syphilis and/or severe nervous strain.

HAEMATEMESIS (Hematemesis) The vomiting of blood most often due to ruptured ulcers in the stomach.

HAEMATURIA (Hematuria) The presence of blood in the urine that indicates an inflammatory condition in a part of the urinary tract.

HEART DISEASE-VALVULAR A condition of the heart in which the movable partition(s) that control the flow of blood through the heart may be defective. These parts may be defective at birth or they may become defective following an inflammation of the heart.

HEMIPLEGIA A paralysis that affects one side of the body.

HEMOPTYSIS The spitting of blood coming from the upper airway and/or lungs most often found in cases of *consumption.*

HEMORRHAGE An abnormal sudden flow of blood from a vein or artery into surrounding tissue and/or body outlets. Generally differs from *bleeding* in that the amount of blood lost is greater in *hemorrhage.*

HEMORRHAGE OF THE LUNGS A loss of blood due to tissue breakdown in the lungs noted by *hemoptysis.*

HEMORRHOIDS Also called *Piles.* Swellings formed within the rectum and around the anus by the dilatation of hemorrhoid veins and thickening of their walls.

HEPATITIS Also called *Bilious Disorder.* An inflammation of the liver noted by the yellowish discoloration of the skin and white's of the eye often is preceded by symptoms of general malaise.

HERNIA Also called *Rupture.* A term generally used to note the protrusion of the intestine through the abdominal wall. A *double hernia* indicates that there is a *hernia* on both sides of the abdomen.

HIP-JOINT DISEASE Also called *Coxarium Morbus, Coxitis, Coxalgia.*

HYDRA-THORAX (Hydrothorax) Also called *Dropsy of the Chest.*

HYDROCELE The accumulation of fluid in the scrotum.

218

HYPERTROPHY OF THE LIVER An enlarged liver mainly due to chronic alcoholism or inflammatory disease

IMBECILE A person who is feebleminded, i.e., mentally defective. They are unable to function as an adult.

IMBECILITY A state of weakness of mind that may be present since birth or acquired through injury or disease.

INFIRMITY A general term indicating a state of physical weakness or *imbecility.*

INFLAMMATION A state in which the infected part is hotter, redder, more congested and more painful than that which is normal.

INFLAMMATION OF THE BOWELS A general term noting a diseased state of the mucous membranes of the small and/or large intestine.

ISHURIA (Ischuria) The retention or suppression of urine.

INFLAMMATION OF THE LUNGS An internal inflammation in the chest that is frequently the result of a *cold.*

INSANITY Also called *Alienation, Madness.* A mental condition that may be caused by developmental problems, disease, or aging. Some of the more common symptoms are a change in character and habits, melancholia, mania, and hallucinations.

INTERMITTENT FEVER Also called *Fever and Ague.* There is a complete intermission of *fever,* i. e., the body temperature returns to normal between attacks of the *fever.* A sign of *malaria.*

KIDNEY DISEASE Also called *Bright's Disease.* A general term for inflammation and/or degeneration of the kidney.

LARYNGEAL PHTHISIS Also called *Tuberculosis of the larynx.* A chronic form of *laryngitis* caused by tubercular ulceration in the throat noted by difficulty in swallowing and hoarseness.

LIVER DISEASE   A broad phrase indicating abnormal function of the organ includes specific common affections, e.g. *hepatitis, jaundice, bilious disorder.*

LOCOMOTOR ATAXIA   Also called *Creeping Palsy. Tabes Dorsalis.* A disease of the spinal cord noted by *lightning-pains* (brief, stabbing pains) and uncoordinated voluntary muscles of the extremities.   Believed to be caused by syphilis or tuberculosis.

LUMBAGO   A *backache* due to *rheumatism* in the loins and the small of the back.

LUMBAR ABSCESS   A collection of pus found in the lumbar region usually at a distance from the original infected site.

LUNG DISEASE   A general phrase indicating a disorder in the structure and/or function of the lung(s).

LUNG FEVER   Also called *Croupous Pneumonia, Lobar Pneumonia.* An acute inflammation of the lobes of the lung usually beginning in the right lower lobe caused by bacteria. The signs and symptoms are chills and fever, rapid breathing, and rust-colored sputum.

MALARIA   Also called *Miasma.* Unhealthy vapors of marshy areas producing fever.

MALARIAL POISONING   Also called *Malaria.* A disease noted by chills, fever, and sweats caused by inhalation of unhealthy vapors in marshy areas.

MALIGNANT VARIOLA   Also called *Black Smallpox.* A severe form of *smallpox* noted by the presence of blood in the pustules giving them a black appearance - often a fatal disease.

MANIA   A form of insanity noted by unusually strong emotional and physical excitement in which there may be a tendency to violence. It is a chronic condition. When an *acute* form is noted, it is generally of alcoholic origin.

MARAMUS   A gradual wasting of the body due to a lack of food or a defect in the body's ability to process food.

MARAMUS TABES   A progressive wasting of the body due to a defect in the body's ability to process food - associated with loco-motor *ataxia*.

MENINGITIS   An inflammation of the membrane covering the brain and/or spinal cord. It is usually due to the presence of some other disease process in the body, e.g., syphilis or tuberculosis. The headache and rigidity of the neck note disease in the brain. And when it is found in the spinal cord it is noted by rigidity of muscles of the body.

MORBUS   Disease or affection.

MORPHINE HABIT   The chronic misuse of morphine or opium for its narcotic effect, i.e., producing stupor.

MYELITIS   A general term most often indicating an inflammation of the spinal cord. The disease is noted by neurological changes below the level of the disease process leading to paralysis.

NECROSIS OF SKULL   The death of bony tissue of the head. A loss of bony tissue of the lower jaw is commonly found in those who have been exposed to the fumes of phosphorus.

NERVOUS EXHAUSTION   Also called *Nervous Prostration*. A condition caused by a disorder of the nervous system due to exces-sive use of the mental faculties noted by many losses, loss of inter-est in all usual physical activities, loss of memory, inability to sleep, etc. – reflecting a deprivation of all the drives needed to maintain life.

NEURALGIA   A condition noted by sharp, brief episodes of pain along nerve pathways found in individuals with such chronic ill-nesses as gout, malaria, diabetes, rheumatism, alcoholism, and hys-teria – the mechanism of the affection is not known.

OLD AGE The last years of life noted by declining physical stamina and mental dullness, i.e., *senility*.

OPHTHMALIA An inflammation of the mucous membranes that come in contact with the eye, i.e., under the eyelids and extending to the anterior portion of the eyeball. It may result from a cold or irritant or by contagion. In extreme cases it may indicate congestion or inflammation of the brain.

OPIUM EATING The habit of misusing drugs containing *opium*.

OSSIFICATION OF HEART Also called *Bony Heart* A change or state of change in the tissue of the heart to bony substance due to deposits of phosphate of lime.

PARALYSIS Also called *Palsy*. A general term for the loss of the power of motion or sense of motion in any part of the body.

PARTIAL PARALYSIS An incomplete loss of the power or sense of motion in any part of the body.

PATELLA The knee-cap or knee-pan.

PERITONITIS An inflammation of the membrane lining the abdominal cavity and enveloping the intestines called the *peritoneum*. Causes include: simple exposure to cold and wet, septic infections after surgical procedures or childbirth, and diseases, e.g., tuberculosis, cancer, or syphilis. It is most often noted by abdominal pain, vomiting, constipation, and moderate fever.

PHTHISIS PULMONALIS Also called *Consumption, Phthisis, Tuberculosis. Tuberculosis of the Lung*. A disease noted by a wasting away of the body and the deposition of tubercular matter into the lung tissue. Although a bacterium was found to be present in the tubercle, it remains a common belief that the formation of the tubercle is due to defective nutrition.

PILES Also called *Hemorrhoids*.

PLEURO-PNEUMONIA An inflammation of both the pleura and the lungs. It often begins with pleurisy and then extends to the lungs.

PLEURISY Also called *Pleuritis*. An inflammation of the pleura – the membrane that covers the lungs and lines the chest cavity. A common cause is tuberculosis.

PNEUMONIA Also called *Pneumonitis*. A general term indicating an inflammation of the lungs. It is most commonly used to mean lobar pneumonia. It is noted by chills, fever, chest pain, cough with purulent and bloody sputum - a frequent cause of death in the young and the elderly.

PROGRESSIVE PARALYSIS Also called *Locomotor Ataxia*.

PROSTRATION Also called *Exhaustion*.

PULMONARY CONSUMPTION Also called *Phthisis, Phthisis Pulmonalis, Tuberculosis,* and *Tuberculosis of the Lung*.

PULMONARY HEMORRHAGE A discharge of blood from the tissues of the lungs noted by chest discomfort, blood in sputum and/or blood in vomit. Often found in the late stage of *Phthisis Pulmonalis*.

PYAEMIA (Pyemia) A form of blood poisoning in which decomposing pus is spread from one part of the body to other parts of the body through the blood.

REMITTENT FEVER Also called *Bilious Fever*. A fever that comes and goes but does not abate completely, i.e., there is only a remission. Occurs in individuals with *malaria*. It is believed by some to be due to quinine poisoning.

RENAL & CYSTIC DISEASE A general phrase indicating a disorder involving the kidney and the urinary bladder – inflammatory in nature.

RENAL DISEASE A general phrase indicating a disorder in the structure and/or function of the kidney.

RENAL DROPSY OF CHEST A *hydrothorax* of the chest cavities due to kidney disease.

RHEUMATISM A general term used to indicate a painful inflammatory disease of the joints and/or muscles, so named from the belief that the pain was caused by *rheum* or humor flowing through the parts affected. It was caused by a diseased condition of the blood. And there is a tendency for it to occur on exposure to cold and wet.

RUPTURE OF THE HEART A hernia of the heart - a protrusion of the heart into the abdomen through a break in the diaphragm. It may be due to a wound.

SCIATICA An inflammation of the great nerve of the thigh. It is noted by pain along the nerve pathway and caused by exposure to cold and dampness.

SCORBUTUS Also called *Scurvy.*

SCROFULA A disease affecting glandular and bony tissue afflicting one-fifth of the population. The signature characteristic of this disease is the formation of tubercles. It varies in its manifestations from the slightest eruption on the skin to the most malignant, pulmonary *consumption.*

SCURVY A disease caused by deprivation of fresh fruits and vegetables commonly found in sailors and the poor. Symptoms begin with bleeding gums and may go on to *prostration.*

SENILE DEBILITY Also called *Senility, Senile Decay.* A weakness of body and mind found in the aged.

SENILE GANGRENE A condition in which there is a death of tissue of the extremities usually found in the aged individual.

SEQUELA TO ERYSIPELAS An inflammation of a body organ, often a kidney, that may follow a case of *erysipelas*.

SMALL POX Also called *Variola*. A disease that is passed from one person to another by a poison that is found in the pustules on the skin and in body excretions.

SOFTENING OF THE BRAIN Also called *Progressive Paralysis of the Insane* or *Progressive Dementia with General Paralysis*. A condition indicating progressive paralysis and dementia not attributed to aging. Cause unknown, severe nervous strain and *syphilis* are believed to be related factors.

SPERMATORRHOEA (Spermatorrhea) Also called *Seminal Weakness*. The involuntary emission of semen occurring without copulation. It is believed to be caused by habitual masturbation when young, or intestinal worms, spinal irritation, and *piles*.

SPINAL DISEASE A general phrase denoting a disease reflecting an abnormal condition of the bones of the spine, e.g., *curvature of the spine*/crooked back and *kyphosis*/humpback

SUNSTROKE Also called *Heat Stroke*. A condition manifested by fever and prostration due to excessive exposure to the rays of the sun.

SYPHILIS - TERTIARY The third stage of *syphilis*, a chronic infectious disease commonly acquired through sexual congress. It is noted by small skin tumors called *gummas* - a term reflecting the tumor's gummy appearance. And believed, at this stage, to be the cause of *tabes* and *dementia*.

TABES A term generally used to indicate *tabes dorsalis*, i. e., *locomotor ataxia*.

TUBERCULOSIS Also called *Phthisis Pulmonalis*.

TYPHOID FEVER Also called *Enteric Fever*. Symptoms are continuous *fever* and *diarrhea*. The poison of the disease leaves the body mainly through the bowels and is passed along in contaminated water and milk

TYPHOID PNEUMONIA Also called *Typhopneumonia*. A *pneumonia* noted by a general weakness accompanied by typhoid symptoms.

ULCERS Sores on the skin or mucous membrane which discharge matter produced by death of tissue.

ULCERATION OF BOWELS The formations of *ulcers* on the lining of the intestine most often the result of tuberculosis.

UREAMIA (Uremia) The presence of waste products in the blood due to the inability of the kidneys to eliminate them. Signs and symptoms nclude headache, vomiting, convulsions, coma, and the odor of urine on the breath.

VARICOSE VEINS A condition in which the veins are permanently dilated and tortuous. They are found most often on legs and commonly caused by standing for long periods of time.

VERTIGO A sensation of dizziness or swimming of the head.

MILITARY TERMS AND RELATED ABBREVIATIONS

Formal rules for abbreviating a word were infrequently applied in military reports of the 19th century. The following is a list of some of the military terms and abbreviations of that time which may provide clues to the shortened word.

1ST ASSISTANT SURGEON
1ST CLASS FIREMEN
1ST SERGEANT
2ND ASSISTANT SURGEON
2ND ASST. ENGINEER
2ND COOK
3RD ASST. ENGINEER

A.
A. A. S.
A. S.
ACT. P. M.
ACTING ENSIGN
ACTING MASTER'S MATE
ACTING VOLUNTEER LT.
ADD. PAY M.
ADD'L. PAYMASTER
ADJT.
ADJUTANT
ADJUTANT GENERAL
AIDE-DE-CAMP
ART.
ARTIFICER
ARTY.
ARTILLERY
ARTILLERY GUARD
ASSISTANT ADJUTANT
ASSISTANT AIDE-DE-CAMP
ASSISTANT ENGINEER
ASSISTANT SURGEON

B.
BAND
BATTALION
BATTERY
BATTLN.
BATTY.
BLACKSMITH
BOATSWAIN
BOATSWAIN'S MATE
BOY
BREVET
B. S.
BVT.
BRIGADE
BRIGIDIER GENERAL
BUGL.
BUGLER

C.
CANNONEER
CABIN BOY
CAP.
CAPT.
CAPTAIN
CAPTAIN & A. Q. M.
CAPTAIN & C. S.
CARPENTER
CARPENTER'S MATE
CAV.
CAVALRY
C. G.
COMMANDING GENERAL
C. PASSER
C. S.
C. SARGEANT
CHAP.
CHAPLAIN
CLERK
COAL HEAVER

COAL PASSER
COL.
COLONEL
COLORED
COM. CL.
COM. SERGEANT
COMSY.
COMMISSARY
COMMISSARY SERGEANT
COOK
CORP.
CORPORAL
COXSWAIN

D.
D. M.
DRUG.
DRUM MAJOR

E.
ENGINEER
ENSIGN

FARRIER
FIFE MAJOR
FIREMAN
FIRST SGT.
FOOT RIFLEMAN

G.
G. P.
GENERAL
GENERAL SERVICES
GUIDON
GUNNER
GUNNER'S MATE
GUNNERY SGT.

H. A.

H. S.
HARNESS MAKER
HEAVY ARTILLERY
HOME GUARDS
HORSE ARTILLERY
HOSP. STEW.
HOSPITAL STEWARD
HV.

INDEPENDENT
INF.
INFANTRY
INSPECTOR GENERAL
JUDGE ADVOCATE

L.& M.
L. A.
L. C.
L. M.
L'DSMAN
LANDSMAN
LEADER (BAND)
LIEUT. COLONEL
LIEUTENANT
LIGHT ARTILLERY
LIEUTENANT COLONEL
LGT.
LT.

M.
MAJOR
MAJOR GEN.
MAJOR GENERAL
MASTER
MASTER ARMORER
MASTER CARRIAGE MAKER
MASTER'S MATE
MATE

MESS BOY
MIL.
MILITARY
MILITIA
MOUNTED
MOUNTED RIFLES
MOUNTED SERVICES
MOUNTED SHARPSHOOTERS
MOUNTED VOLUNTEERS
MTD.
MUS.
MUSICIAN

NATIONAL GUARD
N.G.
NURSE

OFF.
OFFICER
OFFICER'S STEWARD
ORD.
O. S.
ORDNANCE CORPS
ORD. S.
ORD. SEAMAN
ORDINARY SEAMAN

P.
P. MUSICIAN
P. OFFICER
P. C.
P. M.
PAYMR.
PAYMASTER
PAYMASTER'S CLERK
PAY STEWARD
PILOT
POST ASSISTANT ADJUTANT
PRINC. MUSICIAN

PRINCIPAL MUSICIAN
PRIVATE
PROV.
PROVISIONAL
PROVOST
PROVOST GUARD
PROVOST MARSHALL
PVT.

Q.
Q. M. SERGEANT
Q. M. L.
Q. S.
QUARTERMASTER
QUARTERMASTER GENERAL
QUARTERMASTER SERGEANT

R.
R. A.
REGULAR ARMY
R. Q. M.
REGIMENTAL ADJUTANTS
REGIMENTAL Q. M. PAYMASTER
REGT.
RES.
RESERVES
RIFLES

SAD. S.
SADDLE SERGEANT
SADDLER
S. C.
SEAMAN
SERGEANT
SERGEANT-MAJOR
SGT. OF PIONEERS
SHARPSHOOTERS
SIGNAL CORPS
SIGNAL SERGEANT

S. M.
STATE MILITIA
STEWARD
SURG.
SURGEON
SURGEON GENERAL
SURGEON'S STEWARD

TEAMSTER
TOPOGRAPHICAL ENGINEER

U .S. ORD.
U. S. ARMY
U. S. C. T.
U. S. COLORED TROOPS
U. S. DRAGOONS (Mexican War)
U. S. MARINE CORPS
U. S. M. A.
UNITED STATES MILITARY ACADEMY
U. S. NAVY
U. S. VETERAN RESERVE CORPS
U. S. VETERAN VOLUNTEERS
U. S. VOLTIGUERS (Mexican War)
UNASSIGNED

V. S.
VET. SURG.
VET. SURGEON
VET'Y. SURGEON
VETERINARY SERGEANT

W.
WAG.
WAG. M.
WAGONER

YEOMAN

REFERENCES

REFERENCES

Boatner, M. M. III. 1991. *The Civil War Dictionary. Rev. Ed.*, New York: Vintage Books.

Casper, C. N. Compiler. 1903. *Milwaukee, A Picturesque and Descriptive Account of the Present Mercantile and Industrial Interest and Advantages of the Metropolis of Wisconsin.* Merchants' and Manufacturers' Ass'n. of Milwaukee: Wetzel Bros. Printing Co.

Cetina, Judith G. 1977. *A History of Veterans' Homes in the United States, 1811-1930.* Doctoral Dissertation, Department of History, Case Western Reserve University.

Corbett, Richard W., Chief Clerk. 1903. *Souvenir of the Soldiers' Home. Detailed Description of Northwestern Branch, National Military Home for Disabled Volunteer Soldiers.* Milwaukee County, Wisconsin: Burdick & Allen Print.

Dorland, Newman W. A. 1945. *The American Illustrated Medical Dictionary. 20th Edition.* Philadelphia and London: W. B. Saunders Company.

Edwards, Richard. Editor. 1865, 1867, 1868. *Edward's Annual Director to the Inhabitants, Institutions, Incorporated Companies, Manufacturing Establishments, Business, Business Firms, etc., etc. in the City of Milwaukee.* Milwaukee: Starr & Son, Book, Job, and Commercial Printers, 412 and 414 East Water Street.

Farrow, Edward S. 1918. *Dictionary of Military Terms. Rev. Ed.* New York: Thomas Y. Crowell Company

Gould, George M. 1906. *The Practitioner's Medical Dictionary.* Philadelphia: P. Blakiston's Son & Co.

Hartman, William Y. Compiler. 1963. *History of Veterans Administration Center, Wood, Wisconsin.*

Hurn, Ethel Alice. 1911. *Wisconsin Women in the War Between the States.* Wisconsin History Commission. Democrat Printing Co., State Printer.

Jerger, Jeanette L. 1995. *A Medical Miscellany for Genealogists.* Bowie, Maryland: Heritage Books, Inc.

Johnson, Fletcher W. 1891. *Life of Wm. T. Sherman.* Philadelphia: A. T. Hubbard.

Kelly, Patrick J. 1992. *Creating a National Home: The Postwar Care of Disabled Union Soldiers and the Beginning of the Modern State in America.* Doctoral Dissertation, History Department, New York University.

Marten, James. 1996. *A Place of Great Beauty, Improved by Man: The Soldier's Home and Victorian Milwaukee.* Milwaukee, Wisconsin, Marquette University.

Pierce, R. V. 1895. *The People's Common Sense Medical Advisor, in Plain English or Medicine Simplified.* Buffalo, New York: Printed and Published by the World Dispensary Printing Office and Bindery

Roe, E. T. 1903. *Webster's New Standard Dictionary of the English Language.* Chicago: Laird & Lee, Publishers.

Scott, H. L. Colonel, Inspector General, U. S. A. 1861. *Civil War Military Dictionary includes 1855 Rifle Manuel and 1861 Army Cook Book.* Edited and Abridged by Martin Rywell, 1956, Columbia Research Reprints. Harriman, Tennessee: Pioneer Press.

Semple, L., and M. Claus. Fall-Winter 1992. *'Celebrate—National Soldiers' Home.' Preserve Milwaukee.* Milwaukee: A Publication of Historic Milwaukee, Inc.

Taber, C. W. 1970. *Taber's Cyclopedic Medical Dictionary. 11th Edition.* Philadelphia: F. A. Davis Co.

Tallmadge, John J. 1865. Pamphlet. *Permanent Home for Wisconsin Soldiers.* Milwaukee, Wisconsin.

Thickens, John. Compiler. 1869-1870. *Milwaukee City Directory for 1869-1870.* Milwaukee: Paul & Cadwallader, Book and Job Printers.

Thwaites, Reuben G. Editor. 1912. *Civil War Messages and Proclamations of Wisconsin War Governors.* Wisconsin History Commission. Democrat Printing Co., State Printer.

Thompson, Holland. 2000. *'The Sanitary Commission and Other Relief Agencies.' The Photographic History of the Civil War.* Internet. www.civilwarhome.com/sanitarycommission.htm.

Tupek, Karen R. VA Historic Preservation Officer. 2000. *National Home for Disabled Volunteer Soldiers.* VA Historic Preservation Site. Internet. fac.mgt@hq.med.va.gov.

Turner, A. J. Compiler. 1872. *The Legislative Manual of the State of Wisconsin; Comprising Jefferson's Manual, Rules, Forms and Laws for the Regulation of Business: Also, Lists and Tables for Reference, Etc .* Madison, Wisconsin: Atwood & Culver, State Printers, Journal Block.

Weber, G. A., and L. F. Schemckebier. 1934. *The Veterans' Administration, Its History, Activities, and Organization.* Washington: The Brookings Institution.

_____. 1866. *Charter & By-Laws of the Wisconsin Soldiers' Home.* Milwaukee: Daily Wisconsin Steam Printing House.

_____. 1865. *First Annual Report of the Wisconsin Soldiers' Home, Milwaukee, for the Year Ending April 15th, 1865.* Milwaukee: Daily Wisconsin Book and Job Steam Printing House.

_____. 1866. *Second Annual Report of the Wisconsin Soldiers' Home, Milwaukee, Detailed Statement of the Contribution from Each County to the Soldiers' Home Fair.* Milwaukee: Jermain & Brightman, Sentinel Printing House.

_____. 1867. *Third Annual Report and Memorial of the Wisconsin Soldiers' Home, Milwaukee to the Legislature.* Milwaukee: Daily Wisconsin Printing House, Cor. East Water & Huron Sts.

_____. March 7, 1864. Editorial. *Soldiers' Home.* Milwaukee Daily Sentinel.Page. 1.

_____. May 16, 1864, Editorial, *Soldiers' Home,* Milwaukee Daily Sentinel, Page 1.

_____. May 25, 1864. *Soldiers' Home.* Milwaukee Daily Sentinel, Page 1.

_____. 1877. *Annual Report of the Northwestern Branch, National Home for Disabled Volunteer Soldiers.* Milwaukee County Wisconsin, January 19, 1877.Near Milwaukee, Wisconsin: National Home Printing Office.

_____. 1885. *Annual Report, North-Western Branch, National Home for Disabled Volunteer Soldiers.* Milwaukee County, Wisconsin, July 1, 1885. Milwaukee County: National Home Printing Office.

_____. December 22, 1914. *Mrs. Lydia Ely Dies Led Charity Work.* Milwaukee Evening Sentinel.

_____. December 22, 1914. *Woman Patriot Passes Away.* Milwaukee Journal/

_____. Pamphlet. 1967. *Wood, VAC, Century of Service, 1867-1967*

_____. 1992. Pamphlet. *125th Anniversary Historic Walk.* Clement J. Zablocki VA Medical Center.

_____ *Bicentennial Notes, June 1976.* Wood, Wisconsin.

_____ *Bicentennial Notes, July 1976.* Wood, Wisconsin.

_____ *Bicentennial Notes, August 1976.* Wood, Wisconsin.

_____ *Bicentennial Notes, September 1976.* Wood, Wisconsin.

_____ *Bicentennial Notes, October 1976.* Wood, Wisconsin.

_____ *Bicentennial Notes, November 1976.* Wood, Wisconsin.

_____ *Bicentennial Notes, December 1976.* Wood, Wisconsin.

_____. 1870. U. S. Census, State of Wisconsin, County of Milwaukee, City of Wauwatosa.

References for NECROLOGY are noted in that section.

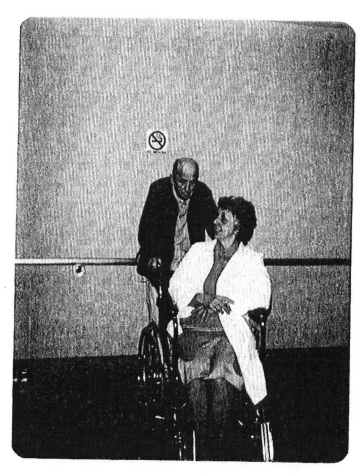

Patient at Veterans Administration, age 101,
pushing author sitting in wheelchair.

Dr. Jeanette Jerger is an educator and administrator of nursing and a past employee of the Veterans Administration of Milwaukee County, Wisconsin. She is a great granddaughter of a Civil War Veteran from Wisconsin, and has been collecting genealogical data for 15 years.

Dr. Jerger is the author of *A Medical Miscellany for Genealogists*, published by Heritage Books, Inc.

Made in United States
North Haven, CT
25 October 2022

25907635R00137